Radio Head Gal

Radio Head Gal

a memoir of hearing loss
and self-worth

Rebecca Knill

JMT Press

Library of Congress Control Number: 2024905125.
Names: Knill, Rebecca, author.
Title: Radio Head Gal / Rebecca Knill.
Description: First Edition. | Minneapolis: JMT Press, 2024.
Hardcover print edition ISBN 979-8-218-33681-3.
Paperback print edition ISBN 979-8-218-33709-4.
E-book edition ISBN 979-8-218-33679-0.
Audiobook edition ISBN 979-8-218-42819-8.
Printed and bound in the United States of America.
Cover illustration by Mark Rook, markrookdesign.squarespace.com.

CONTENTS

CONTENTS

Part I: BEFORE

False Assumptions

Flashback: I am standing in my underwear in a hotel room in Paris, packing for the next morning's departure, when a shadow falls across me. I turn and see my travel roommate, her face livid with outrage, shouting at me in anger.

"I've been pounding on the door for ten minutes!" she fumes.

"What happened?" I ask, puzzled.

"The key didn't work!" she heaves accusingly. "I've been standing here, knocking, like, fifty times! I was pounding on the door!" she repeats. "I had to flag down the porter to let me in!"

I stare at her curiously, wondering why a key card malfunction warrants a full-blown temper tantrum. I travel for work every week, and my hotel keys frequently fail. You walk down to the front desk with the key and ask them to reset it. Done.

It's our last day in Paris, and I'd wanted to people-watch. I corralled a trio of timid seniors in our travel group and led them to a lovely outdoor café where we jubilantly toasted our newfound spontaneity over croque monsieurs and flaming drinks as beautiful Parisians strolled by.

It's a hot day. I have returned to the hotel early to take a bath before our farewell party on the Seine River and threw open the French doors to a tiny balcony like a cartoon princess welcoming avian friends to tidy the room. I had not expected the roommate back for another hour and a half. Yet, here she is, rage mushrooming from her atomic bomb of fury while I pull on my clothes. Her lips move vehemently as I plug in my hearing aid. Loud, negative particles bounce off the walls, sucking up all the oxygen. My magical day rapidly dissolves.

The porter arrives, and she snatches the new key card from him, slamming the door in his face. *Oh my god,* I realize. *She made him go to the lobby for her.* She plops in a chair and kicks off her shoes, glaring as if I had locked her out intentionally.

I don't know her well. We attend the same church and had mentioned a mutual desire to see Paris. I'd even invited her to dinner before the trip to discuss what it was like to travel with someone deaf. I gave her the chance to back out.

"I left the chain lock off —" I begin to say.

"The key didn't work!" she shouts. "I was banging on the door! I knocked seventy times!" Her estimate goes up.

"So, you get a new key," I reply. "Either way, you need a new key —"

"Never mind!" she snaps. "It doesn't matter!" She begins to pack for the next day's departure, throwing items into her bag in a silent rampage. I recognize the familiar flush of shame and debate whether to confront her. I go for it.

"Wait, it does matter," I state firmly. "Don't come in here and suddenly act annoyed because I can't hear. My not hearing your knock is no different than if I wasn't here at all."

"I'm sorry!" she barks, flinging a shoe into her carry-on. It's not an apology. She just wasn't expecting me to call her out.

"We talked about this before we left," I sigh exasperatedly. "What do you not understand about my being deaf?"

The trip had been congenial until her sudden outburst. Earlier that week, she had even confided that her mother was losing her hearing. The roommate wept when she told me her mother refused to talk about it with her. Her emotional tug-of-war struck a chord. My mother and I also kept at a mutual arms' length from each other on matters of hearing loss. Still, I knew her mother's frame of reference — the shame behind the stigma, that vague layer of disgrace constantly looming overhead. And as soon as the roommate unleashed her torrent of wrath about my not hearing, I felt my perspective silently shift: *If I were your mother, I wouldn't talk about it with you, either.*

* * *

It wasn't the first time I'd missed a door knock. I have a hundred versions of this story: Someone knows perfectly well that I'm deaf, knocks on the door, receives no response, and has a dramatic meltdown, venting accusingly, "I knocked really LOUD!" to which I respond pointedly, "I'm deaf."

It's a classic case of false assumption. People imagine everyone can hear exactly the way they do, which is forgivable. It's natural to superimpose your own perspective on others as the starting default. The actual sin is then doubling down, insisting that everyone must hear and that any deviation from an audio approach is unacceptable. Few realize their mistake and exclaim, "Oh, how foolish of me! Of course, you can't hear my knock!" No, the implication is clear: *Only a freak can't hear that.*

False assumptions set the foundation for fearmongering. Deafness is an easy target in the sport of intentionally stirring up worry, typically based on a prehistoric-era principle that hearing sound is the only means to warn of impending danger. For example, a hearing man recently unloaded on social media to express his concerns about his deaf wife. He feared for his own safety because he stayed up late, and she removed her hearing devices at night. "Even if I screamed all night, she'd never hear me," he complained, his choice of words betraying his underlying resentment. However, he had no health issues to provoke such worry. In his mind, he was a victim.

His false assumption was that his wife was required to save him (and more specifically, save him by *hearing*), completely overlooking that an accident could befall him anywhere, anytime, or while he was alone at home. To him, his screaming (and her hearing him scream) were the only options for his safety. Meanwhile, he rejected alternative suggestions, such as carrying a cell phone to call 911 himself (since he clearly could still vocalize in this imaginary hour of need) or wearing a smartwatch that automatically dialed 911 when it detected a fall. Instead, he proclaimed his wife's deaf state unacceptable because it risked his life. Hypothetically. (*Cough* See chapter on gaslighting.)

Validating assumptions has been a critical step in every methodology I've learned in my project management career. An assumption is a statement considered true without proof (for example, "all customers have email capability"). However, an entire project can derail if an assumption is later proven false. Therefore, it's essential to continually identify and validate assumptions to stay on track. In life, too, identifying and validating assumptions are important components of understanding bias.

"Have you ever been with a woman?" I once asked my friend and work sign language interpreter, Mark Alan English, a gay man.

"No," he replied, shrugging.

"So, how do you know?" I asked.

He identified as gay since childhood, he said. He always knew.

"What about you?" he asked, turning the tables. "Have you ever been with a woman?"

"No," I replied, surprised.

"Why not?" he asked.

"I've never been attracted to a woman," I said.

"Exactly," said Mark Alan.

"Oh," I responded, and the moment resonated. I had unwittingly imposed my own preferences onto Mark Alan's life, assuming that his gay perspective must have been secondary after rejecting a straight lifestyle instead of respecting it as his legitimate, equally valid default. Likewise, when weighing deaf versus hearing, we often look at the hearing perspective exclusively and then double down, failing to acknowledge hearing loss as a distinct and valid perspective in its own right for a growing segment of the population.

Unvalidated assumptions follow us everywhere. Hearing people assume that I want to hear just because they can hear. Their flawed logic leads to further assumptions: that hiding my deafness is a goal or that all consumers prefer to receive information solely through audio means. However, if people had validated their initial assumption, they would have understood that I didn't care about hearing and even less about audio.

What I wanted was accessibility.

2

Diversity Matters

I never wanted to be hearing. I said this out loud in my TED talk (*How Technology Has Changed What It's Like to Be Deaf*),[1] and the audience went bug-eyed, struggling to process this heresy. *How could anyone not want to be hearing?* I wasn't anti-hearing. I just felt my life would be simpler if everyone else were deaf.

I was born with hearing loss, so deafness was my normal, the starting point from which I adapted. I saw myself as different but equal, and I thought everyone else did, too. In retrospect, that wasn't true. I didn't know until much later that the world categorized hearing loss like they would a multi-car pileup on the freeway: a calamity that disproportionately impacted everything in its path. But to me, deafness was just a state of being.

The TED audience told me later they had presumed that my problem statement was "being deaf" and my solution was "becoming hearing." However, my presentation focused on society's view of life with hearing loss as being of lesser value, and my idea was to systemically change that outdated viewpoint through consumer power, demanding scientific innovation to level the playing field. "Technology has come so far," I stated. "Our mindset just needs to catch up." After their initial jaw drop, the TED audience adjusted to this unexpected shift and said they left thinking differently. They were eager to learn more.

Embracing one's identity and living authentically are the foundations of diversity and inclusion efforts, but that wasn't always so. I remember when my employer first introduced diversity training in the 1990s. The curriculum was intended to be color-blind and treat everyone the same. Ergo, if we blurred our differences, we could work together more effectively. But something was missing. The '90s version told us our differences didn't matter, yet they were a big part of who we were. Consequently, the one-size-fits-all approach invariably favored the majority by requiring others to suppress parts of their identities to blend in.

In the years since, the concept of diversity has evolved. Today, it's not about ignoring differences but celebrating them. It's about creating a workplace where everyone feels welcome and respected, regardless of their background. When we can be ourselves at work, celebrating our unique identities and perspectives, we are more productive, creative, and engaged. We are also more likely to feel a sense of belonging and connection to our colleagues.

Diversity training also helps us understand unconscious bias. These are the hidden prejudices we all have, which can lead to unfair treatment of others. By understanding our mindsets, we can start to challenge them and build a workplace that's fair for everyone. We can also learn to appreciate our colleagues' unique perspectives and see the value in differences.

Ironically, as I write about the importance of diversity and inclusion, backlash is mounting, desiring to resurrect the one-size-fits-all mandates of the past. Those who see diversity as a threat seem determined to roll back hard-won human rights, which makes me especially sad. I grew up in a world that pressured me to hide my differences, and my younger self did not have the skills to push back on those expectations. Those in power today can choose to mute or support equality. Which way will they ultimately go? Their legacy will tell.

Because the issues have become so politicized, I feel compelled to capture my thoughts in this book before they are silenced forever. "Diversity" and "inclusion" can't just be buzzwords; they are essential for a healthy society in which differences are respected and everyone belongs.

Today's diversity training looks at the sum of our parts — physical ability, faith, family background, race, sexual orientation, gender identity, work experience, and more. Recognizing how multiple factors influence our perspectives and how we process information uniquely helps us find our fit and understand how to include others in our experience.

For example, deafness is a dimension of my physical ability. But deafness is not simply the absence of sound. Deafness informs everything for me — from my choice of checkout aisle, what I worry about, and how I volunteer to which electronics I buy and how I approach problem-solving. It shapes my identity and transforms how I experience the world. Likewise, deafness also affects how others perceive me through unconscious bias.

Prejudice comes in many forms. For example:

- **Racism** is discrimination based on race or ethnicity.
- **Sexism** is discrimination based on gender.
- **Ableism** is:
    - "Discrimination or prejudice against individuals with disabilities."[2] or "... an assumption that it is necessary to cater only for able-bodied people."[3]

Drilling down further on ableism, academic and author Tom L. Humphries[4] (and expanded upon further by psychologist and Deaf advocate Harlan Lane)[5] coined the term **audism:**

- **Audism** is: "The notion that one is superior based on one's ability to hear or to behave in the manner of one who hears."

In public, all but the most stubborn bigots will deny being racist (even while making statements that suggest otherwise) because, deep down, they know that racism is unacceptable. Unlike racism or sexism, however, ableism is rarely acknowledged as discrimination. I spot ableist commentary every day, even from people who would never dream of minimizing someone's race or religious background. Declaring typical ability as superior is so deeply ingrained in society that people fiercely defend it. They might even suggest something is wrong with me for calling them out.

While a person with a disability might not have chosen their condition, that doesn't mean they actively wish for another life. If the disability was from birth, they adapt and modify processes, preferably with the availability of accessible options. If the disability was acquired later, they grieve, process, and hopefully learn coping strategies and behaviors because that's how humans deal with loss. Still, when frustrations arise, the exasperation is almost always due to accessibility barriers and how others treat the person in question rather than the condition itself.

A friend of mine, Michael, was born with undeveloped hands. When asked whether he'd choose to change if he could, he thought about his newly acquired adaptive vehicle and shrugged, "Nah." He didn't think in terms of superiority or inferiority. He just wanted tools to get stuff done.

Those who profess that typical ability is superior perpetuate a harmful mindset that lingers in a cloud of negativity. It would be convenient if every human possessed the same range of abilities for their body and mind, but they don't. Meanwhile, making judgments is never helpful. Many disabilities, including sensorineural hearing loss, do not have a cure today. While hearing devices or other assistive aids can provide considerable correction, they are still limited, and one is not truly "fixed." In addition, some people have supplemental complications, such as ear ringing or vertigo, which further exacerbate their condition. What should someone who lives with hearing loss do then, just wallow in their presumed inferiority? Instead of looking down, society should value and accommodate diverse abilities without prioritizing one over the other.

Identifying ableist commentary is pretty straightforward. Replace the word "deaf" or "disabled" in a sentence with another diverse segment — such as "person of color," "gay," or "female." Repeat your revised sentence and ask: Would you be uncomfortable saying that out loud? Would you cringe if someone else did? If the answer is yes, it's probably ableist.

Models of Disability

How people perceive disability falls under two models: medical and social.

- The medical model, introduced by psychiatrist Thomas Szasz[6] in the 1950s, focuses solely on the physiological condition and considers typical ability the only valid measurement standard. According to this model, success means a medical cure, period, and disability is reduced to a one-dimensional state of brokenness. *Sucks for you,* the medical model seems to say. *You fall outside the norm.*

- The social model emerged during the disability rights movement of the 1970s, and the term was coined by academic Mike Oliver.[7] In the social model, disability is defined as stigma and its barriers created by society — rather than the physical condition itself — and solutions focus on inclusion through accessibility and adaptation. For example, deafness is not a disability if the smoke alarm includes a flashing light.

Design Standards

Accessible design means individuals with disabilities can use a product as efficiently and independently as the non-disabled. **Universal design** extends beyond accessibility; it means optimal functionality is available to everyone — young or old, short or tall, disabled or not — and not just the average user.[8]

I notice a lot of shame-and-blame responses in particular with hearing loss, such as other people's outrage over missed sounds like door knocks. But getting annoyed at deafness is misplaced anger. It's like blaming the Bundt dish when the cake unmolds in chunks because you didn't bother to grease and flour the pan. Likewise, pointing fingers at ability differences to rebuke and shame excuses the fundamental problem of inaccessibility. When product design fails to consider access, it resembles diversity training from the '90s, a one-size-fits-all approach that favors the majority and glosses over the rest. It's as if the unvalidated starting assumption was, "All customers can hear audio notifications," but I'm being kind. The designers knew perfectly well that some consumers couldn't hear the alert and intentionally bypassed solutioning for an accessible alternative because they perceived the market segment was too small or, more likely, didn't matter. However, hearing loss is statistically relevant today by anyone's count; for example, one in five young people. It matters.

Book Summary

This book is intended as a rebuttal to an ableist society. It emphasizes the critical role of self-advocacy and effective communication in asserting one's needs. And finally, it explores the importance of accessibility and inclusivity because living authentically is only possible where space exists for your real self to succeed.

Whether you are personally impacted by hearing loss or work in a healthcare or technology-related field, this book strives to offer perspectives you might not have considered before. While my deaf journey is unique, the stories shared here might encourage you to reexamine your belief structure. I hope they inspire you to challenge personal assumptions and explore potential changes that could benefit you and those around you.

Good luck and Godspeed.

3

Secrets and Lies

I was born at four o'clock in the morning on the bathroom floor of our old house on Belle Avenue, half a block between Lake Erie to the north and the local hospital to the south. My mother had already given birth to four babies plus a stillborn in six years. She had no labor with me, a preemie who nevertheless resembled a bowling ball by eight months.

In kindergarten, I contracted rubella (also known as German measles) during a worldwide epidemic. I can still picture my classroom and its adjoining coat closet, which ended in a small restroom. A girl in my class regularly threw the soap bar out the bathroom window. I don't know why — perhaps it was an early form of social protest. But that is the snapshot forever burned in my brain: The day I was sent home sick from kindergarten, while waiting for my ride, I watched the girl sling the soap and grin like a murderous clown.

In grade school, I was diagnosed with severe hearing loss, initially attributed to my kindergarten rubella. Years later, however, my OB-GYN disputed my medical history, insisting that childhood German measles could not have been the culprit. Rubella was commonplace for decades before the epidemic, a fever and rash that eventually went away. Typically mild, children recovered without complication.

But not fetuses.

When a pregnant person contracted rubella in the first trimester, the virus was potentially fatal in the womb. It even had a name, congenital rubella syndrome (CRS),[9] and caused disability — most commonly deafness — or death to the fetus. Before the rubella vaccine became available, thousands of fetuses were miscarried, stillborn, or born with deafness or deaf/blindness after rubella exposure. The 1960s epidemics spurred the introduction of a new vaccine (later combined into the measles–mumps–rubella (MMR) shot) because of rubella's extreme impacts on fetal development.

I was around twenty-five, visiting family in my hometown, when a relative confided that my mother had been exposed to rubella when she was pregnant with me, which likely caused my deafness. I remember being surprised — this was new information! I brought it up at the dinner table as innocent conversation, with no intention of casting blame, and my mother reacted so angrily that my sister kicked me sharply under the table to shut up.

"Who told you that?" my mother demanded. I didn't want to betray my source, so I replied that it must have been the family doctor. "I don't know why he would talk about that," she snapped. "He should know better."

Things began to make sense. For starters, my hearing loss was evident long before I had rubella in kindergarten. I was a bellowing toddler, often compared to the obnoxiously booming television character Charlie Bratton, originated by comedian Jackie Gleason. In the spirit of disclosure, the character's full nickname was "Loudmouth Charlie Bratton." In retrospect, the moniker seems mean since I couldn't hear myself talk at average volume, but no one knew that yet. The nickname stuck. My mother called me Charlie for the rest of her life.

I never resented my mother for my deafness any more than I begrudged my siblings for passing along chicken pox. However, withholding crucial information about my health history while disingenuously pointing the finger at my own kindergarten rubella instilled a distrust I never quite got past. While knowing exactly what happened in utero is impossible, why leave out the most probable explanation?

If we had been able to talk about it, the situation might have been salvageable. Still, it wasn't surprising that my mother cut off that potential dinner table conversation. Deafness was a touchy subject for her, and she often became impatient when I couldn't hear. Today, when I encounter people unable to hide their irritation at having to repeat more than once for someone with hearing loss, I recognize that tone, the sound of my childhood.

* * *

With a large family, parental oversight tends to loosen exponentially after each birth. As a fifth child, I got different iterations of my parents than my older siblings describe, and the opposite of my younger sister's close bond, born six years after me.

By the time I came into being, my parents were hands-off. I think they engaged mentally for the first few children and then pressed autoplay, at least when it came to me. Deafness gave me no extra guardrails that I recall. With minimal parental intervention, I had the freedom to navigate and discover the world around me. Looking back, I value the independence and strong work ethic instilled by my parents' example. While their approach might seem bloodless, their unwavering mission in life was to push their kids out of the nest to fly on their own and sell the house so they couldn't move back.

I consider myself fortunate to have grown up in a neighborhood of fertile Catholic families who spawned over a hundred grade-school-age children on a single half-block. There were friends of every age from every family. The older kids looked out for the younger ones, and I benefited from having popular siblings. We formed a small army and gathered every night for outdoor games, our playing field spanning multiple front yards and extending to backyards for hide-and-seek. With safety in numbers, our parents pushed us out the door after dinner to give themselves peace, quiet, and presumably cocktails. It takes a village, the saying goes, and I'm grateful that magical place was mine.

I was a smart kid, practically born reading. My father was a writer, and his grandfather was a language professor and playwright, so early literacy was either a genetic bonus or overflow knowledge from my siblings. I wasn't a prodigy, just an advanced reader with a razor-sharp memory for anything I saw, no doubt leaning into my other senses to compensate for limited hearing.

I loved going to the library as much as I loved words. At age six, I walked to the stacks every Saturday by myself. Armed with the library card I stole from my mother, I flashed the adult ID to the amused librarian, who recognized a kindred bookworm and allowed me access to the grown-up section, ordinarily off-limits to children. It must have been peculiar to see me perched on an oversized chair, my feet sticking out, engrossed in psychology manuals bigger than my head, but I didn't care. Being surrounded by books was literary heaven.

Meanwhile, my hearing loss remained undiagnosed until grade school. I wasn't aware at the time that my sound processing was different — you don't know what you don't know — but certain memories tell a different story. In kindergarten, my class performed in a musical program that my mother attended. Minutes before we took the stage, I realized I had zero knowledge of the choreography. I discovered there had been a rehearsal I knew nothing about, so I improvised. Afterward, my mother was furious at my comic performance. "Disgraceful," she uttered, tight-lipped, and she wouldn't make eye contact, embarrassed to be seen with me.

Most likely, I hadn't heard the teacher announce the special rehearsal. Looking back, what stands out is my instinctive reaction. I didn't even try to defend myself. By age five, I had already internalized the notion I messed up at something that everyone else had been capable of, and I needed to lie low.

Despite a few hiccups, my childhood was happy. I liked school, had friends, and was treated well. I heard *some* sound but was oblivious to everyone else's auditory experience. Few electronics existed, so inaccessible design was not yet a noticeable pattern. As a kid, I played a lot of sports at school and home, which were visual enough activities that hearing wasn't an issue.

Teachers at our parochial grade school noticed my deafness early on. The school nurse used to conduct informal (and nerve-racking) hearing tests by lining up a group of students, crouching behind like a cat waiting to pounce, and whispering behind our backs. The school told my mother I had hearing loss, which she vehemently denied. This information was courtesy of my oldest cousin, Sharon, who relayed the story years later. My mother confided in her brother's wife (Sharon's mother), so Sharon always had the inside scoop on family gossip.

My first awareness of accessibility shame came in second grade. My Catholic grade school class was preparing to make our first Communion, and completing the sacrament of confession was a prerequisite to ensure recipients were in a state of grace, cleansed of sin. The confessional space in the adjoining church was three wooden stalls the size of phone booths. The priest sat in the middle chamber and alternated from side to side via small screened windows, which slid open like a fast-food drive-through. A padded step lay under each window for the confessee to kneel on.

To a person with hearing loss, the confession process was a one-two punch of futility: The ritual was conducted in the dark and behind a screen barrier, which made lipreading challenging. To complicate matters, I had to stand on the kneeler just to reach the window due to my short height. However, my body weight wasn't enough to keep the occupancy light steady, which ratted out to the priest that I wasn't kneeling. A gruff and impatient man, the monsignor berated me the entire time for speaking too loudly, asking him to repeat himself, and failing to kneel. When I left the stall, I cried in the pew as I recited prayers, hoping others would interpret my tears as sincere repentance for my sins because I hadn't even heard the penance assignment. I was off to a terrible start.

For my second confession attempt, I aimed to get in and out fast. I asked only for a blessing to speed up my exit. The cranky monsignor accused me of being unrepentant and labeled me the worst sinner of all, a devastating burden for a seven-year-old. Ironically, the audiocentric design of the confession process was so traumatizing that I resorted to dishonesty. In desperation, I confessed to a made-up sin on the spot to end the ordeal.

At least twice a year after that, my class lined up for mandatory confession, during which I continued my deceit. I patiently awaited a larger classmate's emergence from the confessional booth, then seamlessly merged between the crowded arrival and departure lines in the narrow aisle behind him with all the finesse of a jewel thief stepping through a laser security system. I shadowed him into the pew, knelt with head bowed, and recited a fake penance (with honest prayers) to maintain the façade. Perfecting this strategy, I avoided the confessional booth for the next six years until graduation.

A person reading this might wonder, "Why didn't you speak up?" But shame has an illogical effect. Why individuals don't immediately come forward is never self-explanatory. Unless you have personally experienced the stigma surrounding hearing loss (or shame-triggering crimes such as domestic abuse, racial profiling, or sexual harassment), you're unlikely to grasp an individual's decision-making process. However, their viewpoint is still valid even if your reaction would differ.

A hearing family member will never understand their deaf relative's contrary choices in the face of shame. For example, a deaf person asking for a comment to be repeated is a very different experience than someone hearing. It doesn't mean the family member isn't willing to listen and discuss the reason. But context matters. Shame overshadows everything when it comes to fueling a victim's impulse to hide.

Years ago, I had a conversation with a co-worker. It was before smartphones, and I was debating going somewhere unfamiliar. I needed to know exactly how to get there and details about the venue. My preparation process was not that different from someone with low vision who counted steps as a navigation methodology. And the co-worker completely dismissed my deaf perspective as being high-maintenance and said in a patronizing voice, "Just go. Stop worrying about it. Everything will be fine."

The conversation illustrated how much our experiences diverged. In the years before smartphones, texting, or ride-sharing, the prospect of getting lost was entirely different for me. I had no accessible options; I had to rely on my own knowledge and abilities instead of my ears. He could whip out his flip phone or ask someone on a noisy street for help. I could not. The deaf filter of my life experience could not have been more distant.

The school nurse's whispered hearing tests continued. By the end of second grade, the nuns held an intervention with my mother regarding my need for hearing aids. Per my cousin Sharon, the discussion grew contentious, and my mother resisted every step of the way.

Medical procedures followed. I spent a week in the hospital undergoing a barrage of tests. It was a positive experience due to an extensive crafts room in the children's ward and frankly resembled going to sleep-away camp, if a camp also included exploratory ear surgery and an official hearing test (or audiogram) in a soundproof booth. My audiogram scores confirmed severe deafness, meaning I couldn't hear sound — any sound — under 70 decibels (dB).

Eventually, my mother took me downtown to get fitted for analog hearing aids that blasted speech and noise equally. My loss was worse in the low-frequency range. This was unusual but lucky, as speech typically occurs at higher frequencies. As a result, my super-powerful aids helped me more than most people with severe deafness. With enough amplification, I could hear music and the sound of my own voice. With lipreading, I could understand speech. Basically, I could pass for hearing.

On the walk home from the bus stop, multiple kids in the neighborhood excitedly asked about my devices. The news spread throughout the block like wildfire, and I welcomed their curiosity. Their young minds had not yet formed negative opinions about hearing loss, only excitement over a device equivalent to a new toy. The novelty held their interest for maybe a day and then was forgotten.

On the first day of wearing the hearing aids to school, the feedback started — the high-pitched whistling that occurred when the device volume was too high, or the microphone was touched. I began to cry, not sure what to do. My teacher sent me to the principal's office, a scary prospect and my first time inside those fortress-like doors. Although the nuns were not usually known for their empathy, in this situation, they showed mercy. No one in the school office wanted to phone my mother, perhaps remembering the earlier intervention, so the principal herself took on the task. She made the call in front of me, got the needed information, and then gave me simple instructions to fix the squealing.

I still remember how the stern, feared figure transformed into a relatable human being in my eyes, taking the time to chat with me about her aunt's hearing aids and giving me the space to regain my composure. Most of the short stories I wrote featured a superhero/angel mash-up, and I wondered if perhaps her nun's habit was her cape and if her superpower was kindness. Those thoughts evaporated quickly. She resumed her formidable, ruler-wielding ways as soon as the next troublemaker arrived.

Faith and my hearing loss continued to intersect. At ten, my mother took me to an acupuncturist to fix my hearing, a treatment I'm not sure was ever intended for sensorineural loss. As we left for the appointment, my grandmother pressed a scapular into my hand for protection. The scapular was a string necklace from which pictures of Jesus hung on my chest and back, like wearing a tiny sandwich board advertisement under my shirt, and the plastic images stuck uncomfortably to my skin. I was startled by the implication. Divine intervention had been invoked! Yet my sister's eyeglasses didn't warrant scapular protection, which seemed like a double standard.

The acupuncture appointment was a disaster. No one explained why sticking needles into my head and attaching an electric current was a good idea. For an unprepared ten-year-old, the procedure was the equivalent of jamming my finger into an electric socket.

Needless to say, the acupuncture treatment did not fix my hearing. There was no second round. My loss continued to progress. By my teens, it measured 95 dB or a profoundly deaf classification. Despite this, with my powerful hearing aids and expert lipreading, I could still understand speech. For the most part.

I attended the local high school. With multiple new teachers yearly, only three instructors ever referenced my ears. I used the awkward silence on the subject to my advantage. Despite my love for sports, I convinced our family doctor to excuse me from four years of physical education, falsely claiming that taking gym while deaf was too dangerous. (Really, I just didn't want the hassle of changing clothes in the middle of the day.) No one ever challenged this.

I remember all three teachers, but one in particular stands out. In my junior year, she told me I'd probably never get hired in the workforce because of my hearing loss. I think she thought she was doing me a favor by preparing me for the real world, but her words were overly pessimistic, even for that era. I can't recall anyone else making a discouraging statement about my hearing loss during my entire youth and only once as an adult; that's how out of the ordinary it was. I remember being mortified by her omen, not just for the message but because I had a crush on the social science teacher who sat across from her in the teachers' offices, and he was within earshot. Decades later, I still flash back to her doomsday premonition at job interviews. (But the joke's on her since I've gotten virtually every job I've applied for.)

High school meant continuing to do pretty much anything I wanted. Having unrestricted freedom from my parents fostered considerable self-sufficiency. I never had a curfew, was never grounded, and never had conversations with my folks about grades (although I did well academically), course selection, homework, extracurriculars, or what I would do after graduation. My parents never expressed an interest in meeting my friends or asked whether I was dating anyone.

We talked about other things, however. My father taught my sister and me ballroom dancing, aikido, and chess, and we played tennis on Sunday mornings. We threw darts in the basement, and he'd sometimes take us along to pick up the Friday night pizza or visit the wine store, which always meant a pretzel stick from the jar on the counter.

My mother epitomized the value of hard work. From her, I learned the importance of organization and the art of frugality through clipping coupons. She taught me to cook. (My first cookbook was composed entirely of her cherished recipes.) Under her instruction, I learned how to bake, temper chocolate in a double boiler, and make water-bath custard. Sewing was another skill she imparted, and to this day, I'm grateful for her passing down this expertise. Her repertoire also extended to old-school household wisdom, like the beauty of cleaning windows with vinegar and newspaper. Her resourcefulness was put to good use as my Girl Scout troop leader for a short time, at least until she dumped a plate of spaghetti sauce on a misbehaving scout's head during a campout.

My parents were complete opposites: My father was a tall, fairhaired German, and my mother was short with black hair and olive skin. He was intellectually gifted and grew up poor, a reserved and introverted scholarship student. In contrast, my mother was an extroverted sorority girl with an Irish mother who came from wealth and an immigrant father who established himself as a successful banker in the local Romanian community.

A journalist, my father was a man of few words and comfortable with silence. I inherited his introversion, physical attributes, and aversion to sentimentality. I often wrote short stories and plays on his manual typewriter and borrowed his books. His library was open territory regardless of whether the material was age-appropriate. One time, I picked *The Rise and Fall of the Third Reich*[10] for a school book report, causing the nuns to call our house aghast. Unconcerned, my father mentioned the call to me and asked whether I thought the author's lack of objectivity had compromised the book's credibility. I was eight.

My mother was the social manager of our family, a chatty contrast to my father's reserve. Despite our cone of silence about hearing loss, she was not unfriendly or neglectful. I remain amazed at her tireless work ethic with few of today's modern conveniences. She was the only girl amongst three brothers, and she hosted all the family parties and cared for her widowed mother when she was dying. I can only imagine the challenges of her married life, raising five rambunctious kids under the age of seven (and later, six children under the age of twelve) without, in those early years, a car or dishwasher, no mobile devices, and a husband who traveled constantly for work.

It's easy to take someone so selfless for granted, which is unfortunate. I have only the best memories of the annual rituals my mother orchestrated, which I still honor today. Cumulatively, she baked hundreds of tins of Christmas cookies for us to decorate, hard-boiled eggs for coloring, compiled Easter baskets, and wrangled Halloween costumes. Stockings were hung, and we decorated trees with cherished ornaments every year. We displayed the flag on patriotic holidays, and family picnics were routine. She always asked what kind of cake I wanted for my birthday: lemon meringue pie, which she made from scratch.

While we clashed on matters of hearing loss, I still have many good memories of my mother. She was a football fanatic; my siblings knew not to call during games on Sunday, and many of her Christmas gifts from her children were squishy toys for her to throw at the television screen during tense competitions. She played bridge and did crossword puzzles. She was a loyal friend to childhood classmates and stayed in touch with former neighbors. I think of her often; she smelled like suntan lotion and cherry almond moisturizer.

Despite our shared love for the written word, my father and I were cordial but not close. His frequent travel kept him from most of my significant life events like school plays and graduations. Even when his work brought him to my town after I relocated, he didn't necessarily feel the need to connect. I'd find out a month later, think it odd, and then shrug. That was my father.

I never took his absences personally, as he was consistent and predictable. He did participate in a high school Career Day event one year, which my sister must have arranged since I played no role in his involvement. I remember the excitement from the teachers and students about his presence and the lines that formed to speak with him. And if caught in the right mood, he could be exceptionally witty. He was a gifted singer in his church's choir. I told him my friend Heidi performed as a soloist at funerals, and he promptly coined the term "mor-sician."

Regardless of my father's travel, he was still present in a number of good memories: Carving Halloween pumpkins. Cooking stinky preparations of octopus and squid, eaten with chopsticks. He was generous, and when he spoke, which wasn't that often, I thought he was the smartest person alive.

I also have warm memories of my school years during the 1960s and 1970s even though students with hearing loss had few options back then: attend specialized schools for the deaf or keep up with their peers at mainstream institutions through lipreading like me. Assistive technology, including mobile devices, was decades away from invention. In fact, my family had only just acquired a three-channel, black-and-white television.

It was a different time. For someone with hearing loss (but not recognized as deaf), the playing field wasn't level, not even a little — although I only realized this in retrospect, years later. My situation was not a shared reality. I was the lone boat on the water, the missing sock in the dryer.

When it came to deafness, I was on my own.

4

Superheroes

Flashback: I am in the emergency room surrounded by medical professionals in superhero attire: Catwoman, Spiderman, a Ninja Turtle. Also, a clown, a grape bunch, and Tiny Tim. I think I'm hallucinating until Elvis wishes me a happy Halloween, and the context becomes clear.

For a minute, being in the presence of heroic defenders feels familiar. Since I was a kid, my fantasy was to be an introverted superhero who read minds and rescued people with kindness while flying through the air, cloaked in anonymity. I wanted to know what was going on in their heads to understand their motivations. I fancied myself as an interceptor between heaven and earth — an angel in training — helping people in need from above.

It wasn't lost on me that virtually every superhero and villain had a physical disability or defining trauma. This is an actual cliché upon which comic book geeks write dissertations. Disability is routinely used as a catalyst for writers to illustrate their characters' tortured souls, reveal flaws and vulnerabilities, manufacture sympathy, and generate obstacles to advance the story.

However, those dramatic narratives also reinforce the unfortunate message that individuals with disabilities need to overcompensate for their limitations through extraordinary achievement (or supernatural powers) to justify their worth. In other words, someone with a disability must perform better than everyone else to be thought half as competent as someone non-disabled. It's probably the same lens through which women have historically been measured against men, only multiplied for disability. Even though no one ever said this out loud, the awareness always lurked in the back of my mind.

But today, I need a superhero of my own. I am lying on a hospital bed, admitted through an urgent care center referral. A doctor bends over me, trying to insert a central line into my chest while a specialist stabs my hands and feet, competing to strike blood first to get an IV going. I desperately need to cough. My lungs are bursting with fluid — double pneumonia — and my veins have collapsed. The overhead lights burn. I've been shot in the head, or so it feels, from the blistering fever I've been trying to shake for over a week.

The doctor pushes the needle hard into my chest, a railroad spike plunging through the skin. The clock on the wall ticks in slow motion, and I focus on it, watching time stretch and elongate. He pushes harder, and I can feel the bed's metal springs give way under my buttocks as the pressure of his hands crushes my chest.

He's going to break my ribs, I think, alarmed, but I can't speak without coughing. I've already been admonished to hold still twice after half-hearted wheezes. The clock ticks to ten minutes, then fifteen. I cough weakly, eliciting murderous glares from the doctor hovering over me and spitting saliva on my face as he talks. My neck spasms, and I finally speak, asking them to please turn off the bright overhead light, which feels like an acid shower scalding the skin off my face.

A medical student with a costume arrow through his head attempts to complete the intake interview as I lie prone. "If your heart stops beating," he reads aloud, "do you want to be resuscitated?"

I wheeze out a response, "No ... God, no." My heart is the least of my worries. The doctor will suffocate me first.

As the clock ticks away, reaching the twenty-five-minute mark, I pray for relief. *This is it. This is the absolute limit of what I can bear.* I think about my health care directive, relieved that it specifies cremation and not open-casket viewing, sparing mourners the sight of my head attached to what will surely end up as a pile of mangled bones. Just when I feel like giving up, the medical student places his hand over mine and gives it a reassuring squeeze. For a moment, I visualize his cape of kindness. He smiles just a little, and everything changes. The needle finally slides into my chest vein. The central line is in.

A week earlier, sick with a hacking cough and fever, I had snagged a walk-in appointment at my regular clinic. The random physician who attended to me was aloof and dismissive. Maybe she thought I was a hypochondriac. Maybe she had been counting on that canceled appointment to catch up on paperwork. Or maybe she took me less seriously because I told her I was deaf.

The fever had roller-coasted for over a week, spiking at 105°F. She listened to my chest and heard me cough hard enough that I couldn't finish my sentences. She said she didn't hear anything in my lungs and didn't need to order a chest x-ray. She seemed disappointed I had a measurable fever that she couldn't chalk up to my imagination. She hedged that perhaps, maybe, it might be mono. But no antibiotics for me, she declared, pointing to the pill bottle diagram on the wall with a prominent "x" in a circle, indicating that her office prescribed them sparingly.

That was Friday. On Saturday, I called the clinic again, coughing uncontrollably. The on-call physician was worried and advised me to go to the emergency room if I couldn't breathe. She was dismayed by my hacking and horrified that her colleague hadn't prescribed cough syrup and, frankly, antibiotics. I told her I could breathe, but the fever had risen, and the cough was worse. On Sunday, I went to the urgent care center for a chest x-ray.

"Pneumonia in both lungs," diagnosed the urgent care center physician. "I'm going to admit you to the hospital overnight for intravenous antibiotics."

I dashed home to grab my laptop just as the on-call physician at the family practice called back to check on me, worried her colleague had dropped the ball. I told her the urgent care center was admitting me to the hospital and that I needed to go.

"I'm sorry," she said. "For everything."

The overnight stretched into eight days in the hospital, with new complications appearing daily. But I already knew what was coming: I was going to lose a critical chunk of my remaining hearing.

Even though I was classified as profoundly deaf, I always had some sound left to lose. While a person can go a very long time without noticing their initial hearing loss, subsequent progression feels quite dramatic toward the end, like the cascading chain reactions in a nuclear fission experiment. (The less you have, the more you notice.)

The pattern certainly was familiar. In my late twenties and thirties, I came down with a respiratory virus every year after Christmas travel. "It's a regional germ that you don't have immunity to," explained a physician, "coupled with an allergy of some kind." Following each bout of illness, I would notice a drop in my hearing, a change in pitch or volume, or a decreased ability to understand speech, which my annual audiogram would confirm. It was consistent, predictable, and measurable.

Needless to say, progressive hearing loss sucked. It was the entire cycle of grief played out in an endless, downward spiral. Losing my remaining hearing all at once would have been preferable. Jump to the end, accept it, and get on with life, but the reality was far more agonizing: years — no, decades — of perpetual breath-holding, always waiting and wondering when the next slide would come. Every day became a delicate balancing act, constantly recalibrating because my hearing differed from the previous week, like grasping a high ledge and feeling my fingers slipping. Dread, uncertainty, and worry were constant companions, boxed into an overwhelming package. And no one ever believed me when I forecast the next drop.

"Respiratory infections don't cause deafness," said every physician I've ever asked. Medically, bronchitis and pneumonia were not established causes of progressive hearing loss. Yet I knew. Every time my lungs engaged in battle, whether from a virus, antibiotics, or nonstop coughing, tiny gremlins snuck into my ear canals, tossed a few Molotov cocktails, and left carnage in their wake. The medical community dismissed it as nonsense, but I knew. Every single time. Of course, I knew.

And you will know when it happens to you.

5

Hearing 101

When it comes to hearing loss, false assumptions abound. For example, most people think the term "deaf" means a complete inability to hear or involves someone who relies on sign language for communication. However, deafness is rarely an all-or-nothing proposition, and sign language is not a prerequisite. Hearing loss encompasses many variables: limited volume, gaps in frequencies or pitch, and difficulty understanding speech. While a tiny percentage of deaf individuals are indeed without any sound at all, most profoundly deaf people still have some remaining hearing (also called "residual hearing"). I couldn't hear a jet plane scream overhead with just my natural hearing, yet I could hear or guess most speech when amplified by powerful hearing aids. Go figure.

The physiological process of hearing is not limited to the ear canal. Hearing is controlled by the brain, thanks to the cochlea, a small organ in the inner ear, lined with thousands of receptors called hair cells. When sound enters your ear, those hair cells convert that sound to electrical signals and transmit them to your brain via the auditory nerve. The brain then interprets those signals as sound.

Sensorineural hearing loss occurs when the fragile hair cells of the cochlea are damaged, usually through noise exposure, aging, genetics, or illness. People sometimes refer to this as nerve deafness, but that's misleading. With sensorineural hearing loss, often there's nothing wrong with the auditory nerve but damage to the hair cells of the cochlea, which send the signals to the nerve.

Progressive loss means hair cells die in splotches. As a condominium board member, I like to compare sensorineural hearing loss to our building's mutilated front lawn. Our grass has patches of damage from where neighbor kids rode their bikes, dogs urinated, and chipmunks dug burrows. Twice now, hit-and-run autos have plowed gaping holes in the metal fence surrounding our property, leaving telltale skid marks on the sidewalk and lawn, dragging down the anchoring cement posts. Progressive hearing loss is just like that.

Snail-shaped, the cochlea functions like a rolled-up piano keyboard. As sound waves travel through the cochlea, different areas vibrate based on frequency (or pitch).[11] Hearing loss is typically classified as low- or high-frequency, depending on where the damaged hair cells have splotched. Low-frequency sounds cause vibrations in one area of the cochlea, while high-frequency sounds cause vibrations in another. Location matters.

Even though I was born with limited hearing, it took over forty years to progressively lose the rest as patches of hair cell damage crept indefinitely like lopsided weeds. I often visualized my deafness as a movie villain writhing from bullet holes and multiple stab wounds, crawling through an air shaft, bleeding through the ceiling tiles, yet refusing to die.

The biology of cochlear hair cells starts at conception, which is why fetal exposure to rubella in the first trimester is a critical risk for deafness. Thanks to the MMR vaccine, rubella was eradicated in the United States decades ago. However, as the population of unvaccinated individuals reaches childbearing age or travels abroad (where rubella is still common), it seems inevitable that German measles will make a reappearance in the US. Invariably, unvaccinated pregnant people (or those with weakened immune systems who are expecting) will be exposed to rubella once again, which in the past caused fetal deafness or death.

By the tenth week of gestation, a fetus has all of the hair cells it will get, around 16,000.[12] Cochlear hair cells in mammals do not regenerate; interestingly, they do in birds, fish, and reptiles.[13] Note: As long as I've been aware, scientists continue to research the prospect of regenerating new cochlear hair cells in humans.

Deafness has multiple levels of classification, defined by ranges of the softest sound a person can recognize without a hearing device or amplification:

Classification	Softest Sound Recognized (measured by decibel (dB))
Typical hearing	0 – 25 dB
Mild hearing loss	26 – 40 dB
Moderate hearing loss	41 – 55 dB
Moderately severe deafness	56 – 70 dB
Severe deafness	71 – 90 dB
Profound deafness	91 – 130 dB

Compilation from multiple sources.

Hearing aids are typically recommended after diagnosis of mild to moderate sensorineural hearing loss. Devices range from simple models amplifying sound to advanced digital devices using sophisticated processing and technological capabilities.

Once hair cell loss advances to severe or profound deafness, however, hearing aids may no longer provide sufficient benefit since the devices still rely on the damaged hair cells to transmit sound to the auditory nerve. At that point, an individual with significant hearing loss might be considered a candidate for cochlear implantation (often shorthanded to "CI").

Cochlear implantation is a surgical process in which computer chips are installed inside the skull and cochlea to recreate hair cell stimulation and send signals to the auditory nerve. The CI process also leverages an external processor and proprietary software. It is not an implantable hearing aid, nor does it restore natural hearing. In fact, the full-insertion CI surgical procedure generally destroys the remainder of the natural hearing, although hybrid preservation strategies exist today for certain scenarios. Once activated, the electronics take over communication with the auditory nerve, thereby recreating the sense of hearing.

Hearing loss differs by individual. Likewise, not all deaf are the same, so it's helpful to know the various classifications:

- **Deaf** (with a capital "D") are individuals who identify as culturally Deaf and members of the Deaf community.
- **deaf** (with a lower-case "d") are individuals with significant hearing loss who do not identify as culturally Deaf.
- **d/Deaf** (spelled with a lowercase "d," slash, then capital "D") is an inclusive term that encompasses all people with hearing loss.

- **late deafened** are individuals who experience deafness as adults, sometimes called "oral deaf," meaning they use verbal speech for communication.
- **hard of hearing** are individuals with mild to moderate hearing loss who generally do not identify as deaf.

Note: Use "d/Deaf" or "hard of hearing" when referencing individuals with hearing loss. The term "hearing impaired" has negative connotations and should be avoided.

Culturally Deaf

The Deaf community (with a capital "D") refers to individuals who identify as members of a language-based culture. American Sign Language (ASL) is the primary language used by the Deaf in the United States and Canada. (Other countries have their own Deaf culture and corresponding sign language, such as British Sign Language.)

In Deaf culture, deafness is a source of pride rather than disability. The passing down of stories, rituals, shared experiences and history, and a unique language is highly valued and comparable to the preservation of any ethnic legacy. The birth of a Deaf child is a cause for celebration, an opportunity to pass this cultural heritage to the next generation.

Many culturally Deaf are physically deaf, having been born deaf or lost their hearing at a young age. Hearing members of a Deaf family typically identify as part of the Deaf community, as well. Ninety percent of deaf children are born to hearing parents[14] and typically are not members of the culturally Deaf community. Relevant terms are:

- **DOD** means Deaf of Deaf (or a Deaf child born to Deaf parents).
- **CODA** means Child of Deaf Adults (or a hearing child born to Deaf parents).

Late-Deafened

Individuals with hearing loss who become deaf later in life are classified as "late-deafened." The late-deafened enthusiastically embrace technology to reconnect with the hearing world but might also learn sign language. Unless they have a previous association with the culturally Deaf community, their perspective generally views deafness as a physical condition; they were born with the ability to hear and speak, developed a dependence on hearing, and subsequently lost it. However, deafness becomes an acquired piece of their identity.

Hard of Hearing

Those with mild hearing loss are categorized as "hard of hearing." Interestingly, within the Deaf community, anyone not part of the Deaf culture is labeled "hard of hearing," regardless of the level of their hearing loss. From the Deaf perspective, labeling someone "hard of hearing" is a faint insult, meaning, "You are not one of us. You are not Deaf."

Individuals who are hard of hearing often suffer the most from harassment from their hearing peers, as their loss is generally viewed as not trying hard enough. My friend Lee used to say being Deaf (with a capital "D") was preferable because the general public felt no remorse over treating hard of hearing like an inflatable clown punching toy. To society, hard of hearing was still "hearing," just defectively so. By contrast, most hearing people were too intimidated by language barriers to openly jerk around the culturally Deaf, although they might do so behind their backs.

* * *

Like diversity, deafness is not one-size-fits-all. Nor is my journey, either then or now.

6

You Can't Even Tell!

Almost every week for as long as I can remember, someone learns I'm deaf and exclaims, "You can't even tell!" — or its fraternal twin, "You'd never know!" I respond that the statement is not a compliment because, conversely, it means that "being able to tell" is bad. Their words imply that disability, like dirty dishes, should be hidden before guests arrive.

I've had this conversation too many times to count. The comments might appear harmless on their own, but in bulk, they're called microaggressions. Microaggressions are tiny digs that occur constantly from multiple sources and directions, ultimately creating an avalanche of social pressure. The individuals claiming the phrase firmly believe they are paying a compliment and that my objections are false modesty. However, their words betray their belief that passing for a hearing person is something to strive for, never mind that it's only for appearance's sake.

Praising someone for their disability being less visible is like complimenting a biracial person for having ambiguous skin color. You would never say, "You can't even tell!" to a girl in a STEM program because you know that would perpetuate a harmful stereotype. It's no different for hearing loss.

When you praise someone for appearing non-disabled, you minimize their experience. Yet, their situation could be far more complex than you imagine. They might also struggle with asking for access. Meanwhile, your remark reinforces that visibility is something to be embarrassed about, even if that's not how you meant it. The bright spot of "you can't even tell" is false assumptions are brought to light, which hopefully leads to an educational opportunity.

Other false assumptions pertain to hearing loss demographics. Hearing loss has always affected older individuals in particular and is the third most common chronic health condition facing seniors today:

- **1 in 3** senior citizens has hearing loss.[15] [16]
- **1 in 2** older than seventy-five has hearing loss.[17]

However, times have changed. While aging was the number one cause of hearing loss in the past, noise exposure is the primary culprit now, and it disproportionately affects young people. Teen hearing loss cases have increased by 30 percent in the last twenty years due to excessive sound levels.[18] In fact, children are now losing their hearing faster than their parents.

- **1 in 5** teenagers (20 percent) already has significant hearing loss, according to The World Health Organization (WHO).[19]
- **1 in 6** American adults (15.5 percent) has trouble hearing, according to the Centers for Disease Control and Prevention (CDC).[20]

- **1 in 8** people (12.5 percent) aged twelve years or older has hearing loss in both ears, according to The National Institutes of Health (NIH).[21]
- **1 in 4** people (25 percent) worldwide will have hearing loss by 2050, according to WHO.[22]

How did this happen? Environmental noise levels have exploded in the modern world. Specifically, earbuds at high volume, thunderous concerts and sporting events, buzzing lawnmowers and other loud machinery, exploding fireworks, and roaring traffic are all contributing factors. The CDC indicates exposure to sound levels at 70 to 85 dB or higher for extended periods can damage hair cells (and even quicker when noise gets louder).[23] By reference, 70 dB equates to the sound of a washing machine. Once hair cells begin dying, the human response is to increase volume to compensate, creating a vicious death spiral.

The emergence of hearing loss amongst Millennials and Generation Z, who have been the driving force behind many cultural changes in recent years, is a significant shift. Youth represent a new and influential demographic in this area, like baby dinosaurs hatching: unthreatening at first but capable of transforming into powerful, snarling beasts. They don't romanticize their sense of hearing, don't view themselves as disabled, and don't feel they need to be fixed. Instead, they want cutting-edge technology, and they want it now.

I take great interest in knowing that hearing loss has expanded to the influencer generations. As changemakers, I believe they are well-positioned to advocate for a more inclusive society. I particularly admire twenty- and thirty-somethings as a political force because they can be somewhat self-centered, which is necessary to disrupt long-standing social stigmas. They reject the notion of shame and demand authenticity on issues that matter to them. They are also digital natives, unaware of life before mobile devices or accessibility features. They have high expectations for societal change but also presume that stuff will be given to them. These very traits are what give them a strategic advantage. They represent a large voting bloc and can wield their purchasing power to demand technological progress. Those of us who grew up before accommodation laws lack that sense of entitlement, which is our disadvantage, truly. We accepted the status quo because no other options existed.

The younger generations are also crucial allies in the fight against ableism. Their schools were/are diversity proponents, and they're not afraid to show their individuality. They see the world as nuanced and know the importance of inclusion.

Case in point: Recently, my friend Danica's preteen daughter quite matter-of-factly told her mother she was going to have three children, "A him/his, a her/hers, and a they/theirs." I did a double-take when Danica told me this story, but I loved it. Her daughter's mindset automatically defaulted to an inclusive state where traditional gender roles were not mandatory.

I'm also inspired by how readily younger generations accept diversity without judgment. Danica's daughter's class includes students who have bipolar disorder or experience panic attacks, and they openly discuss their stories and accommodation needs. This transparency normalizes these issues as visible and unremarkable. The other kids say, "That's just Paul or Ringo in the corner having a panic attack, and they need us to give them space." No stigma. Everyone belongs.

What if everyone thought that way?

7

Belonging

B elonging means a lot in grade school. You want to be accepted just like everyone else. But when you're the only student with hearing aids, it's hard to feel like you fit in.

As a child, I dreaded my annual hearing test. Back then, audiologists were my nemeses, a fate worse than going to the dentist. That's saying something, too, considering my childhood dentist shunned Novocain and eventually quit because he disliked kids.

To be fair, I don't think the audiologists liked me any better. In my mind, they saw me as a grim disappointment as they tracked my profoundly deaf scores on paper, bamboozled by my lack of a deaf accent. I bristled at how appointments ended with the audiologists' tragic reactions. They stared at my test results like I had flunked out of school, shook their heads, and pursed their lips with chagrin because the scores were progressively worse.

After a series of rueful sighs, they'd muster all their energy to summarize: "At least your speech is okay." "It's good that you don't need glasses." Or the old standby: "You can't even tell!" — as if those were the only redeeming aspects of my presumably miserable life. Usually, I scowled, wishing the floor would open and swallow them whole ahead of their conclusion: "Well, the only stronger hearing aid is a body device with long cords, and you don't want to wear *that*."

I wish I had been brave enough to call out their negativity back then. All their overly dramatic reactions did was make me feel bad about failing a medical diagnostic test and convince me to cheat. I resorted to turning up my hearing aids past an appropriate level, stealthily reading lips through the soundproof window, and figuring out a logical pattern for pressing the button in the sound booth to confirm I had heard something (when I hadn't).

I didn't know that my type of sensorineural hearing loss didn't get better; it's permanent and progressive. Yet every year, I went to my appointment and told the audiologist that maybe, just maybe, my scores had improved, and every year, I went through the same cycles of grief and shame when they had not.

Fortunately, not all was disastrous on the Ear Nose Throat (ENT) Clinic front. I had an enlightening experience with an audiologist in my early twenties. On my first visit, I asked her to not react when reviewing my previous audiograms. I said I was aware that my unaccented speech was a cruel decoy for audiologists ambushed by the depth of my deficit on paper, the *Ripley's Believe It or Not!* freak that I was. And could she please not register dismay on her face if my scores dropped from the last time? Because I knew already, okay, and I needed her to be objective.

And to her credit, she was. She conducted the test professionally and never once betrayed any emotion or judgment at my declining scores, as if she saw this kind of thing every day of the week — which, of course, she did.

After the test, she asked me several questions:

"Do you know how to sign?" (No.)

"Do you know any other deaf people?" (No.)

"Do you want to know what I think?" (Yes.)

"You need to give yourself a break," she said. "Aren't you exhausted?"

There was a distinct explosion in my mind, a Pandora's Box popping open, followed by reels of eels slithering out and hissing. I didn't know what to say.

"I'm not sure what you mean," I finally remarked.

"Don't get me wrong," she said. "You've chosen to live in the hearing world, but that doesn't have to be exclusive. You could level out the playing field if you knew how to sign. You could just be yourself."

The eels slithered out of my ears and wrapped around my neck, choking me. "I don't ever get to be myself," I said, clearing my throat. "I'm not exactly sure how that works."

Until then, I had never met another person with hearing loss. While several deaf students attended my high school, we didn't connect until decades later, courtesy of social media. It was a big campus. We never had any classes together, and I wasn't looking to find them, either. I never gave any thought to it because why would I? You don't know what you don't know.

After that audiology appointment, I decided to learn sign language for real. I began attending a weekly ASL social in a decaying mansion owned by a nonprofit. A disillusioned Deaf theater actor taught the class, and the content often pertained to biological warfare and dystopian themes. I was never quite sure if the course was some sort of performance art piece, so I approached it with skepticism and focused on acquiring conversational signing skills. It felt awkward at first, but the more I used it, the more natural it became.

Through the social, I became friends with a hearing man in a tangled marital situation, which informed our conversation topics. He lived in a rooming house near me while his goth wife lived in a different state. He was both afraid of and excited by her. He shared with me that a resident in the rooming house would barge in when others took their baths, and if his wife was ever there, he knew she would hurt the intruder. She wore a vial of blood around her neck and carried a knife.

We met often that first year to practice, and I vividly recall the man's stories, wringing every drop from the concept of "fear" in ASL with dramatic expression and body language. I told him he needed to open a Halloween Haunted House for the Deaf because he thrived on terror and darkness.

I, on the other hand, did not, so I switched to taking more traditional ASL classes at a local college and connected with several Deaf social organizations. Still, it was only after joining a group of Deaf campers on a week-long wilderness trip that I experienced what it was like to communicate manually, twenty-four/seven. It was an eye-opening experience and made me realize how different my life could have been.

Being around people like me created a palpable feeling of belonging. I felt liberated from the pressure to hide my deafness. I stashed my devices in a plastic bag while canoeing and rarely used them once we reached shore. For the first time in my life, hearing was irrelevant. Every sound, every conversation defaulted to sign language. Even though I lipread well in the hearing world, the camping trip highlighted how much easier human interaction was in a truly inclusive environment. It was life-changing.

Embracing a manual mode of communication was like entering a magic kingdom. It was a way of life for one town in the late 1600s. Jonathan Lambert, a Deaf man with Deaf offspring, relocated to Chilmark, a secluded community on Martha's Vineyard.[24] As the residents intermarried and reproduced, the proportion of Deaf individuals to hearing individuals increased. The town adapted its own sign language to communicate, and everyone was fluent. Signing was required to conduct business, socialize, and live. Parents passed down the language to subsequent generations. For the town's inhabitants, both Deaf and hearing, manual communication (and deafness) was the norm.

For the people of Chilmark, deafness was not a disability but a component of their identity — who they were. The community was a testament to the power of language to unite and affirm, a precursor to a future where visual modes of communication would transcend boundaries and create cultural connections that spoke volumes, even in silence.

8

Cultural Membership

Approximately 90 percent of deaf children are born to hearing parents. However, the hearing and culturally Deaf hold conflicting viewpoints on many subjects, including cochlear implants.

Most hearing individuals view deafness solely through a medical lens. By contrast, the (capital "D") Deaf are members of a community strongly aligned based on shared experiences and values. This cultural tribalism serves as a vital support network for the Deaf, similar to subgroups pertaining to indigenous peoples, the LGBTQ+ community, or even Parrotheads. The Deaf culture is distinct from others, defined by a unique language with its own grammar, alongside separate schools, professional and social networks, sporting events, theaters, and gathering places. Members proudly embrace their Deaf identity.

When I began researching cochlear implants in the late '80s and early '90s, I was aware of the Deaf community's protests that CIs threatened to erase Deaf culture and disrupt the continuity of the language. I followed the debate closely. It was a major moment in history and spawned multiple documentaries and think pieces due to the polar opposite perspectives of the parties involved. Specifically, the Deaf community fiercely disagreed with hearing parents who chose to implant their deaf children.

For context, early cochlear implants focused on sound recognition, with less success in speech comprehension. Implanting children with the aim of achieving minimal oral speech proficiency (while withholding sign language) generally resulted in the child not being fluent in either language. They were also stuck in cultural limbo, deprived of full membership in any community. The procedure was equated to attempting to change an adopted child's race by altering their skin color. Tellingly, the ASL sign for "cochlear implant" reflects that original concern: a claw-like handshape thunked against the side of the neck, like the bite of a vampire's fangs, forcibly and irrevocably transformed.

Cochlear implantation also conflicted with the Deaf community's values. The culturally Deaf did not view themselves as broken; they didn't want or need to be fixed. Although a handful of Deaf adults opted for cochlear implantation during that era, they were not the subject of protests as they were capable of providing informed consent. Nonetheless, they still encountered ostracization from the Deaf community.

Conversely, hearing parents viewed deafness without the cultural or social implications. Typical hearing was their measurement standard, and they believed the child would have greater opportunities and face fewer challenges if they had even sound recognition. Therefore, cochlear implantation was the closest means of assimilating the deaf child into their hearing family.

In the decades since, cochlear implant technology has dramatically improved, and its reach expanded. Cultural concerns have receded over time, and the controversy around implanting children has mostly faded. Additionally, sign language's appeal has broadened beyond the Deaf world. Bilingual households have become more common. Even the website for Gallaudet University (the national university for the d/Deaf and hard of hearing) acknowledges the shift, stating:

> "As cochlear implants for children have become more widely used, the emphasis of the debate has changed. The focus is more on the type of support and educational services provided and the child's exposure to visual language." [Gallaudet University website.][25]

Not everyone recalls the Deaf community's protests against cochlear implants. Without that reference point, however, many hearing individuals dismiss cultural concerns or even self-acceptance as valid perspectives for why any d/Deaf person would decline the opportunity to implant today, often rationalizing, "They just don't know any better."

There are many examples of cultural practices that might not align with one's beliefs or experiences, but we acknowledge and respect differences for harmonious co-existence. For instance, the Amish community abstains from using power grids to bring electricity into their homes. Yet, it would be disrespectful to chalk up their practice to unawareness. Similarly, dietary prohibitions such as abstaining from consuming pork or animal products have deep-seated cultural and religious significance. These choices are deliberate and meaningful in upholding particular beliefs. Likewise, a decision by d/Deaf individuals to not pursue implantation warrants respect as well.

Cultural respect can be a thorny subject when values don't align. While writing my TED talk, I stumbled into an argument with a politically conservative acquaintance. I told her I was thinking about contrasting the parallels between implanting children in the early 2000s versus providing gender-affirming care for minors in the 2020s, as both issues involved parental rights in making life-altering decisions in the face of cultural opposition. My acquaintance believed that gender was firmly established at birth and that supporting even counseling services on the subject meant rejecting God's design. I disagreed, so — partly to aggravate her — I questioned why her argument covered only specific aspects of physical identity, adding that babies born deaf were just as much God's design. I looked up a specific scripture on my phone:

> "The Lord said to him, 'Who gave human beings their mouths? Who makes them deaf or mute? Who gives them sight or makes them blind? Is it not I, the Lord?'" [Exodus 4:11 (NIV).]

For the record, I don't interpret the scripture to mean that God intentionally creates disability during the process of creation in the womb. In my view, this passage acknowledges that a range of abilities exist within God's creation, and God simply helps us scale applicable challenges, such as with Moses and his fear of public speaking (as the context for that scripture).

I told my friend that physical and cognitive attributes were such an essential component of identity that it seemed hypocritical to pick and choose which changes meant rejecting God's design while others were exempt. Shouldn't the standard be applied consistently or else admit that humans were empowered to make their own choices? For example, did her beliefs prohibit expanding leg bones to extend one's height? Rhinoplasty or proactive mastectomy due to genetic code handed down over generations? Who was to say a person had to accept certain characteristics or markers if they didn't fit who they were?

"What about cochlear implants?" I pressed on. "In your perspective, would that also be rejecting God's design?"

"I don't know," she said in a tone that implied she didn't care because she was locked into the politics behind prohibiting gender-affirming care and didn't want to get sidetracked by the fact that humans (or parents on behalf of their children) make decisions to alter and/or align their physical identity all the time without requiring anyone's permission.

By this point, I felt my comparison had missed its target, so I began to wrap up. "Two decades ago, the Deaf community saw cochlear implants as the equivalent of cultural genocide. However, their opposition has evolved over time. Do you think your objections toward gender-affirming care will change eventually?"

"No, it's completely different," she insisted. "Being deaf is a mistake. Trans is going against what God intended."

Being labeled a medical mistake did not sit well with me. I told her that I considered disparaging any diverse segment to be interchangeable with besmirching the d/Deaf. Communities needed to stand up for each other because the majority would continue to steamroll over the minority otherwise.

Despite attempts to share our thoughts, my friend and I found ourselves at an impasse. Recognizing the futility of further debate, we agreed to disagree, acknowledging the complexity of the issues at hand. Though our viewpoints may differ, the dialogue served as reminder of the ongoing struggle for inclusivity and understanding in society.

9

Faking It

According to the medical model of disability, hearing loss is framed as my problem — mine, alone — and my only path to success is getting fixed. While hearing devices provide some assistance, they are not perfect, and the struggle to comprehend speech in challenging situations still snowballs. Occasionally, the temptation beckons to just fake it.

Faking is not the same as guessing. Guessing is a valid hearing strategy involving stringing together clues based on probability and using snippets of actual words. Damaged hearing is all about filling in the blanks, which is why audiogram scores are higher for repeating back sentences than single-syllable words; speech is easiest to comprehend in context. For example, "coal" and "cold" might sound the same, but even a three-year-old knows Santa leaves coal in a stocking for naughty kids, not Mucinex and tissues.

For a writer like me, hearing tests are basically playing *Name That Tune.* As a deaf person, I have managed to get by my entire life by hearing a little, lipreading a lot, and relying on the statistical probability that certain words follow other words. Over time, guessing becomes second nature.

This practice frustrates one of my sisters in particular. "You have to tell me when you don't hear something," she sighed when I visited and had responded incorrectly to a question she asked.

I replied that guessing based on context is how all deaf people hear. I did not invent this myself.

"Are you guessing right now?" she asked.

I said yes, and we both laughed.

For my dear hearing sister, speech comprehension is a binary concept. She either hears it or she doesn't. And if she doesn't, she asks for a repeat. She was overlaying her hearing experience onto my deaf reality and assuming the context was the same. (It's not.)

"Look," I finally replied. "I don't ever hear things the way that you do. I am also not going to ask you to repeat every single thing you say. Trust me, you don't want that either. Just tell me when I'm wrong, or move on."

Another friend says that all the time — "Just tell me if you don't hear something" — but that request is based on a false assumption. Hearing loss does not deal with absolutes but rather probabilities. Virtually every sentence has ambiguous consonants, vowels, or entire words, which means all conversation requires unconscious guesswork. My friend only notices when I guess wrong; she has no idea how often I guess right.

I understand where objectors are coming from. They think guessing is a discretionary activity and don't want me to miss out. However, that expectation comes with a mandate to process information in the same manner that they do — to hear as they do — because that's the only valid approach for them. There's a hint of indignation, too, when they realize I treat a portion of what they say as expendable. It's as offensive as if they prepared an elaborate four-course meal, and I only ate the salad. (But that still would have been okay in a vegan context, so another example of how we assign validity to only some viewpoints.)

Despite the grumbling, guessing is a standard comprehension strategy for those with hearing loss. Faking, on the other hand, is a conscious detour into calculated deception based on a total blank slate. It's a desperate attempt to offer a "yes" or "no" response that hopefully aligns with what was just asked, whatever that was. Faking happens when the level of shame baked into hearing loss has taken over or more than two repeats have been requested. Maybe the speaker seems annoyed or impatient, or the conversation has become too much work.

Everyone with some degree of deafness has faked comprehension, including me. It's a familiar instinct that truly baffles hearing people, whose frame of reference is that one time they missed something or a group scenario where everyone strained to hear. It can never be truly explained; unless they have walked in my shoes, they won't ever understand. They don't experience the constant exasperation, snarky slights, or disgruntled disdain. For them, the concept of not comprehending is a single-use application.

No one starts out with an intent to fake. It begins as a temporary stall to regain lost context, often due to someone speaking before the recipient is aware. Best case scenario: The fake goes undetected, the conversation gets back on track, and the process feels seamless. But after a bunch of tries, if the situation seems hopeless (or the speaker seems impatient), faking can easily go off the rails. It can also become habit-forming, like finding solace in overeating or resorting to self-harm. It provides a fleeting sense of relief, but it's always dishonest, regardless of whether the individual gets caught.

I've gotten caught faking, big time. It involved a neighbor couple who alternated between treating me as a friend and as persona non grata. I never knew which side of their face I would get with each encounter, which made interactions stressful even without the added pressure of mangled comprehension.

The notorious faking incident still haunts me. It was a cold, windy Christmas Eve, and I walked into a parking lot just as they were leaving. The man rolled down the driver's window to say something but then turned his face to his companion, speaking away from me. I asked for a repeat, but I didn't catch a single word of what he said over the roar of the wind. His exasperation was visible, and I could feel my anxiety rising. I assumed they stopped to wish me a Merry Christmas — what else could it have been? — which is what I said back. Apparently, I faked wrong. Inappropriately wrong, as if they had just told me someone had died. (I had met one of their friends who was a cancer survivor, so that was entirely possible.) Their faces reflected pure horror, mouths agape, clearly conveying that my response was thoughtless and rude, and I was the jerk they obviously thought I was. (I never did learn what he said.)

Privately, I called them The Chagrin Twins as their dramatic facial responses when I incorrectly guessed pieces of conversation were the hallmark of almost every awkward moment during that time in my life. They rarely looked at me while speaking and often seemed irked, so piecing together what they said was sometimes challenging. I would drift further from comprehension until I'd finally shut it down by faking, invariably incorrectly, and they'd stare at me in disbelief as if I'd just confessed to murdering their pet while they slept.

The Chagrin Twins weren't bad people. They just gave off mixed messages. We shared plenty of positive interactions where they greeted me enthusiastically, or mutual friends would mention they had spoken highly of me. But their intermittent friendliness complicated things. I'd get lulled into a false sense of security by the last chummy interaction and be startled by their irritability the next time. They produced a seesaw of emotion that left me on shaky ground.

They even invaded my sleeping hours. I sometimes dreamt about them in what I called my Getaway Dreams. These were similar to Anxiety Dreams, but instead of being naked at the SATs, I unexpectedly found myself inside their house and had to flee before they returned. What was most infuriating was that The Chagrin Twins weren't even in the dreams! They were merely referenced as being nearby, which felt insulting. They were too important even to make a cameo appearance! In my dreams!

They knew I was deaf. They asked about my hearing loss often, according to friends. Other people just told me when my response didn't match or proactively restated their question to get back on track. The Chagrin Twins did not. They never gave me the benefit of the doubt (that I hadn't heard them) when I replied out of context. But I never asked them to, either.

In retrospect, I should have taken ownership during the Chagrin Twins' era. However, their exaggerated double takes were so withering that my mortified body practically sank into the ground like the wicked witch melting away. Whenever The Chagrin Twins pointed their fire hose of shame in my direction, I flashed back to the cockroaches that would scatter when I turned on the kitchen light in my old apartment on Third Avenue. That was me, a skittish insect that needed to flee quickly. In their presence, I was an utter, complete failure in life, and their intermittent disapproval felt like a sudden downpour of reproach that I couldn't escape.

Needless to say, my self-advocacy skills with the Chagrin Twins were nonexistent. I felt any effort to educate them on how to converse with someone with hearing loss would come across as criticism. Who was I to judge?

"Just be grateful they're not The Chagrin Quints," huffed my friend Geoff, bless him, and I agreed. I actually enjoyed interacting with The Chagrin Twins when comprehension flowed smoothly. However, it took a lot of internal cheerleading to muster the courage to face them. Other times, I avoided them and waved from a distance.

The incident was a wake-up call. Faking is a very real consequence of the perpetual "you can't even tell!" merry-go-round; it encourages a pattern of dishonesty to extend the illusion of appearing to be hearing. I'm glad about the Christmas Eve debacle now, although I wasn't at the time. It was a habit I needed to break.

That particular mishap with The Chagrin Twins was a significant milestone on my personal path to self-advocacy. From them, I learned two valuable lessons: First, nothing good comes from faking, so avoid it at all cost; and second, if I encounter that horror-struck reaction again, to swallow my pride and own up to it by saying, "I can tell from your face that I misheard you."

After all, avoiding embarrassment is an excellent motivational tool.

10

Unconventional Challenges

M y journey into adulthood took a less-traveled path. My parents had a rule: After finishing Catholic grade school, my siblings and I were no longer obligated to attend Sunday church. However, we had to participate in some sort of faith-based program, such as weekly catechism classes. Actually, my parents never told me this directly. It came from my cousin Sharon (or, as I called her, "The Parental Newsmonger").

By high school, I was open to alternative philosophies. My typing class partner was a lovely boy who happened to be a Jehovah's Witness. He invited me to attend his congregational meeting, which served as both my first date and an opportunity to save my soul. Soon after, a Mormon man asked me to attend his weekly gathering. I attended both and vowed to keep an open mind. Meanwhile, I tagged along to Young Life events with my sister.

As a rebellious teenager, I probably sensed that matters of faith were a ripe landmine for aggravating my parents. I told a family friend about my spiritual experimentation. She insisted on equal time, inviting me to the weekly prayer meeting at her house. Her family members were former neighbors who still lived on our old block, so my parents knew their parents, and we were good friends with the siblings. I visited, liked the people in the group, and kept coming back. I dubbed them "the Cult" because, in some respects, their behavior and characteristics aligned with the definition. I had just turned fifteen, while most of the group were fun singles around twenty-five.

It might seem strange as cults go, but I loved it, at least in the early years. One of the best memories of my life was camping amidst thousands at a Woodstock-like music festival on a farm in Pennsylvania on my sixteenth birthday, watching a midnight meteor shower from the roof of a car. It was the mid-'70s, so communal experiences were in vogue, and everyone brought their unique talents and expertise to create a cohesive and interconnected community. The Cult became a surrogate family to me, attending my school plays, encouraging my writing, helping me with homework, and treating me like a beloved younger sister. I was officially initiated into the group. I thought I was all in.

My parents were aware of my Cult participation but never inquired about the details. Years later, my cousin Sharon told me my mother had had a private meltdown about it. While my grandmother had raised my father and his siblings under her Catholic doctrine, my paternal grandfather observed non-mainstream religious principles. Specifically, he rejected conventional medicine in favor of holistic approaches, which complicated his already unstable mental health. As a young man, my Dad had to step in to make decisions about his father's competency, which caused much family turmoil. I never knew my grandfather. Sadly, he died from untreated cancer. His practices and mental health were something of a dirty family secret, discussed in whispers.

Apparently, I struck a nerve with my faith journey, scraping up troubling memories of my late grandfather's alternative beliefs. My mother confided her fears to my aunt (who shared the information with Sharon). Sharon also said that my mother bitterly resented that the Cult's influence was stronger than my parents' in taming my teenage rebellion; both of my parents begrudgingly acknowledged the Cult's positive impact, although they never said anything to me. Despite my parents' discomfort, the Cult was profoundly important in my life, and I still hold them dear.

After high school graduation, I took a job at a law firm in my hometown, preparing legal documents for lawsuits concerning the unauthorized use of copyrighted material. The work seemed routine for the first few months, processing shipments of bootleg merchandise from private investigators and preparing cease-and-desist letters for the perpetrators. Everything changed when the investigators began sending boxes of amateur pornography, not to be confused with avant-garde art or even the slick artificiality of drugstore publications. The content contained hard-core, illegal use of a comic strip represented by our law firm. At only seventeen, I was too young to join my colleagues at the discos at night. Instead, I worked behind the locked doors of a photocopy room, where I cataloged stacks of pornographic materials and drafted boilerplate complaint documents with exhibits.

Immersed in XXX-rated material by day and touched by the Holy Spirit at night, my life spanned both dark and light. Eventually, I made peace with the paradox: I was no longer surprised by the contents of the boxes arriving daily and grew equally guarded regarding the teachings of the Cult.

Initially, the Cult was a good match for me: God + the Ten Commandments + the Good Samaritan + Community. Above all, they radiated grace and service. I still imagined my superhero alter ego as an angel in training, blessing others without revealing my face, and the loving environment seemed like an essential piece to the puzzle. I found it especially meaningful that we shorthanded the term "random acts of kindness" to the acronym "RAK," coincidentally the same initials as my name.

Faith had always been part of my life, even as a kid. The play *Godspell* by John-Michael Tebelak had premiered locally. It was based on the Book of Matthew in the New Testament, from which I took great inspiration: Love God and your neighbor. Care for strangers. Give to the poor. Do unto others as you would have them do to you. Show humility. Give generously. Champion inclusion. Seek nonviolence. Forgive. Repent. Promote unity. Love unconditionally.

After a couple of years, however, the Cult's teachings gradually shifted to conspiracy theories pertaining to the Illuminati, Jimmy Hoffa, corporate Satanism, and forecasts about the end of the world. Armageddon date predictions came and went. A farm compound was acquired. Someone from a canned goods company came and spoke to the group about stockpiling food. Weapons were purchased. Firearms training ensued.

My reasons for joining the Cult had been rooted in my desire for connection and a sense of belonging within a community. The people and their genuine beliefs in the teachings of Jesus drew me in. Still, I could see the survivalist rabbit hole ahead and knew this detour was not what I had signed up for. It was time to leave.

I wanted to attend college but had no means to pay for it. On a whim, I requested a Gallaudet University catalog and entertained the idea of immersing myself at the national school for the d/Deaf. I had no previous exposure to the Deaf community, however, so my contemplation was brief. But one of my last memories of living at home was leafing through the Gallaudet brochure in the kitchen as my mother cooked dinner. I told her I was considering applying but felt I'd be disadvantaged because I didn't know sign language.

It was one of the few occasions I'd ever brought up the subject of deafness with my mother. She remained silent, and the moment passed. My sights quickly changed to Minnesota, where a few people from the Cult had relocated. I could move there, find full-time work, establish my residency (to reduce tuition costs), and attend college at night to achieve my goal. The Cult respected education and knew that a diverse mix of chosen professions formed a complete whole. I received nothing but encouragement when I shared my plans (although I did leave under the pretense that I would return).

I was nineteen and had just bought my first car. One of the Cult members, a mechanic, gifted me a complete set of custom automotive tools and spent an afternoon teaching me to change my oil and fix a flat tire. That's how I'll always remember their spirit of generosity and care. And on my last night in my hometown, the Cult threw a farewell shower to send me off.

At the party, my friends surprised me with a homemade blanket and a blue ribbon that read, "You're brave!" It never occurred to me to be scared. I felt ready to take the next step. I was tired of cataloging porn, and with my peers off pursuing their paths in college, it was time to get on with my life.

Even though I relocated to another state with just $400 and no job, I didn't see myself as exceptionally brave. Instead, I viewed myself as practical and risk-averse, always careful to know the outcome of everything upfront because that was how I navigated life with limited hearing. Spontaneity was not my friend. Rather, I was a cautious observer, always conducting thorough research before taking action. However, despite the potential danger ahead, I felt a strong sense of confidence in the direction I was headed with this move.

A week after relocating, I was hired by a progressive, respectable law firm as the recruiting coordinator for the summer clerkship program, which included the day-to-day management of the law students' work, plus event planning for new attorney socialization. The hiring partner liked my organizational skills, but it was my subscription to my hometown's daily newspaper that gave me the unexpected edge. As an Ohio football fan, he coveted my sports section. I felt a genuine connection with the attorneys and staff from the start. I quickly developed close friendships with the law students whose internships I curated. I worked long hours, attended college in the evenings, and socialized with colleagues regularly.

People at the law firm knew about my hearing loss. Since my former high school teacher had branded me as unemployable, I preemptively added deafness to my resume to divert the alleged tsunami of employers who might be closed-minded. For efficiency's sake, facing rejection up front was better than being surprised later, I thought, and the proactive declaration opened the door for others to ask about hearing loss in a positive, receptive manner. My speech comprehension was still fair with lipreading, and my super-powerful hearing aids enabled me to get by on the telephone. I blended into the workplace seamlessly. Or so I thought.

After several years at the law firm, the managing partner — who might have been going through a mid-life crisis — hired a new office administrator. Their frequent meetings were often accompanied by giggling and took place behind closed doors, quite noticeable in a quiet office with its own law librarian. Rumors flew.

All of the attorneys participated as mentors in the internship program, so I knew them well, and they seemed to like and respect me. It was also fair to say that the partners, twice my age, loved me like a daughter. After all, my job required me to ask about their cases, inspect their personal lives for crossover marketing possibilities, and find fascinating slants to update in their Martindale-Hubbell directory profiles. Who wouldn't love someone so keenly invested in promoting their brilliance?

The new administrator, for one.

Upon her arrival, she quickly ruffled feathers amongst the attorneys, Ivy League graduates who silently calculated the risks associated with an inexperienced professional with the potential to blackmail the collective partnership over tawdry details. At the same time, she alienated the support staff by implementing change fast and furiously without regard for professional relationships established between admins and attorneys, many of whom had been paired since law school.

My role now reported to the new administrator. Although the hierarchy shift didn't change my job responsibilities, I was wary. I knew the drama she caused because everyone told me. As their sounding board and confidante, I listened and tried to be supportive.

I began to notice petty incidents in which she undermined my work, such as deprioritizing my jobs in the centralized word processing pool without telling me, canceling my conference room reservations, misplacing phone messages for me from the front desk, and interrupting my backlog meetings with the law clerks for manufactured reasons.

A couple of the younger attorneys sat me down, worried. They told me she was bad-mouthing me behind my back. They said she harbored a grudge due to my close relationships with the lawyers, a hostility which intensified dramatically after two of the partners decided to escort me to a company event by boat, where we arrived like royalty on the waterfront.

The younger attorneys continued their warning: The administrator disliked that I handled event planning, which involved a substantial budget for attorney socialization. In contrast, she had only limited funds to organize an annual Christmas lunch for the support staff. I was an obstacle in her path, and I needed to watch my back because she was gunning for me. She was from the Mean Girls' School of Politics, and I needed to be ready.

Until then, my only real brush with Mean Girls was a shunning in eighth grade. I had misread some signals, and when it became clear that a popular clique was, in fact, *not* inviting me into their ranks, I retreated. But it was too late. I had just made the school basketball team, and a girl in the clique had not. Boom! The unbridled vindictiveness of thirteen-year-old girls, unleashed.

It was a stunning display of getting canceled, so arbitrary and disloyal. We had been schoolmates for eight years! Amidst the storm, however, moments of grace prevailed. I particularly remember the kindness of my sister's friend, Kitty, who was a year older than me and lived next door. The eighth-grade girls went to the Catholic high school first thing each morning for cooking and sewing class. Kitty was a regular student there and aware of my predicament, so she insisted I walk to school with her. In a sense, she became my first ally, a high school freshman who outranked the eighth-grade visitors, and her presence muted the Mean Girls when we arrived each day.

After class, I still had to make the return trip to the grade school five blocks away. To avoid conflict, I zigzagged the back alleys near my house instead of taking the school-designated route. The rest of the day followed a predictable pattern of name-calling and note-passing. While relatively mild compared to modern bullying, the experience left scars, specifically, a perpetual wariness towards forming new connections and constantly scrutinizing people's intentions.

I wasn't unpopular. Up until then, I sat solidly in the invisible ring of good students who didn't cause trouble. Fortunately, grade school graduation beckoned that June, and our small class went our separate ways. Some of the Mean Girls headed to the Catholic academy while I followed my siblings to the public high school, welcomed into a vibrant student body of thousands. Meanwhile, I kept my head down and hung out with my sister's friends.

I was never mocked in school for my hearing loss. Once, as a joke, a boy sitting behind me tried to lower my hearing aid volume without my noticing. I didn't take it as a slight. He was just a goofy kid distracted by a shiny object and failed in his attempt. I had forgotten the incident until his sister mentioned it at a school reunion many years later. As an adult, he had told her the story and expressed regret.

Context was everything. I remembered the Mean Girls' shunning in detail because of its intentionally predatory vibe. However, I only vaguely recalled hearing-aid-gate because it was a spontaneous prank that ended seconds later once the jig was up. I even thought it was a different boy. Still, it was disconcerting to learn that the man had felt guilty enough to confess the act to his sibling decades later. It made me wonder whether the situation had been worse than I perceived. Was I now an unwitting object of pity?

* * *

The showdown with the new administrator came to this: I rarely went into her space. One fateful day, however, the front desk asked me to drop off phone messages to her empty office. As I left the pink slips on her desk, my peripheral vision caught my name scribbled on a purple notepad. Curious, I glanced at the page and saw that she had written my performance review with the words "CAN'T HEAR" scrawled in capital letters. My radar snapped to attention.

Sensing something sinister afoot, I glanced into the hall and quickly snatched the document. I hurriedly made a photocopy and slipped the original back in its place. I read the review carefully at home that night. As I digested the pages, I realized in horror that the administrator had been tracking my conversations for more than eight months to tally up how often I asked for clarifications or repeats. She wrote that she was increasingly uncomfortable working with me because I couldn't hear "normally," and she concluded that I was a liability to the law firm. In her assessment, I would never succeed at my job, be promoted, or rise to the required level of training. She said my hearing loss was an embarrassment to the company, and I would inevitably become disgruntled and disengaged.

Ouch.

If I were to read that performance review today, it would sting. However, I think I could successfully separate the emotion from the content and articulate how the administrator had foolishly crossed a line into overt discrimination. In her own handwriting! At a law firm! But that performance review occurred several years before awareness of disability rights laws, plus I was in my early twenties with no self-advocacy skills. The emotional punch got me. I was utterly devastated. I confided in a work friend (I'll name her Stephanie) but could barely speak. The shame was staggering.

Which was precisely the point.

In classic Mean Girl mode, the administrator twisted information to sow doubt. She used a fact — my hearing loss — but misrepresented it to create a narrative far from the truth, absurdly so. The clerkship program had just been named the best in the country by a prominent industry magazine! Distorting reality was a Mean Girl staple, to find a vulnerable point to exaggerate and push to inflict pain and foster doubt because she viewed me as a threat to her popularity. She was planning to blindside me. I felt lucky to have stumbled upon the write-up in advance, as it gave me several days to prepare.

When the day of the performance review arrived, the administrator pulled out her purple pad and read it aloud without giving me a copy, so I had to look at her as she spoke. I was steeled and ready. She got to the hearing loss section and watched me closely. She expected me to crumble or react defensively, apologize, or weep from embarrassment. I did not.

"Do you understand what I mean?" she asked after each sentence, as if I was incompetent and unable to grasp the insult.

"That's inappropriate content for a performance review," I replied evenly because, in a million years, I didn't want to give her the satisfaction of a reaction. "You need to take it out."

She was surprised, and I could tell she was disappointed by my lack of emotion. She reiterated her points several times, looking at me with false concern. I kept my face blank and stuck to the line Stephanie had scripted. "That's inappropriate content for a performance review. You need to take it out."

I was pleased I could respond calmly because I had cried privately many times up to that point. I spoke as matter-of-factly as if we were discussing the weather. Ultimately, she removed the content from the final review. But I still had a copy of the original in her handwriting.

I debated what to do. At that point, the job had been my entire world, and it didn't seem fair to be chased out by a Mean Girl. I loved the attorneys, but the damage was done, and the joy was gone. I contacted a former colleague at another firm to discuss the possibility of pursuing a legal case. Ultimately, I withdrew the request because I couldn't talk about it. Literally. I was so overcome with emotion that I could barely squeak and had to cut the call short.

I found a new job elsewhere and submitted my resignation. The attorneys were bewildered, and the hiring partner was devastated. On my last day, I composed a detailed summary of my performance review experience and left it for the new managing partner, whom I considered a friend. The position had recently changed hands, and I felt obligated to outline the risks of the administrator's behavior to the company. My report was written like a constructive performance review, without emotion. I attached a copy of the handwritten review, as well.

After my departure, Stephanie called periodically with unofficial updates. Her position was such that she had access to confidential files and covertly shared the information with me. The company engaged outside counsel to handle the matter and took my feedback seriously. And justice was served: Eventually, the firm and the new administrator parted ways.

In this case, overt discrimination was a gift. The handwritten document validated with 100 percent certainty the exact words the administrator had conveyed. Though painful, I preferred its lack of ambiguity. Subtle discrimination, on the other hand, is much more challenging to bear as it mingles the indignity of being wronged with no way to prove it.

"Your life was fine," a relative once remarked in the context of a general discussion about people we knew who had faced discrimination. The comment struck me as wildly presumptuous; it seemed to imply deafness had no impact on my life because she personally saw no evidence of overt bias. Her statement dismissed the possibility of hidden barriers simply because she had not experienced them first-hand. Yet prejudice almost always lurks in the shadows, subtly influencing words and actions, insidious in its presence.

Hearing people don't see this. A lack of overt bullying doesn't mean an absence of societal stigma. While shame can be a vicious swipe at what you are, it's also the steady-drip calling out of what you're *not*. It lurks in the design choices favoring audio-only experiences, in the implicit criticisms of "discreet" hearing aids in advertisements, and in casual statements that subtly label any visible aspect of disability as undesirable or consider only typical ability as normal. The silent judgment weaves itself into the fabric of daily life and creates a pervasive blanket of disapproval that envelopes those affected. It's impossible to escape.

The law firm evaluation was harrowing and pivotal, the milestone where my deaf journey began. It was the first time my hearing loss had been used against me, and except for a random stroke of luck, I was utterly unprepared. I needed to learn how to talk about it because, whether I hid it or not, deafness was a significant part of my identity. Yet, up to that point, I never thought of myself that way.

11

The Art of Pivot

How you view disability varies based on whether you were born with it or acquired it later. Likewise, how others perceive your disability often influences how easily you adapt. Since my hearing loss was from birth, it was my standard frame of reference, my normal. But it also progressed throughout my life, so I continually needed to pivot.

"Pivot" is one of my favorite words. It comes up often in business. The most successful companies can quickly pivot — change direction and take a different approach — in response to industry shifts or unexpected challenges. "When life gives you lemons, make lemonade" is a pivot, and so is "cutting your losses" and "switching to Plan B."

With any loss, the natural tendency is to want back what you had. But hair cell damage isn't reversible, yet getting a hearing device and simply calling it done is not an equivalent substitution.

I applaud those who embrace sign language and the d/Deaf communities, and I equally commend those who seek hearing aids or implants to help bridge the gap to the hearing world. But I get nervous for individuals who continue to rely solely on hearing, digging in their heels and insisting on doing everything the same and inevitably becoming frustrated. As excellent as many devices can be, there are always limitations. A guaranteed solution does not yet exist. Meanwhile, they reject supplemental visual tools to enhance accessibility — such as captioning or speech-to-text technology — because they believe audio is the only valid choice on which they must rely. They don't want to adapt. Even though it might simplify their lives, they refuse to pivot.

Often, it's due to basic stubbornness. For example, my late neighbor Ruth (not her real name) frequently misplaced her house keys and credit cards. I saw or spoke to her multiple times per week for almost thirty years. We lived in the same building, and I eventually became her regular driver when she had to hang up her car keys. We went to brunch and happy hours, plays and concerts, sporting events, the State Fair, and cast our ballots to vote. Once, we ventured to Wisconsin for a cheese curd festival. I genuinely enjoyed her company and vast intellect, and she was happy to resume her life. Ruth was of my mother's generation, and I considered her a local surrogate, trying to mirror the selfless care my siblings bestowed upon our parents. Moreover, our solo life trajectories bore striking similarities. When I approached Ruth's age, for example, I hoped to have a similar emergency contact nearby.

Anyway, in virtually every conversation, Ruth would express alarm as she struggled to find the specific items she had recently set down. She insisted her tendency to lose housekeys dated back to childhood. She wasn't neurodiverse or losing her memory. She didn't lose other items. She just couldn't find her keys and her credit cards. But she did nothing to rectify this pattern.

Ruth adamantly resisted the pivot. She hated it when people (me) tried to tell her what to do, and I did all the time. As soon as we paid at a restaurant, I'd put my credit card back in my wallet and remind Ruth to do the same. She'd outright refuse, glaring, annoyed. Ruth's most deeply held conviction was that she shouldn't have to put her charge card away or keep her keys in a consistent location. She wasn't forgetful or overwhelmed. She made a conscious choice on the spot to disregard. She just had this weird sense of entitlement, like it was beneath her to follow any strategy of organization even when given the prompt and opportunity.

You would think someone who historically misplaced those objects would get used to them going missing. *Wrong.* Ruth would call me in a state of panic, and we would spend the next half hour searching, retracing steps in a restaurant, as if it was the first time she had lost something, as if she had tried everything in her power to prevent it from happening.

Once, she casually tossed her ring of house keys to the floor of my car, and I discreetly pocketed it after I dropped her off to go park. Later, as she frantically rummaged through her purse, searching for her keys, I handed them over and was met with a steely-eyed death stare.

"I won't remind you if you don't want me to," I said. "But then you forfeit the right to complain when something goes missing." In thirty years, she never once said, "I'd better put these away so I don't lose them." The cycle never varied. She refused to pivot. Even when prompted, her resistance to change prevailed.

Similarly, lots of people resist the pivot when it comes to hearing loss. For example, family members routinely complain about needing to shout so a spouse can hear them. Yet, out of the same stubbornness that Ruth demonstrated, the shouters decline to switch to a more accessible option for the conversation, like employing mindful methods of speaking to enhance comprehension or, barring that, then texting, a speech-to-text app, a whiteboard, or God forbid, learning sign language as a long-term solution. No, they keep tossing their figurative keys to the floor of the car, stuck in a prison of their own making, yelling.

Ruth's temperament was not unique. When dealing with loss, many repeat the same failed approach — the way they did things before — and refuse to pivot. But the old way is no longer sustainable and will only cause frustration. Fortunately, accessibility options continue to expand, and simply keeping pace with the times might influence change even if the reality of hearing loss does not.

For example, in the last decade, (visual) texting has supplanted (audio) voicemail as the messaging app of choice. My cell phone automatically transcribes my voicemail now, and just the other day, I discovered a button for "Use RTT" (real-time text) on my keypad, which live-captions my telephone calls without the need to dial through a third-party app. Video calls also default to subtitles. The world moves forward even without my asking.

Trying to pivot can be particularly challenging when facing opposition. Giving up driving, for example, is a classic example where resistance is natural, either from the driver not ready to give up their independence or the relative unwilling to serve as a future chauffeur. Asking others to accommodate your hearing loss is equally hard.

Meanwhile, I had my own pivot to navigate. After my pneumonia, my ability to understand speech deteriorated quickly, and I needed to stop using the voice telephone altogether. My loss had progressed beyond any previous level, and even though I didn't particularly value what I was losing, I was trapped in a perpetual cycle of grief, an anxiety spiral from which I wanted off. Despite my efforts to communicate my needs and pivot, certain people continued to leave voicemails. Finally, I took action.

For my birthday that summer, I made an appointment with a psychologist. I had started to imagine what it would be like to live completely deaf, although not capital "D." Like a domesticated animal returning to the wild, the window of opportunity for me to integrate into the Deaf community was long closed. No, my entry portal now was the late-deafened world, lowercase "d."

The year was 1999. I had been using a Teletypewriter (TTY), a primitive phone for the d/Deaf that allowed callers to type messages back and forth via a keyboard plugged into a phone jack, like texting on a landline but way less sophisticated. I stopped answering voice calls at home. Since I could no longer hear well enough to use a traditional telephone, I told people without TTYs to call me through a third-party relay operator. Or email me. (Email was new enough then that not everyone used it regularly.)

Months passed. I needed to keep my telephone line for the TTY. Many folks, including my family, opted for email, which was ideal. However, a small subset continued to leave detailed voice messages venting about how inconvenient it was not to be able to reach me by telephone.

It was pretty inconvenient for me, too. To pick up the voicemail messages, I had to call the relay service, give them my voicemail login name and password for retrieval, and ask the operator to type the translation into the TTY. (Voicemail autotranslation would have been handy back then, but it was still decades away from reality.)

In hindsight, I should have put my foot down and stopped picking up the voicemail messages, but I didn't, at least not right away. Mostly, I was dismayed that despite dealing with the soul-sucking cycle of hearing loss, a few acquaintances forgot or ignored everything I said, didn't even try to help, and then scolded me for something beyond my control. Asking for help was difficult enough, and being continually disregarded was a slap in the face.

For me, the voicemail situation was the tipping point. The psychologist and I talked it through, and she provided me with an invaluable piece of advice: Always remove the emotion — the shaming stinger — from the equation.

"If you were out of town, people wouldn't be able to reach you by phone either," she said quite reasonably, a decade before mobile phones. "So, why is that okay but not because you can't hear?"

Her words sunk in.

"People impose on you what they want you to be," she continued. "Coming to terms with your hearing loss is not unlike coming out of the closet. The resistance people face when they announce they're gay is the same resistance you face by asserting your deafness. You are basically coming out of the closet as a deaf person, and hearing people don't want to know. People will try to shame you into apologizing. Some people will even act offended and try to put you on the defensive. And some people," she shrugged, "are just never going to accept it. You need to move on."

On New Year's Eve, I changed my telephone greeting. I announced that my voicemail was no longer monitored and that callers should use email instead. I stopped picking up the voicemail messages. It took six months (and a lot of unretrieved calls) for everyone to adapt. I forced them to pivot.

Drawing the line on voicemails was an essential step toward accepting my reality. It was a new day, decade, and even century, but I still had a long road ahead.

12

Cycles of Distortion

We all know a gaslighter, someone who generates doubt by distorting reality. The term comes from the 1944 film *Gaslight,* in which the main character's spouse intentionally brightens and dims the gas-powered lights to convince her that she's going insane. Classic gaslighting is where one party exploits a power imbalance, like a dominant spouse, authority figure, or boss. The negative performance review I received from the law firm administrator was a textbook example of gaslighting. By twisting my hearing loss experience, she undermined my confidence and made me doubt my competence, even though I was a top performer.

Gaslighting ranges from subtle exaggeration to outright lies. Following my experience at the law firm, I landed a job as a research grant proposal writer for a man I nicknamed the "Psychotic Psychology Professor," or "PPP" for short. The school afforded him far too much privilege, mainly due to the gobs of research funding he brought in. Money changes everything, and in this case, it persuaded the administration to overlook the PPP's dubious accounting practices and a staggering pile of harassment complaints.

The PPP was darkness personified, a creepy stalker who sat in his car in the parking lot and followed me sometimes when I left for the night. He called 911 twice on my predecessor and said she hadn't shown up for work and might be suicidal. Both absences were pre-scheduled vacation days.

On a professional level, he used his position of power to question the mental stability of his students, both male and female, to mess with their minds and spread derogatory rumors. He would abruptly end advisee relationships via letter right before an important milestone, leaving the sealed termination envelope on my desk to hand off. A few months in, I discovered copies of the letters in the common area filing cabinets and realized in horror what I had delivered.

I thought it was my dream job in academia, but it only lasted five months. It was winter, and I constantly nicked my dry skin on the sharp edges of the research papers I thumbed. Every day, the PPP inspected my scratched-up hands, implying that I was purposely slashing my fingers, and he cited the black turtlenecks I wore in the chilly office as evidence of my presumed depression. I knew he was setting the groundwork to fire me. For paper cuts!

Not long after, a colleague mentioned that the PPP had abruptly downgraded my job position. I approached the PPP confidently, thinking it was a misunderstanding, and he suddenly turned vicious. He disparaged my understanding of my job and then belittled me for getting upset. (I actually wasn't yet.) He claimed that in all his years of experience, he had never seen anyone as emotionally disturbed as me, a bold statement from someone who regularly committed violent patients to mental institutions. He spat at me with venom and disdain, leaving me completely shaken. I walked to the bathroom calmly, locked myself in a stall, and bawled. Life was too short. I gave my notice the next day.

After my departure, I was invited to join not one but two dedicated support groups for the numerous students and employees whose careers the PPP had run aground. Unlike the law firm experience that gnawed at my soul for months afterward, I was so over it. I declined.

Instead, I channeled my revenge into a creative outlet. I wrote a play about a gaslighting academic who met a gruesome end at the hands of an emotionally fragile employee who wore black turtlenecks. To my surprise, the script earned a playwriting fellowship for the following year.

Why am I talking about gaslighting? Gaslighting is a classic method used to shame people, including those with hearing loss. Even though my experience with the PPP wasn't about deafness, it opened my eyes to how easily another person can manipulate someone with even mild people-pleasing tendencies by wielding scorn.

It's easy to see how gaslighters pinpoint and amplify stigma to undermine your confidence. They convince you that your hearing loss is unreasonably burdensome, which makes you less worthy. Gaslighters go beyond basic complaining. You might express how you feel, for example, and instead of acknowledging your concerns, gaslighters flip the script to point the finger at you and then groom you to not challenge them through intimidation or withholding.

Like discrimination, gaslighting manifests on a scale from subtle to overt. The PPP was the perfect example of the latter. In fact, he holds the dubious distinction of being my measurement standard for extreme gaslighting. However, most folks hover at the subtle end of the gaslighting spectrum when it pertains to hearing loss. They mindlessly mirror something they've heard somewhere else and aren't aware that ableism is real discrimination. They don't recognize their behavior until it's called out.

That doesn't mean it's harmless, though. It's crucial to understand how gaslighting causes your confidence to shrink. Ideally, families make adjustments to accommodate loved ones with hearing loss, yet gaslighters act as if these steps are unreasonable when, in reality, they're not beyond the average person's capabilities. That is, if the gaslighter even tries at all. More likely, they shift the blame to you — the person with hearing loss — and shame you into believing you make life unbearable for everyone around.

People with hearing loss inadvertently engage in psychological manipulation, too. They erase themselves with constant apologies and proactively declare themselves unworthy as human beings because they are unhappy about their loss of sound. Unfortunately, as they fish for validation through exaggeration and repetition, they reinforce the idea that their condition is unacceptably burdensome to others, perpetuating the cycle of distortion until their statements are perceived as true.

Loads of phrases are gaslighting triggers:

"Why do you need the volume so high?"
"What I said was not that hard to understand."
"I shouldn't have to repeat myself."
"Would you just listen?"
"It's not that hard to hear."
"Why should everyone change how they speak just because you have trouble hearing?"
"You're too young to have hearing problems."
"I'm sure you can manage without special treatment; you're being too sensitive."
"Stop expecting us to adapt to your needs all the time."

It's reasonable to discuss how hearing loss affects you and others. However, when opinions veer into distortion, specify how sound or hearing "should" be, or blame things on hearing loss (rather than inaccessibility or their own reluctance to adapt), that can cross into both ableism and gaslighting. It's quite easy to fall into the habit of downplaying the significance of making adjustments for inclusivity and accessibility.

* * *

After the PPP, I was thankful for the playwriting fellowship that allowed me to do what I loved most: write. When the year was over, I applied for a position at a Fortune 500 company (referred to here as "The Firm"). As it happened, the general counsel at The Firm went to school with an attorney from my previous law firm, who gave me a great reference. I got the job and loved the friendly co-workers and fun environment.

In my new job, I was fortunate to have a supportive manager who encouraged me to use sign language interpreters in meetings even before accommodation laws went into effect. I worked in project management, and meetings were conducted via conference calls connecting multiple office locations. Since I couldn't lipread across telephone lines, having someone sign the spoken content face-to-face bridged the gap between my hearing colleagues and me — basically, it leveled the playing field.

I found a referral agency that sent a steady parade of sign language interpreters for project meetings. I explained to each that I voiced for myself and was deaf (with a lower-case "d"), as that changed their interpretation method. I was familiar with ASL, but I personally used Pidgin Signed English (or PSE), an ASL-English hybrid most commonly leveraged by late-deafened signers or people who were lipreaders, not to be confused with Signed Exact English.

PSE loosely follows an English sentence structure alongside ASL shortcuts, whereas pure ASL is a recognized language of its own and adheres to its own distinct syntax rules separate from English. For work, I needed to know the actual words uttered, not a conceptual translation, so PSE was the best fit for me.

The interpreters were always professional and followed my instructions precisely, although some of the more extroverted souls offered a Broadway performance, playing to the crowds in the balcony. Still, I don't remember any interpreters not doing their job well. They were exceptionally talented, given the many industry-specific acronyms my work used, the Sorkin-like rapid pace of meeting dialogue, and the number of people talking over each other.

My colleagues enjoyed having interpreters at meetings. I was the only deaf employee in my early years at The Firm, and the interpreters were met with only favorable reactions. Their presence quickly became routine, which encouraged diversity awareness. I can't understate how accepted I felt. It was a large firm that grew to a hundred thousand headcount throughout my career due to explosive growth and acquisitions. Even the hiccups that served as lessons learned involved essentially decent people. I loved working there.

I quickly became the go-to resource for any hearing loss or accommodation discussions. However, not all requests reflected good judgment. A colleague once emailed me to ask if he could skip requesting an interpreter for a deaf job applicant because he didn't want the trouble. It didn't occur to him that, as a deaf person, I might find this offensive. I gently reminded him of his responsibility to provide reasonable accommodations under the law. (Yes, he had to request the interpreter.)

While my Deaf acquaintances always slyly introduced me as "hard of hearing" (since I was not culturally Deaf), The Firm embraced my deafness as a gift from the Equal Employment Opportunity gods, particularly in the early 1990s when diversity training was beginning to spread through corporate America. Even though efforts at the time focused on race and gender, my employer was excited to showcase sign language interpreters in the workplace and welcomed any chance to put me on the diversity pedestal. With the enactment of the Americans with Disabilities Act (ADA) in the early '90s, this opportunity became even more potent.

Was that spotlight genuine or opportunistic? Their intentions were good, but the execution was sometimes awkward. I felt responsible for representing my diverse segment and paving the way for future hires, and my superhero fascination still compelled me to compensate for my shortcomings through overachievement. In return, the company always appreciated and recognized my hard work. It felt like a win-win.

When Human Resources announced they would be filming an in-house video for their first diversity training series launch, I knew they would ask me to be part of it. "They're going to want sign language," I told my manager when the memo came out. Sure enough, two enthusiastic videographers made a beeline for my desk and asked to film me, thrilled to have some visual action to feature.

"Sure," I said, "but I don't have an interpreter here right now, and obviously, I voice for myself."

"Your speech is perfect," said one, dumbfounded. "You can't even tell."

"I wear hearing aids," I replied warily. "I can hear the sound of my voice."

"How about just you on a conference call, then?" asked the other. "Could you do some sign language?"

"You want me to sign?" I clarified, perplexed. "While I'm talking on the telephone?"

"Oh! Well, what if you just sign to the camera for a little bit?"

"The thing is," I said, "there aren't any other deaf people here for me to sign with. I'm happy to be filmed with an interpreter signing to me, which is an accurate representation, but I don't want to simulate something fake."

Ultimately, the final video struck a balance between authenticity and a low-key style despite the videographers' initial desire for more flash and sparkle. I kept waiting for them to pull out a Braille document for me to rub, but thankfully, they did not.

* * *

Human beings are complex, and a critical ally can also be an obstacle. For example, the boss who encouraged me to use sign language interpreters also battled his own demon: anger management. To his credit, the Angry Manager was one of the most supportive bosses I've ever had. Except when he wasn't.

It was easy to tell when the Angry Manager was upset because his face would visibly change: His mouth would tighten, and his words would come out in a literal spit. Fortunately, his anger was rarely directed at me. He felt overlooked and being left out of the loop always set him off. He wasn't imagining things either. He was a straight white male whose female superiors didn't take him seriously — an intriguing role reversal — and I guess he found that concept exceptionally hard to digest.

I once went to Human Resources when the Angry Manager threatened to fire me because I asked him to calm down during an outburst. Despite this incident, I would still greet him warmly if I saw him today. I genuinely liked him as a friend, and the feelings were mutual. However, we had conflicts, particularly when his demon and the corporate disability pedestal collided head-on.

In the '90s, The Firm had solicited new business ideas from employees. I submitted a proposal to an executive vice president I'll call Jeremy, who was the CEO's right-hand man, outlining a plan to expand and market an existing program to the Deaf community using TTY communications. The proposal moved forward as a modest initiative. Jeremy's response was particularly receptive — to be honest, over-impressed — and he personally wrote me many effusive notes of thanks.

The Firm hosted an all-company reception at a hotel every year and gave out several awards based on co-worker nominations. The trophies were large, massively heavy Lucite columns with a pointy tip and jagged side. (I often visualized them as impromptu defense weapons when completing emergency preparedness training classes.)

The day before the awards reception, the Angry Manager informed me with more than a little edge that Jeremy had nominated me for — and I had won — one of the prestigious awards. However, when Human Resources notified the winners' supervisors to confirm eligibility, the Angry Manager preemptively rejected my award — he told me this to my face — because he hadn't been in the loop on the nomination. He said I had won the previous year (although back-to-back wins were not prohibited), so he instructed Human Resources to grant the award to a different employee on our team whom the Angry Manager had personally nominated.

I was acutely aware that I was a pawn caught between two men manipulating me for their own agendas. Jeremy had put me on the disability pedestal after several brutal mass layoffs, knowing that recognizing the deaf team member would be a feel-good choice to end the year on an upbeat note. It would have been interesting if the Angry Manager had said, "He's using you, and I'm calling off your award because it smacks of tokenism." But in reality, the Angry Manager was reacting to being left out of the award selection process (and the bypass of his nominee), so he responded by denying my recognition.

We attended the awards reception grouped by team, with a couple thousand local employees in attendance. Jeremy repeatedly dropped my name and business idea in his keynote speech and then announced a surprise: I was the first-ever recipient of a new spot bonus, personally selected by the CEO!

The event felt like a game show with an embarrassing avalanche of prizes. However, no one had informed the Angry Manager about the spot bonus either, and he sat beside me, clenching and unclenching his fists. I couldn't enjoy the moment. The excessive attention didn't feel genuine, particularly with the Angry Manager giving off nuclear reactor meltdown vibes at my side.

The awards ceremony began. My name was called! On top of the other acclaim, Jeremy had intervened to reinstate the annual award despite the Angry Manager's interference, which infuriated him even more. (The other team member also received a trophy.)

I stood with the Angry Manager at the reception afterward when Jeremy suddenly bounded into our circle. Jeremy greeted me effusively by name, turned to my boss, and extended his hand in introduction. The Angry Manager's jaw tightened in fury when he realized Jeremy had no idea who he was, a vice president in his own right. But Jeremy knew me, his new BFF.

Did I receive the recognition because I was deaf or because of my hard work and dedication? Had anyone else even been considered for the CEO's spot bonus? The company had been through a significant upheaval and needed a morale reset. Who could quibble with choosing someone with a known disability? Was it grandstanding or justified because I had a decent concept and pushed it through? Either way, the recognition felt disproportionate to the business proposal.

Still, better to be put on a pedestal than thrown under it.

* * *

I worked in project management at The Firm for almost thirty-three years, the last half as a people manager and vice president. Due to ongoing acquisitions, reorganizations, and departmental restructuring, endless opportunities fell into my lap, which meant constantly acquiring new skills and juggling multiple responsibilities. I felt fortunate to work with people I loved and found the work interesting. As The Firm grew, project meetings morphed into larger and larger calls, sometimes with up to 100 participants. I continued using signers to interpret the same.

Several bosses after the Angry Manager, I worked on a high-priority effort involving mainframe systems controls. My regular job was to oversee change requests related to data-driven rules on the mainframe systems, so my role on the project was as a subject matter expert.

The individuals leading the initiative didn't work in project management and weren't aware of standard protocols. They would call meetings with only ten minutes' notice despite nothing urgent to discuss. While I could usually get an interpreter assigned still within that day, ten minutes wasn't enough time to even drive to our office campus. (Remote options were not yet available.)

I talked to the project leaders several times, informing them that the immediate timeframe precluded getting an interpreter assignment. I requested they establish a recurring weekly meeting invite (same day/same time) so I could schedule an ongoing interpreter job in advance. They refused. To the project leaders, every meeting was of drop-everything urgency. Unfortunately, they believed that the priority of their project gave them a pass on providing accommodations. The ADA was still young, and ambiguity existed regarding how the laws were applied, which further complicated the situation.

When the project leaders called the first urgent meeting without the possibility of an interpreter, my boss at the time chose to attend in my place, essentially serving as a seat filler. Although he probably thought he was doing me a favor, reassigning an inaccessible task — for example, substituting a less-qualified individual to participate — was actually not acceptable under company policy if a reasonable accommodation was available. It didn't matter that our team was not the meeting organizer.

The urgent invites continued. I skipped the ones if I couldn't get an interpreter. The project leaders complained, but I felt that I had no choice. Fortunately, that particular boss was reasonable, and we could always discuss disagreements. He was smart and ambitious, although new to people management. Interestingly, I had previously worked for *his* boss, who told me he thought my boss was afraid of me, and he wanted my feedback for my boss's personal development. I didn't think my boss was intimidated; he was just low-drama and avoided conflict. I'm sure he rolled his eyes and sighed each time the project leaders escalated their complaints.

When it became evident that the last-minute summonses would continue, I offered to step down from the project. In hindsight, this was absurd because I was considered the business owner of the content being discussed. (While the technical partners could provide the raw data and programming logic, I managed the knowledge of the business reasons behind the rules.) Additionally, a company acquisition had just occurred. I was one of four team members given a bonus contract to stay with the company for at least two more years. Our role was to provide continuity to the new management on the systems' business rules, which was precisely what this project addressed.

Getting an interpreter assigned was not hard. The project leaders just couldn't see beyond what they perceived as unnecessary inconvenience. However, ADA accommodations are not required to be convenient to be considered reasonable, and they are not always a one-time, straightforward request, like procuring a particular piece of adaptable equipment. Some people need a different work schedule that deviates from company hours. Others need a desk configuration that doesn't match the rest of the office design. I needed advance notice to line up interpreters.

When the technology manager, Ching, learned of my offer to step out of the project, she voiced her solidarity: "If Rebecca's not on the project, then neither am I." That was the epitome of allyship, to lend her power in a situation where my voice alone wasn't enough to influence change.

Ching's reinforcement reversed the direction of the tide. Technology resources were in demand, and a systems project couldn't proceed without them. Ching's unwavering support validated that my participation was essential and that my request wasn't unreasonable. Knowing that the technology team had my back was honestly one of the best affirmations I've ever received.

Bolstered by Ching's support, I pushed back. I emailed the senior leader of the compliance division at the time, who also happened to be the project sponsor. He had tried to recruit me for an open position several years earlier, so I felt comfortable reaching out to state my case.

To be ADA-compliant, job descriptions had to identify any physical capabilities required by the work, for example, being able to lift fifty pounds. To my knowledge, none of the job descriptions within the company excluded candidates based on their ability to hear.

I facetiously suggested to the compliance leader that his team would naturally want to revise all of the company's job descriptions to reflect that team members with disabilities were not eligible to apply for postings because the "urgent" nature of assembling their meetings would always outweigh the responsibility to provide reasonable accommodations. It was a bluff (and maybe borderline extortion), but my point was this: No department was above the law. He said he would see what he could do. I gave myself a fist pump.

I contacted the accommodations department at the corporate headquarters for clarification. They were flummoxed, saying they were unaware of any other team member who had requested sign language interpreter services, so no procedural precedent existed. They said they would discuss and get back to me.

I want to acknowledge that The Firm wholly supported federal laws and paid for my ongoing sign language interpreters without complaint. It wasn't that management or the accommodations department weren't willing to help. However, it was an earlier time, and the real-life details of how to apply accommodation policies had not yet been fleshed out. So, more discussion was needed.

Meanwhile, the project leaders continued to complain to my boss, and his low-conflict response was that I simply attend the meetings without an interpreter to keep the peace. Basically, rely on lipreading for the project leaders present in the room but still miss what was being discussed by everyone else on speakerphone. I said no. My boss and I spent an hour debating the tenets of the ADA.

"If I use a wheelchair, and the project meeting is on a floor accessible only by stairs, then I am prevented from participating," I argued. "A reasonable accommodation request is for the project to move that meeting to an accessible room so that I'm included." He agreed.

"How is my situation different?" I asked. "If I don't have enough notice of a meeting to line up an interpreter, I'm excluded from participation. You would never ask someone who can't navigate stairs to just suck it up and answer questions being shouted down a stairwell."

He didn't feel it was a direct comparison. We were at an impasse. I ended up leaving for the afternoon. I didn't storm out dramatically. I'm not sure anyone even knew I was gone. It wasn't like I was planning to quit. I loved my job, but I needed to take a step back and recalibrate on how to proceed next.

Apparently, a lot happened while I was gone. I don't know who was involved or who said what, but when I returned to work the next day, ready to resume the discussion, my boss informed me that yet another senior leader had authorized an extremely generous solution for me to have a full-time interpreter at work. I was speechless.

On the one hand, I was grateful for how the debate unfolded. While the initial discussion was uncomfortable and slightly heated, it uncovered gaps in understanding how to apply accommodation laws. I appreciated that there was room to discuss and disagree. I gave myself a back pat for sticking it out and advocating for my rights, especially considering the devastating experience I had at the law firm where I simply gave up. Gutting it out was a significant step forward for me. Progress!

Moreover, the discussion remained professional and respectful without shaming or a traumatic aftertaste. No one was saying I wasn't good at my job or disparaging my hearing loss. We just had different understandings. Our exchange of legal interpretation was almost clinical, trying to define where the accommodation yardstick began. No one took offense. I continued to think highly of that manager even after he moved to other roles, and I still consider him a friend.

On the other hand, I had mixed feelings. I wanted a basic policy interpretation and got the Cadillac of accommodations in return. A lot of money was being spent to make everyone happy. But what if my regular interpreter got sick or stuck in traffic? As grateful as I was for The Firm's generosity, I couldn't help but think that the solution was mostly about not inconveniencing anyone else. I just needed a recurring meeting invite, which was already standard for most projects, so the solution felt a bit overblown.

But this was how my interpreter, Mark Alan English, came into my life, so I wasn't going to split hairs.

13

Mark Alan

first met Mark Alan at a Deaf Culture Salon at a local college in the 1990s. The Salon was a hip social opportunity — like a pop-up nightclub but with lectures — that brought together various corners of the Deaf community to discuss important topics. This particular event was about the persecution of the Deaf during the Holocaust.

The Deaf community was highly interactive. I watched the crowd signing wildly in ASL and felt intimidated by their fluency. Amidst the attendees, I spotted Mark Alan holding court, all eyes focused on him with rapt admiration. He was the alpha dog in the group and wickedly amusing, based on the laughter coming from that area.

"Who, question mark," I signed to the Deaf psychologist sitting beside me.

"Mark Alan English," she fingerspelled. She knew him. Everyone knew him.

And I remembered because of his last name — "English" — which is the first question every interpreter asks: "Do you sign ASL or English?" It struck me as hugely ironic that an interpreter's last name would be "English," considering that within the Deaf community, signing in English meant you were "hard of hearing" — the ultimate insult — meaning, not Deaf.

When the agency randomly assigned Mark Alan to interpret for me one day, I remembered having seen him before. His signing was as fluid as if we were old friends just chatting away, and I specifically asked the agency to assign him to a two-day computer training class. We talked during breaks, and Mark Alan's sense of humor made the time fly by. His exceptional interpreting skills also impressed me. I began requesting him for all of my agency jobs.

By that point, I had been assigned a million interpreters, but none compared to Mark Alan. He was by far the best, molding seamlessly into the conversation as if he knew what people would say next. It was hard to get on his calendar, though, as he was a popular choice and booked solid. My best option was to schedule him for recurring invites stretching months into the future.

When The Firm gave the green light to schedule a full-time interpreter, I immediately asked Mark Alan if he was interested. He agreed. We then penciled him in and blocked off a few months at a time. Periodically, I asked, "Is this okay? Are you sure you want to spend so much time here?" He said he did. After all, it was a good gig, being booked all day without gaps for transit and having time to work on his own business between calls.

I can't emphasize enough how critical Mark Alan's interpreting was for me at a time when my hearing was rapidly spiraling. His presence leveled my playing field and proved I was as capable as anyone. I owe him an enormous debt. I owe him my career.

I also felt grateful to work for an employer that genuinely believed in fairness. The Firm (as Mark Alan tagged it) tried to ensure everyone had an equal chance of success from the start. The only discernable difference between myself and my colleagues was that I couldn't hear.

On a personal level, Mark Alan and I were a good fit. We were freakishly alike, six weeks apart in age, former Catholics with red hair and freckles, borderline hypochondriacs, and similar preferences for weather, food, music, and art. We owned the same dining room table sets and curtains, acquired before we even knew each other. We swapped book titles and movies, liked the same authors, and often had the same reactions. With two exceptions: I was single and straight, and he was married and gay.

Mark Alan is one of the most compelling people I have ever met. He is a natural attention seeker, the life of the party, the one to whom everyone turns for witty insights and thoughtful commentary. He has impeccable ethics and a strong passion for combating injustice. I have learned so much from him.

Aside from medical professionals, Mark Alan was the only person with whom I ever debated cochlear implants. He was my impartial sounding board and the person I trusted most concerning a critical life decision.

So, consider yourself introduced.

14

Mother 1.0

My relationship with my mother was complicated. "Arms length" was the description that came to mind. I thought we co-existed just fine with 751.4 miles between us. My parents were solid, upstanding people, but neither was particularly sentimental. For example, during one annual visit, my mother declined to commit to meeting up with me at all because her water aerobics class at the Y might be rescheduled. (We eventually connected.)

Our visits were polite and pleasant, usually involving group gatherings like family picnics or birthday celebrations. The dynamic between my mother and me mirrored that of many mother-daughter combos, equal parts love and driving each other batty. I never knew quite what to think: whether my presence was as out-of-sight-out-of-mind as I perceived or whether my mother felt slighted because I booked time with my siblings first. She never commented one way or the other, and I wasn't angling to spend more time alone with her either.

My mother and I were basically strangers, given that I had spent my teenage years mostly with the Cult, then moved out of state at nineteen. Deafness was also a contributing factor: I struggled with using the voice telephone, and she didn't use a TTY or relay service, so we rarely spoke outside of visits. I saw her in person at most twice a year. We were good for about an hour of conversation, ticking off distant relatives' doings but never discussing much about ourselves.

A friend once asked if it was difficult growing up in an awkward relationship with a parent, and I said no, not at all. That's just how we were, and I didn't know any different. Our primary struggle was a disparity of context. When my mother expressed frustration, she didn't distinguish between typical childhood grievances and the challenges posed by my deafness. At that phase of my life, neither did I. It was only later, after venturing out on my own, encountering other d/Deaf individuals, and observing how their parents communicated with deliberate visual cues (even without sign language), that I realized the difference. Their proactive efforts to accommodate and adapt reinvented their parent-child relationship. They flipped the script and made space for deafness in their daily routines instead of the other way around. Who even knew that was an option?

My mother wasn't a mean person. Like many others, she mistook hearing loss for not listening. It's extremely common. Consider the frequent usage in television and movies of the phrase "Are you deaf?" as an expression of anger, meaning "Why aren't you listening?" Society pretty much conditions us to view hearing loss as a character flaw rather than recognizing it as simply another aspect of human diversity.

I get it. It's incredibly frustrating when you think someone isn't paying attention. You feel disrespected and irrelevant, and it makes you mad. But hearing loss is not the same thing. Unfortunately, many people fail to grasp this. They express annoyance at having to repeat themselves but disregard common-sense strategies for better comprehension. Invariably, they speak louder and louder until they snap. Like the Hulk, their impatience transforms into real anger.

They dismiss the context because they personally are not deaf. All of their energy has been channeled into their absolute conviction that they have been defied without considering the recipient's inability to hear.

How do I explain this? Parents raise their voices at their children all the time — to clean up their mess, do their homework, and get ready for school. But in a fair society, reprimanding someone for their hearing loss should be off-limits. I sometimes see online posts from mothers who sheepishly admit they lose their temper when their deaf child doesn't hear them, always with a chuckle and a sense of amusement as they relay the story. Their cluelessness is evident. When you scold or snap at someone because they can't hear you, you shame them, even if you're not yelling or angry. And most of the time, people won't tell you how belittled and small you made them feel because then it's shame squared — the shame of being shamed. They will shut down to get you to shut up, yet the layers of shame still accumulate, unforgotten, because you are not the only person who makes them feel this way.

It's a harsh, unvalidated assumption to believe a person with hearing loss isn't listening. I often remember the Crabby Cookie Guy, a curmudgeon who ran a little shop near work. It was such a great paradox — cookies and an ornery owner — but the cookies were a welcome afternoon treat even if the vendor wasn't.

A co-worker and I went to get cookies one day. I asked for a chocolate chip *pecan* cookie, and the Crabby Cookie Guy replied he didn't have any. I pointed to another cookie and said, "Okay, just chocolate chip then." Apparently, the cookie I pointed to wasn't chocolate chip, and he screamed in rage, "I JUST TOLD YOU I DON'T HAVE ANY! ARE YOU DEAF OR JUST DUMB?"

Everyone in line was shocked at his angry outburst. He didn't know I was deaf. I was already pointing to the cookie I wanted. All he had to do was hand it over and ring it up. The co-worker with me was speechless.

"He just yelled at you," was his shaky, stunned reply as we walked back.

"He did," I agreed. "Some people think that's an acceptable way to behave."

I run into people like the Crabby Cookie Guy all the time. My mother, too, had a rising temper. She'd call my name from other rooms, unanswered. Instead of coming to find me, however, her volume would escalate until she reached a state of fury. It would end with me finally hearing her at 100+ decibels or my sister alerting me.

My mother and I didn't always clash. For example, several years after I moved away, she tagged along with my father on a business trip to Minneapolis. My speech comprehension with hearing aids and lipreading was enough to get by. My mother was a frequent sunbather, so I took her to a nearby beach while my father worked. Their stay was brief, and the sun was out. The visit was uneventful, mainly because my lack of hearing didn't intrude.

The peace was short-lived. That same year, I ended up in the hospital in Minneapolis with a medical issue but in no danger of dying. A week after discharge, I felt I needed to disclose the incident to my mother. I was struggling to hear the voice telephone at the time (the reason I didn't contact anyone from the hospital), and this call was no exception. Even at home with a handset amplifier, I had to ask for multiple repeats, so she was already irate before I shared the news. I told her I had been in the hospital, and she blew up, furious that I hadn't called her sooner so she could have come, which was a noble impulse but not a natural assumption based on our hands-off relationship.

"I didn't want you here!" I blurted out amidst her yelling, probably too bluntly for courtesy. I was keenly aware that my way of doing things as a deaf person collided squarely with her hearing-centric routines and unwillingness to bend. She hung up on me, and while we never talked about it again, I knew what I said had hurt her.

Fast forward ten years. My speech comprehension had deteriorated so far that I had stopped using the voice telephone completely, and our communication was limited to letter writing. (My parents were not using email yet.) My mother wrote and said she was coming to town by herself for a convention. The timing could not have been worse. Hosting anyone hearing would have been tough, but the combination of her strong will plus my inability to stand up for myself spelled disaster.

I had bought a condo, and she asked if she could stay in the building's guest room just across from mine. I played out the scenarios in my mind: My mother would probably ignore my request not to knock on my door, which I wouldn't hear, causing a commotion in front of my neighbors. Since I usually left early for work, she'd have to navigate the bus route downtown to the convention center. If she got lost, she'd call using a voice phone instead of TTY. Each scenario felt inevitable; there was no compromise or pivot.

I wrote back and lied, saying that my company kept a hotel room downtown for guests, which just happened to be open that week, only a block from the convention center. She could use it for free! I didn't tell her I booked a random hotel room and had it directly billed to me. Technically, I didn't leave her homeless, but I still felt guilty about the deception.

I wished we could have talked about things. She really was a very caring person. I distinctly remember her sympathy when I smashed my finger as a kid, necessitating a trip to the ER. I also recall finding an amplified handset on the upstairs telephone when I was twelve, which my mother presumably had acquired for me. It was a kind gesture that also didn't change anything in her own daily routine. (She used the downstairs phone exclusively, as my parents' bedroom was on the main level.) We just never talked about it. I discovered it accidentally one day when I picked up the phone but stayed quiet, like acknowledging it might open a portal to an underwater abyss.

So, we had highs and lows. My mother was a hard-working and selfless parent who cooked family dinners every night and took us shopping for school uniforms. I never felt like she saw me as inferior due to my deafness, but the inconvenience wore her down. Her frustration was evident, and I walked on eggshells to avoid making her angry. She was unable to change her behavior to accommodate my deafness. But I never asked her to either. In fact, I never even thought about it until after I moved away and was exposed to differences in approach.

I didn't experience the same tension with my father, who instinctively faced me when he spoke. He was responsible for buying my hearing aid batteries, which back then were a specialty product only sold downtown at an audiology office near his work, so we routinely had check-ins on inventory. While we never discussed deafness either, I can't recall a single instance where he snapped at me due to my inability to hear. That's not to say he didn't have his own quick temper (which, to be honest, was sharper than my mother's), but deafness was just never the trigger.

* * *

My mother liked trying new restaurants and arrived in Minneapolis bearing a list of dining destinations. While I worked, she went to the convention, and I chauffeured her around town at night. Our friction resumed as we drove the city streets: little explosions volleying back and forth. She talked nonstop from the passenger seat, and for the first time in my life, I tried to self-advocate. I repeatedly told her that I needed to lipread and couldn't look at her while driving.

Undeterred, she kept talking, growing angrier by the minute. I finally remarked sharply that I couldn't hear her and would not respond until we arrived at the restaurant. I had no idea what she was saying. I was close to tears, having forgotten how demoralizing it was, feeling powerless to confront her.

The week felt like a distressing flashback to a previous life, except for one significant moment. On the first night, after dinner, I escorted her back to her hotel. As we located her room, her demeanor shifted. She confided in me, admitting that she'd never stayed alone in a hotel before and was afraid. She asked if I could stay with her. It was a rare instance of vulnerability, and I betrayed her. I begged off, saying I wouldn't have time to go home and change before work the next day.

I wanted to be gracious, I honestly did, but kindness failed me. How did I ever think it could be my superpower? I was overwhelmed just spending a few hours together. I desperately needed to take off my hearing aids for the day, but we had no history of co-existing in a deaf state. So, I helped her move the hotel room furniture in front of the door to make her feel more secure. Then I left.

I replayed that moment on an endless loop for years. What if I had chosen to break the cycle of mutual rejection? The door between us was ajar, and I closed it with my own hand. When I told her I needed to go, I saw it on her face: the realization that I couldn't bear to be alone with her, even in her moment of need. I saw myself through her eyes and cringed at the reflection.

Our saga continued. Each day, I resolved to start over. After all, my hearing was much worse than what my mother would have remembered. Meanwhile, I had been working at a progressive company and had gotten used to talking about accommodations. I was able to tell her what I needed from her for communication. But what I couldn't do was take the next step to confront her outright and say, "Why are you ignoring everything I just said?" I was frustrated and exhausted. *Was it possible that I was invisible?*

On the convention's final day, she told me to drop her off at the airport and not come in. I reminded her that we were going to have dinner before she left. She said she was tired and wanted to sit alone before her flight. For five hours! I asked if she was sure. She said yes. I did not argue. I dropped her at the airport.

Needless to say, it was a terrible trip for both of us. My mother never visited again, except when the whole family converged for a holiday weekend a few years later. However, she continued to write letters and send birthday gifts as if nothing had happened. She seemed glad to see me during my annual hometown visit. My hearing loss was just a separate compartment we couldn't navigate, like the hidden partition inside my computer that I couldn't access, even when my hard drive was full.

My siblings undoubtedly see things differently from me, but even when our experiences aligned, their context differed; they were not deaf. I hesitated to include my mother in this book at all — old patterns of remaining silent die hard — but her role is a key part of my story, and it probably resonates with yours, too. Maybe you find yourself frustrated when your deaf child doesn't hear you, conveniently forget when a spouse tells you what they need, or subtly shame them when their deafness is visible. Or maybe you have hearing loss but struggle to communicate your needs or hold others accountable for accommodating you.

Despite our challenges, we can still work toward creating a more inclusive and supportive environment for everyone. We might not have all the technology or answers yet, but simply recognizing the need for change is the first step in the right direction.

15

Getting Started

B ack to Mark Alan, who had been interpreting for me for a few years by now. In a workday packed with multi-attendee meetings, a bit of time was spent waiting for conference calls to connect or resolving technical difficulties. Mark Alan and I always chatted on mute as we gave organizers the opportunity to success-fully launch calls (or, if necessary, reschedule). On this particular day, he casually mentioned that he had interpreted cochlear implant evaluation sessions and wondered what I thought.

I knew about cochlear implants. For fun, I used to spend week-ends at the Biomedical Library while working for the Psychotic Psy-chology Professor. From everything I'd read, CI experiments back then yielded partial success at best. However, a decade had passed, and my impressions were based on outdated information.

The Deaf community's protests had peaked by the time Mark Alan and I began discussing implantation. While I considered my-self borderline anti-implant, my reasons differed. I wasn't a member of the Deaf community and culture. No, my objections were more squeamish: Images of the early transcutaneous CI procedures — metal prongs protruding right through the skull — horrified me.

Insane, I thought. *Not in a million years.* I told Mark Alan adamantly that I would never consider snaps sticking out of my head. Impeccably neutral, Mark Alan said he thought the processors were now connected by a magnet.

Since I already had noise recognition with my hearing aids — which I could take or leave — I replied that I didn't value anything less than understanding speech. Mark Alan mentioned that some of his clients with CIs used the telephone, a point to consider.

I asked him where someone would even get an implant, and he told me about a local CI clinic and teaching hospital where he had interpreted many times. He even had the telephone number in his planner. I said I'd think about it.

The winter dissolved into spring. I decided to call the CI clinic to inquire about a consultation. I told myself it was only for research purposes and probably would go nowhere. Without any discussion, the person who answered the telephone immediately replied that I didn't meet the qualifications to score an appointment with the CI audiologist.

"Oh, okay," I said, surprised. "Goodbye."

In hindsight, the voice on the other end probably assumed my hearing loss wasn't severe enough to meet the eligibility guidelines for a cochlear implant, given my unaccented speech and that I was using the telephone. However, she didn't know the call was on speakerphone with an interpreter signing. Even though I got shot down for an appointment, I wasn't disappointed. The research on cochlear implants then seemed uninspiring, which added to my reservations. The detour bought me more time.

I moved the idea to the back burner. While I enjoyed debating pros and cons with Mark Alan, I found it annoying to receive unsolicited newspaper clippings about cochlear implants from casual acquaintances — always with a cheerful note attached: "You should try this!" — as if they not only had an exclusive scoop on a revolutionary new technology but seemed to think the invasive skull surgery was as trivial as wash-out hair color. I'm sure they meant well, but out of the blue, I didn't appreciate their input. It was like gaining pounds and people sending brochures for weight loss camps. "How helpful," I would say brightly. "Thank you for bringing this to my attention."

Being able to hear was their center of reference. It was the foundation upon which their world revolved, and they couldn't imagine life without it. They projected those assumptions on me, certain that I felt the same way, too.

They assumed wrong.

* * *

From what I see on social media, most people believe that all cochlear implantees experience equally successful results. Unfortunately, that's not true. CI outcomes can vary from imperfectly excellent to good to mediocre to downright disappointing. Speech comprehension usually doesn't materialize at activation either; progress takes time and effort. Even with hard work, long-term success is still not guaranteed.

I quizzed Mark Alan about his other clients with cochlear implants.

"Why do they still need an interpreter?" I asked.

He shrugged and said they just did.

Months passed. I noticed another drop in speech comprehension. Finally, three years after my bout with pneumonia, I decided to give the CI clinic another call, with Mark Alan interpreting. This time, the response was different. "Fax me a copy of your current hearing test from your ENT clinic," responded the voice on the phone. "I'll check with the CI audiologist to see if you might be a candidate for evaluation."

> Note: My old Ear, Nose, and Throat (ENT) clinic and the new CI clinic were separate, unaffiliated organizations. While the ENT clinic provided general hearing tests, it did not offer any services related to cochlear implants.

"I'm having an audiogram soon," I offered. "I'll fax the form over as soon as I have it."

That was a lie. Thanks to the chamber of horrors that my old ENT clinic had been in my life, I hadn't had my hearing tested for a couple of years and had no plans to do so ever again. What was the point? Most audiogram equipment couldn't even register my right ear and barely picked up sounds on my left. As for the CI clinic, I didn't believe I met the criteria for receiving a cochlear implant — although I didn't actually know what the requirements were.

Still, I was a tiny bit curious. My hearing changed weekly, and time spent on audio-dependent tasks was tedious. Many late-deafened adults describe their descent into silence as unbearably lonely. This is the sad side of hearing loss — the isolation. Family and friends often exclude their loved ones from conversation out of laziness, a sense of entitlement, or an unwillingness to pivot. Sometimes, the exclusion is intentionally cruel, a punishment meant to prod the deaf individual into taking action, but that only creates a bottomless sinkhole of shame. Either way, the person with hearing loss often feels too embarrassed to ask for what they need.

It's heartbreaking to read the online posts from people losing their hearing. Many are so despondent they can barely breathe because their social structure has collapsed. I wish I could think of a parallel, like being diagnosed with cancer or one's house burning down, but there is no comparable loss for which otherwise decent human beings wouldn't shower the victim with compassion and accommodation or where the victim wouldn't ask for and get help. For example, if you broke your arm, you'd expect a ride to the family picnic.

Isolation carries its own nuances as well. Acquaintances flatter themselves by presuming that individuals with hearing loss would always prefer their company, oblivious to the fact that feeling lonely within a group can be worse than being alone. Solitude isn't necessarily a retreat into self-pity; it can signify a deliberate act of empowerment — a choice to reject situations that fail to accommodate one's access needs.

I felt lucky to be a cautious observer of life with an introvert's ability to recharge within myself. Since I had no family obligations nearby, I micromanaged social situations to my liking by meeting up with friends one-on-one. As my audio experience shrank, I embraced being bossy and selfish about where I sat for optimal logistics. Eventually, anything that required me to hear was just not a good use of my time. I also genuinely liked spending time alone. Writing was best in solitude, a respite rather than a hardship. I tried to be purposeful and less frustrated in my approach — to adapt *away* from hearing — because the indisputable fact was that virtually nothing was accessible to the d/Deaf.

I daydreamed about leaving the hearing world behind completely. Living in silence seemed like such a hopeful prospect. Wasn't it better to leverage strengths instead of limitations? Deaf people with zero hearing were some of the most confident people I'd ever met. Cocky, even. And they navigated through life with such grace and charm that their lack of sound seemed like no barrier at all.

But I had one more task to accomplish: to explore the potential of a cochlear implant. Even if I was eligible, I knew the outcome might not be better than the little hearing I had. Nonetheless, I wanted to cover every base. So, off I went to suffer the last audiogram of my natural hearing at my old ENT clinic.

* * *

There weren't many things in the world that I truly hated. I could count on one hand the people I severely disliked (four, to be exact). I wasn't fond of parallel parking or the taste of coffee. However, visiting my old ENT group topped the list of things I absolutely detested.

I resented everything about my annual visit. I begrudged every second of the day on which I would be informed the measurement of my hearing had once again dropped. The pretentious, oversized ear sculpture on the front lawn was a source of loathing. Once, I saw a dog urinating on it and smirked. I cursed that there was no parking even remotely close by. I dreaded the audiologist's dramatic disappointment in my scores, knowing their exaggerated reaction would only add to my discouragement. But mostly, I hated that the staff seemed completely unprepared that a patient might be deaf. At an ENT clinic!

"It's not inconceivable that a patient might not be able to hear," I had vented to the technician at a previous appointment. "In fact, this is where people with hearing loss are supposed to go. Why is my name being called behind a closed door, where I can't see what you're saying? And wouldn't it be a good idea to put a note in my file that says I'm deaf so we don't have to repeat this conversation every year?"

But now, in the autumn before my cochlear implant assessment, I was back at the dreaded ENT clinic, sucking it up because an official audiogram was my admission ticket to even get my foot in the door at the CI clinic. I scheduled the appointment at the suburban ENT office location, hoping a change of scenery would lessen the misery. Upon arrival, I discovered their less-robust testing equipment maxed out at 100 dB. *Did profoundly deaf people only live in the metro area?* I needed 110 to 120 dB to repeat any words back accurately, which meant I failed all of the speech tests, eliciting frantic reactions from the audiologist behind the soundproof window. It was everything I hated with a vengeance.

It was my first audiogram since the pneumonia. Sitting in the car afterward, I realized I probably wouldn't have gone if I had known the sadness it would cause. As I suspected, the sound recognition in my good ear had significantly declined. My bad ear? Zero percent recognition across all frequencies.

I sulked for a few months before calling the CI clinic to find out where to fax the dreadful audiogram results. In the meantime, I stashed the document away in a drawer, like a child with a failed report card, reluctant to show anyone. Finally, with Mark Alan interpreting the call, I shared my latest audiogram scores with the receptionist at the CI clinic. She immediately scheduled an appointment. I felt ambivalent. I told myself that I was only researching the possibilities. Deep down, I didn't think I was going to proceed.

Sensing my malaise, Mark Alan told me about the last time he interpreted for a proctology exam. Mark Alan described it in detail: Patients were positioned facedown with their heads in a hole in the exam table. Therefore, Mark Alan had to lie on his back *underneath the table*, with the d/Deaf patient peering down at him through the opening. This made me laugh and cheered me up to no end.

A couple of weeks later, I met with the audiologist at the CI clinic for the first time. I felt the difference immediately, a complete lack of condescending judgment. Extreme hearing loss was welcome here! The audiologist didn't show the slightest bit of disappointment in my audiogram scores and, frankly, seemed delighted. It was a significant turning point. I was not a freak! I wasn't even atypical, given that only people with profound hearing loss made it through her doors. How strangely the tides had turned.

The audiologist explained how the cochlear implant worked and outlined the surgical procedure: A small part of the mastoid bone behind the ear was removed, and a CI receiver and magnet were placed inside the skull, slightly above the ear. A strip of electrodes was wound snugly inside the cochlea. A magnetic headpiece connected an external sound processor to the internal magnet. Sound streamed to the receiver in the skull via radio waves.

At the CI clinic, the audiologist tested my hearing again as a formality to ensure that my loss met the eligibility guidelines. Based on the ENT audiogram, she predicted I wouldn't be able to respond at all since her test capped sound at the eligibility threshold.

Eligibility requirements differ by clinic, country, or insurer and have loosened as the implant procedure has improved. At the time, my CI clinic required a hearing loss of 70 dB or greater, a prior memory of speech, suitable skull physiology as confirmed by imaging, and the ability to communicate orally (through speech and lipreading).

Adult cochlear implant success favors those who lose their hearing after learning to speak, as their brains have a baseline memory. This allows for a quicker learning curve for unscrambling the signals once the electronics are activated. Additionally, recent exposure to auditory stimulation, whether through natural hearing or hearing aids, also benefits a CI candidate. Just like a car plugged into a battery charger is more likely to start compared to one kept in storage during a frigid Minnesota winter, the auditory nerve is more responsive if it has had timely activity.

The audiologist told me to make myself comfortable and handed me a magazine. I stared at the soundproofing and squinted my eyes intently, even though I had probably never registered sound at 70 dB before in my life. I caught myself thinking that the average success rate for speech comprehension with a CI at the time (50 percent) was still better than zero.

We concluded our first visit. I had mixed emotions. I met the test score criteria for candidacy, at least on paper. Yet, I was cautious and struggled to keep an open mind. I didn't know anyone with a CI and didn't trust the procedure would be successful. I needed time to process the audiologist's information and come to terms with the possibility that — dared I say? — cochlear implantation was a possible option.

Thanks to a same-day cancellation, I met with my family physician that afternoon to discuss a medical referral for the cochlear implant if I chose to proceed. She and I had a tortured relationship, thrust together after my long-time physician retired and referred her caseload in bulk.

My history with physicians was highly polarized. Our relationship was either wonderful or terrible, with nothing in between. The negative ones contradicted everything I said, a trait I recognized in myself with people I disliked. I knew I needed to find another doctor, but deafness made me a creature of habit. I was familiar with how things worked at this office. I knew how to watch the chart bins to confirm when my name was called from the waiting room. I knew the sequence of questions the lab tech would ask. So, I tolerated her.

The physician said she didn't know a lot about cochlear implants but couldn't imagine a life worse than being deaf. I raised my eyebrow. She didn't seem to register the insult. I ignored her comment and told her what I knew about CIs: that there was a slight risk of either meningitis or facial paralysis and that the surgical procedure destroyed all the natural hearing in that ear. I mentioned, perhaps too darkly, that a CI seemed like a sacrificial backing-into-a-corner, like having a proactive mastectomy for someone with the breast cancer gene.

She was concerned. She wanted me to see the psychologist in her practice to discuss. I thought it unnecessary since a psychological evaluation was already ahead as part of the CI clinic's formal evaluation process. However, I needed my physician to start the referral paperwork to my insurance company, so I caved to her quid pro quo and said I'd go.

As we scheduled the appointment, I decided to treat the family practice therapist as a dry-run for the CI evaluation. Back at the office, I asked Mark Alan what I should say. Mark Alan's background was psychiatric interpreting, after all, and he thrived on the adrenaline of lockdown wards despite his squeamishness over the sight of blood. He mentioned that psychiatrists listened for code words, such as "overwhelmed" or "heaviness," as a basis for prescribing drugs.

Did I need drugs? I had no ongoing anxiety, melancholy, or despair. Accessibility angst, sure, mainly relating to having to hear my name called from behind closed doors in medical waiting rooms. My dissatisfaction wasn't with life but with feeling like an imposter in a world created for everyone else. I wondered what it would be like to live authentically. Was there a drug that could make that happen?

A few days later, I met with the family practice psychologist. I explained how my perception of the CI procedure had evolved: initially viewing it as the equivalent of a proactive mastectomy, then a pacemaker, and now a hip replacement — each comparison became less emotionally daunting.

The psychologist said she liked the progression and asked whether I felt "overwhelmed." I stifled a laugh, thinking about Mark Alan's code words for drugs. I told her no but that I was tired of the endless loop of hearing loss followed by the cycles of grief. She thought de-escalation was a reasonable means of coping and emphasized the importance of validating my feelings rather than dismissing them. We talked about why I hadn't told anyone other than Mark Alan that I was considering the CI, and she assigned me a writing task to complete the following sentence: "If I tell people, then <dot> <dot> <dot>."

Back at the office, Mark Alan rolled his eyes dramatically and crossed his arms jokingly as I explained my missed opportunity for drugs.

I decided I needed to meet real-life implantees next. I attended a social gathering for potential candidates at the CI clinic. I made two key contacts: One of them I'll call Bill. He had already undergone implantation and displayed an American flag decal on his headpiece. We swapped business cards and made plans to have lunch. He invited me to feel the bump on his head. I declined.

The other individual I'll call Linda, a late-deafened school teacher. Her sister had been taking notes for her during the presentation portion of the social gathering and glared at me suspiciously. The sister seemed ticked that someone else was talking to Linda rather than applauding her for transcribing the meeting content. (I guessed that Linda was also looking for a support system.) When her sister turned her back, we made plans to meet.

Linda and I clicked immediately. We were close in age and even lived in the same neighborhood. Neither of us knew anyone with a CI, and we compared lists of questions and answers received. She hoped to have the surgery and rehabilitate during her summer break from teaching but was worried whether it was enough time. We agreed to meet regularly for coffee and information.

After the social, I met up with Bill, whose implants were two years old. As I had hoped, he was a fount of CI information.

"Cochlear implants have always worked," said Bill as we sat down. "It's just that the target candidate pool has changed."

Bill told me many things about the cochlear implant surgery: that he worked from home for a week; that he couldn't wash his hair for a few days; that in the Midwest, the head shaving was done as a thin strip compared to other parts of the country where half of the head was shaved; that the process for closing the incision varied by the surgeon, from stitching to stapling to gluing; that when he was in pain at the hospital, ringing and ringing for a painkiller from the nurse who never came, it turned out she had been talking to him, unheard, over the intercom; that I was the ideal candidate and that Susan — the deaf teenager at the CI social who wanted an all-in-the-head implant — was not.

Some post-surgical discomfort was expected, said Bill. Dizziness, a headache, some bleeding. He did not sleep on that part of his head for a few weeks afterward. He mentioned head rushes and tongue-tingling. He said taste disturbances were expected after the surgery due to the proximity of the procedure to a facial nerve, but they typically went away.

Bill was profoundly deaf, like me, although his pre-implant audiogram scores were better than mine. He told me that he had often cried from happiness since his implant and that I would cry, too.

"What's that noise?" he asked his wife repeatedly.

"Crickets," she explained. "Rain on the roof." "The ceiling fan."

His best speech comprehension score, post-implementation, was 96 percent. He cried afterward, he said. He heard it all.

Bill told me about the psychological evaluation and that he and a friend went in together as candidates. His friend's hearing loss was slightly more profound, but only Bill was approved because the friend had unrealistic expectations.

"Time and patience," intoned Bill, and I wrote it down on the work papers I had brought with me to the restaurant in case I got stood up. He tapped the table repeatedly. "Time and patience. Your brain has to work at its own pace. If you expect too much, you will get frustrated. It has to happen on its own."

Bill recommended books on tape as a good training tool and also attending audio therapy. Bill again offered his head to touch, and I did, stroking the hard bump of his scalp and noticing that his hair seemed different there, like a patch of grass re-seeded from another source.

Back at the office, I kept thinking about the conversation. I asked Mark Alan if I had a deaf accent like Bill, and he said no, unblinking. I was quiet. Sometimes, Mark Alan and I were so in sync that I wondered whether he was mirroring back what he thought I wanted him to say.

I told Mark Alan about potential side effects, and we howled with laughter. "I don't need the implant, but I'm here for the tongue tingling," Mark Alan drawled, pretending to be me as a slacker. "I originally wanted a stud in my tongue, but like, this is so much better."

16

Evaluation Day

After completing a round of counseling at my regular physician's office and gaining valuable insights, I felt better prepared for Evaluation Day, when the CI clinic would determine whether I was a medically and psychologically stable candidate for cochlear implantation.

I spent the morning with the CI clinic's psychologist, who was warm, witty, and helpful. Straightaway, she asked how she could accommodate me in communication. I pulled out my FM system, which was a small box that transmitted her words directly into my hearing aids from a microphone clipped to her lapel.

God bless whoever invented the personal FM system, one of my first assistive listening devices, a precursor to Bluetooth. As an adult, my FM system made the difference in everything from taking computer training classes at work with my back turned to understanding speech in noisy restaurants. Completely by accident, I discovered the pulpit microphone at my church had been wired for FM use, which enabled me to follow the sermon from the last row of the balcony, 150 feet away.

Back then, my friend Dave was the church's music pastor. The person who set up the sound system had probably assumed that all FM users used the lightweight headsets provided at the front desk and thus could still hear the choir and other sounds in the background with their ears like the rest of the congregation. However, I carried my own FM receiver in my purse and used a neck loop (not a headset) that transmitted via my hearing aid's t-switch (or telecoil) setting. To eliminate background noise, the t-switch blocked everything except direct sound from the FM microphone.

This meant that, unless I intentionally turned off the FM system during the music portions of the service, I received only the voice at the pulpit microphone, not the choir behind Dave nor the congregation next to me. And Dave trilled exuberant melodies, humming, scatting, and playful "la la dee dee boop boop" improvisations, completely diverging from the choir's performance (obviously thinking no one else could hear his personal accompaniment). It was an unexpected private concert that was pure joy, the highlight of my Sunday.

After Dave left, another pastor, Joel, conducted the singing from the pulpit mic, and he had the loveliest voice imaginable. Hearing him sing (and once again, only him) through my FM system felt like being serenaded, and I loved it. I absolutely loved it. Eventually, someone from the church must have figured it out and wired more platform microphones into the FM system. After that, I heard the choir and congregation singing like everyone else. Sigh. I missed the magic of my private radio frequency.

But back to the psychological evaluation.

So much was riding on this day! I wondered if I had gained an unfair advantage by bringing my FM system, like an athlete doping before a sporting event. I asked the psychologist whether using an assistive listening device was considered cheating, and she assured me it was not. She explained that her role was not to evaluate but to define expectations and to advise of surgery risks. I pretended I was being interviewed on a talk show and tried to be as articulate and charming as possible so they would invite me back.

Right out of the gate, she asked whether I had a significant other, presumably to assess whether an intimate partner was pressuring me into the surgery, a common red flag. I see this situation all the time in online forums: "Do it for me," the spouse says. "I'm tired of always having to repeat myself." (*Cough* See chapter on gaslighting.)

The psychologist probed for details on romantic relationships. I told her about my great unrequited love, a hearing man I'll call "Z." We hung out for several years but were only ever close friends. She asked what it was about Z that I admired. I smiled and replied that he was the kindest person I'd ever known. I thought we could be a superhero duo for service.

He was the standard by which I still measure accommodation. The two of us had dinner at a friend's house, and afterward, he washed the dishes while I sat at the kitchen table. His back was facing me, but he made a point of turning his head toward me every time he spoke so I could lipread. That was what I always remembered about him, I said, the gestures. I never felt like an imposition.

I sometimes questioned whether I had romanticized his courtesy or if my decades-old recollection had been saved through an overly idealistic lens, but he really was a good soul. I wanted to marry the type of person I wished that I could be. I thought he was The One, but ultimately, he wed someone else. When the psychologist asked how I felt about this, I shrugged and said I was disappointed, but I loved him so profoundly that I genuinely wanted him to be happy, regardless of whether that was with me.

I never asked why Z turned me down for a first date. But I was a different person then and lacked the tenacity for follow-up. I had just started my job at The Firm and hadn't yet been exposed to training and coaching that strongly influenced my professional and personal development. For a while, I let myself wonder. There were a million possible reasons, arbitrary and ordinary, yet I always assumed that deafness factored into his hard pass, although he would have been far too polite ever to have said so. Did it matter why? He had the right to choose what he wanted.

I had to confront my own disability mindset not that long after. I had joined an online dating site that matched prospects based on a detailed questionnaire, with no option to run my own searches. After a few weeks, in the spirit of transparency, I decided to add deafness to my profile. Instantly, my algorithm changed. All of my recommendations thereafter were men of every spot and stripe of disability. It would have been fine if those matches had been interspersed randomly based on obvious mutual interests. However, my profile had clearly been punted to an entirely separate classification tier, like the Arboretum's discounted bags of utility apples — blemished but still good. I removed the deaf reference from my profile, but it was too late. The algorithm pursued me as doggedly as if I had been shot with a paintball gun. I canceled the membership and never checked the app again. Was my reaction that different from Z's?

The psychologist asked whether I thought about romantic prospects in the future. I said sure. After all, my dating relationships had been largely positive. Deafness was like truth serum; people with bias tended to show their hand before they could advance to boyfriend consideration. In hindsight, this was a blessing since I had no idea who I was back then or what I wanted and probably would have erased myself out of a desire to seem lower-maintenance.

I wasn't opposed to future marriage or a long-term partnership, I said. I just didn't want to be the minority in my own home. My husband either needed to be deaf or willing to meet halfway. Actually, more than halfway. Defaults always tilted in favor of the majority, so equality as a deaf individual in a mixed partnership would never happen on a fifty/fifty autopilot. It would require a conscious commitment by a partner to reject the standard gravitational force through which the hearing orbited. Meanwhile, living authentically was more important to me than being married, so I wasn't holding my breath.

She asked whether I had always felt this way. I said no, that my priorities shifted once I realized how liberating it was to let go from constantly struggling to fit into the hearing community. I told the psychologist about a friend I'll call Robert, a building contractor, who was quite short and had built a stunning house precisely measured to his height. I was inspired by Robert for bucking convention and customizing his environment for himself, even requiring his taller roommate to stoop to wash the dishes. I began fantasizing about accessibility. The concept was a novelty at the time, before accommodation laws. At a party at Robert's home, I caught myself thinking that I could do this. I could create a deaf-centric home that worked for me. Deafness was my normal, not a deviation from it.

The psychologist seemed to understand. We discussed hearing loss as a parallel to a mixed race or interfaith family, straddling two worlds but not truly belonging to either. I told her that while socializing with others like me had been a revelation, my other foot was still in the hearing community out of necessity. I aimed to wring every possible benefit from making electronics recognize and interpret sound for me because I wanted a reliable bridge. I needed more than hearing aids or cochlear implants. I needed portable technology to pick up the slack and unravel spoken language into written form in any circumstance, for example, when my devices were off.

She asked what I would do differently if I could hear, post-implant. I had to think hard. My life would not revolve around the implant, I replied stubbornly. The CI might bring convenience, but it wasn't a stand-alone solution. I still wanted choices. More than anything, I wanted technology to convert words into visual output. I already had sound with my hearing aid, and it wasn't enough. Accessibility was coming. It had to.

She said she was impressed with the answer. She explained that part of her job was identifying candidates with unrealistic expectations of how a cochlear implant would change their lives. Some candidates, for example, pinned all their hopes on a miracle cure and felt disappointed after successful surgery and activation because the implant didn't take them back in time. Beneath the bionics, they were still deaf. Their families wanted them to be hearing.

When the psychologist wondered if implantation could improve social interaction, I reluctantly agreed. But, I argued, why was that burden always on me? If hearing individuals couldn't muster enough effort to communicate with me now, wasn't our relationship superficial? And if so, why would I value social interaction with people who could only accept me on conditional terms?

But there were exceptions, I hedged. I told the psychologist about Chad the Computer Guy, a sweet but marble-mouthed suitor I met at an electronics store and how our relationship ended solely because of my inability to understand him. I told him I was deaf while chatting, and he asked me out, intrigued. Our first three dates were in restaurants, seated across from each other. Although he did everything right (within the constraints of his natural speech), understanding him was a lot of work. *A lot.*

I never even knew his last name. He told me twice, and I asked him to spell it, hoping that would shed some light, but I still didn't get it. By the third date, it felt rude to bring it up again. Today, we would bump cell phones to share contact info straightaway, but this was before mobile devices and speech-to-text apps, plus I figured I was bound to stumble across his surname organically, somehow.

We went to the zoo on our fourth date. Trying to walk and talk simultaneously was impossible. Chad proposed a fifth date. I was honest and said I didn't think so. He asked why. I explained that I didn't have even a basic level of speech comprehension with him, plus my hearing would only go downhill in a more challenging environment. He said that was a very, very good reason.

He was sweet, and I liked him a lot. I didn't want to offend him by belaboring his mumbly style of speech. He took the rejection well and seemed visibly relieved that it wasn't because I wasn't interested or because of any boorish behavior on his part. We shared a hug, and he walked me to my car.

Okay, I conceded to the psychologist. If the implant worked, it would most likely improve social communication. I hated admitting this on principle, but that didn't mean it wasn't true.

She asked what I would do if the surgery failed since it would destroy my remaining natural hearing in that ear. I acknowledged that the procedure was a sci-fi crapshoot. Yes, I could end up worse than where I started, but I was prepared for complete silence. If it failed, I thought I might open a pastry shop since I used to work at a kosher bakery and liked it. Her jaw dropped. Secretly, I was pleased.

The psychologist asked how owning a bakery pertained to losing my remaining hearing. I explained that I would consider making a change to a career with no dependency on the telephone, that's all. Baking had been an accessible outlet since I was a kid, a celebration of all my other senses: the smell of the bread, the sight of the dough rising, the touch of the punch-down, the taste of the vanilla bean. Hearing was irrelevant. I could see the minutes on the timer and tap when the cakes were done. She laughed and said that she never thought of that.

She asked me to describe my mood. I told her I was happy. I explained that I had started a gratitude journal after my bout with pneumonia, and it prompted me to form goals, think about kindness, and be grateful. When I mentioned that I loved my job, she seemed surprised. I wondered why. Was it a prerequisite for everyone to come in unhappy?

We talked about grief, and I think she understood that I couldn't continue like this, hemorrhaging my hearing in spurts. I'd rather just be completely deaf than constantly grieve and readjust. It was time to make a proactive change. The direction it went didn't really matter.

Our interview concluded. I felt good about it overall. It seemed like the psychologist had given me the green light. I was one checkbox closer to the end!

Next was the CAT scan. I checked in forty minutes early in case they could fit me in. They could! A technician escorted me to the scanner.

"You're gonna get a cochlear implant, are you?" he asked.

"Maybe," I said, removing my earrings and metal hair band.

"Sweetheart," he said. "You can't even tell."

I sighed and took off my hearing aids, lay on the scanner, and let it suck me in. The CAT scan department gave me my films, and I carried them around like an art portfolio for an hour, killing time before my appointment with the surgeon.

I arrived at the surgeon's office. The nurse had already sent me to an exam room and popped in again to say the surgeon was still at the hospital and wouldn't arrive for another forty-five minutes. That was fine, I said. I brought work to do, and there was a desk in the exam room, so I was just happy not to be in the waiting room, on edge, listening for my name. I noticed that she glanced at my legs twice as we spoke. I looked down and saw why.

It was April, but the day was unseasonably warm. Earlier that morning, I threw on a pair of shorts without glancing in the mirror. My friend Geoff and I had been experimenting with bronzing gel the previous night. And on this morning, the momentous day I was being evaluated for cochlear implantation, each of my shins was sporting a bright orange stripe down the front while my calves were as pale as a pina colada. As I sat in the examination room, the fluorescent lights exposed the tiger-orange cast of the bronzer, causing it to glow like radiation.

The nurse's eyes flickered to my knees and back to my face, snickering as I desperately tried to pull my shorts down and cross my legs, tucking them discreetly under my chair before the surgeon arrived. I was extremely nervous. The amount of hysteria I had absorbed from the online bulletin boards had led me to believe that the approval process for cochlear implantation was arbitrary, like a sorority rush or country club admittance.

It wasn't.

While the evaluation process did indeed weed out those who had unrealistic expectations, had medical constraints, or were under duress from family members, the reality was that anyone who met the current eligibility guidelines concerning their degree of hearing loss and oral speech history was likely to be CI approved, assuming they were emotionally stable and had a clean CAT scan, no extenuating medical circumstances, and health insurance to pay for it.

I wish I had understood that because it would have removed 99 percent of the anxiety I experienced on Evaluation Day. On paper, I met all of the necessary criteria. However, the online bulletin boards seemed to indicate that evil snipers picked off a constant stream of potential candidates from approval lists. Were they even real people behind the screen names? Were their denial tales even true, or had pertinent facts been omitted? Their desperation and anguish should have been red flags. Still, I believed a mysterious initiation process was ahead, requiring a password or secret handshake. And I honestly thought it was all in the surgeon's hands.

It wasn't.

He arrived forty minutes late. I didn't know what to make of him. His natural facial expression was a cross between a squint and a frown. I had a list of questions and began asking them a bit defensively, thinking he was challenging my qualifications. His answers seemed abrupt and evasive, which added to my uncertainty.

"How long after the surgery can I go back to work?" I asked.

"I don't know. It varies," he hedged.

"Ballpark," I said.

"Whenever. A week."

I asked whether the implant could make me more susceptible to other illnesses.

"No," he replied, squinting at me with his odd expression. "Why would you say that?"

"Well," I reasoned, "you're putting something inside my head that wasn't there before. Maybe it gets infected."

"No," he said, frowning. "It doesn't."

I relaxed as the time passed. The frown was the surgeon's natural facial expression. He asked to see my written list but didn't offer any proactive commentary or sales pitch. After answering my questions, the surgeon lapsed into silence. I found this unsettling, especially for an evaluation. I finally blurted out: "Look, are you approving me as a candidate?" He asked whether the psychologist had approved me. I said yes (although she never came out and said that, exactly).

He held my CAT scan films to the light, said my mastoids looked good, and that either ear would be fine for implantation. My eyebrows shot up in surprise. I wasn't about to belabor that my approval was basically the absence of denial. I met the criteria. Why wouldn't I be approved?

At that time, implantation was limited to one ear. Even though the audiologist had recommended implanting the better ear, I told the surgeon I preferred implanting my worse ear because it had zero comprehension to lose if the outcome was poor. Instantly, I bit my tongue. Did I just imply I had minimal confidence in his surgical abilities? (He didn't seem to take offense.)

Implant success generally favored more recent hearing loss (i.e., the auditory nerve was active recently, and the brain had a timely memory of speech), which was the basis for the audiologist's recommendation. However, I was not a risk taker. CIs were still relatively new, and I didn't trust the procedure would work. Even though it had been thirty years since I understood speech without lipreading in the worse ear, I had heard the sound of my voice with a hearing aid my entire life, so I felt rehab was doable. I planned to keep my mildly better ear as a backup, and if it turned out to be a lesser companion to the implanted ear, then so be it.

The surgeon and I waited for each other to blink.

"What's next?" I asked to break the silence, although I wanted to shake him and say, *stop leaving me hanging!*

The surgeon said we could schedule the operation.

"Oh, okay," I replied, surprised that it was that simple. "Yes, let's do it."

He called back his nurse and secretary, and we compared calendars. At this clinic, cochlear implant surgeries were scheduled only one day per week, and the first opening was nine weeks later, on Mark Alan's birthday. I already knew Mark Alan would be out of town, so I picked the following week, July 7th.

Lucky seven, I thought. Seven-seven. It didn't get better than that.

17

Telling People

The weeks after Evaluation Day were a fog. I was conflicted and thought I might still cancel the surgery if cold feet prevailed. Two and a half months seemed like an eternity, but it was a standard wait from what I understood.

Linda, the teacher I had met earlier at the CI clinic social, had become my hearing loss twin. She lived right down the street from me, and I rode my bike past her house every day. Also, her procedure was scheduled with the same surgeon a week before mine. As we approached identical stages of preparation, we agreed that only fellow CI recipients or candidates understood our unique fears and mindset. I looked forward to our coffee talks as we compared notes. It was like looking in the mirror.

I immediately informed Mark Alan of my surgery date but was stumped on how to tell others. I dreaded their reactions, remembering how a friend exhaled relief after I threw away a favorite T-shirt. "Oh, thank God. That hole in the armpit was huge. I was so embarrassed for you." I wanted to avoid similar retrospectives.

A month went by. Finally, I confided in my friends Rob and Jan, a beautiful and musically talented couple who radiated positivity.

I knew they would offer unwavering support without judgment. I motioned them into a huddle when I saw them at church that Sunday. They seemed to sense the magnitude of what I was about to say and leaned in.

"Hey, can I tell you something?" I began, not sure how to convey the news. Thankfully, Rob and Jan were the perfect people to tell. I made a mental note to contact them first for any exciting updates I might have ever again. Their enthusiasm was contagious and sincere, and I instantly felt reassured. They were like professional listeners, engaged with rapt attention.

"You are the only people I've told," I confided, and they seemed flattered. I mentioned I still had doubts, and they promised to pray.

After Rob and Jan's preview, I felt ready to share the news more widely via mass email. I knew everyone would be happy for me because — let's face it — hearing people want everyone else to hear as a matter of principle. I don't say that meanly. It's grand if a person has the ability to hear, of course, but that perspective often assumes hearing as the solitary acceptable scenario, deeming any other variation as inferior, which is a form of ableism. Suppose you replace the phrase "want everyone to hear" with "want everyone to have your specific skin color," "your specific gender," or "your specific faith," and you can see the problem.

First, I needed to tell my family. I knew they'd give me a thumbs-up without judgment. Frankly, that relaxed approach was preferable to people fussing with wide-eyed emotion or that downgrade in reception you can feel and see when others discover you're deaf. My siblings never treated me differently because of my hearing loss. No, they went with the flow and made good-natured jokes when I flubbed.

I doubt my siblings ever thought about my hearing. For example, when my brother brought his wife to meet the family, he didn't tell her that I was deaf. So, when she and I first spoke, I asked her to face me directly because I needed to lipread, to which she graciously obliged. She asked my brother later why he hadn't given her a heads-up, and he responded that it never occurred to him. I think that was true for everyone in my family, particularly my sister Barbara, a year older than me, with whom I shared a bedroom growing up. While Barb probably never thought about my deafness either, she didn't need to. She just adapted instinctively. To her, my hearing loss was a part of who I was. I was *her* normal.

With no disrespect to my sister, I recently saw a canine version of this online. A family had an older dog, then brought home a puppy who was blind. The older dog figured it out quickly and simply adjusted, nudging the puppy and placing toys under the puppy's nose to smell whenever the older dog wanted to play. I thought it was sweet, but it bugged me that the comments highlighted readers' tearful reactions instead of recognizing the older dog as a role model for how families can acclimate to disability without emotion or entitlement. The older dog grasped the situation without judgment. He didn't continue waving toys unsuccessfully in front of the sightless puppy's eyes. He didn't whine about unfairness or the unreasonable burden of his little brother not being able to see. No, the older dog saw the big picture — he had someone new to play with! — so he pivoted to non-visual signals that worked equally well for both dogs.

It wasn't difficult to tell people my news. However, I didn't expect anyone to understand my dilemma: my disappointment with the inaccessibility of life, despite existing in a so-called electronic era with an accommodations law that had been in effect for over a decade at that point. The clock had ticked away years with only minor technological advancements from a d/Deaf point of view, and my options for fully engaging with the world were few. There was no family pressure to implant, no gun pointed at my head, just the glaring fact that no other alternatives were available.

I had been dragging my feet on the announcement because I didn't want unsolicited opinions or teary congratulations regarding my decision to undergo the procedure. While I welcomed discussions about the technical aspects and potential outcomes, I sought objectivity. The acquaintances who made pronouncements in hindsight about my hearing loss having been "a lot of work" (for them) were never the people who made any effort to accommodate me. The prospect of their happiness over my impending surgery felt like an implicit agreement that I wasn't an acceptable time investment unless I was "fixed." It was one thing if people unselfishly worried I was missing out on a beautiful experience. However, they had no way of knowing that beyond comparing me with themselves. They just didn't want to pivot, and I was over it.

Around this time, my mother started using email, and her response to my news pleasantly surprised me. While she avoided mentioning my hearing loss directly, her message still conveyed warmth and hometown pride while discussing aesthetic solutions to cover the incision. She wrote:

> "Terrific news, babe. Do you have a preference as to the type of headgear you will prefer? How about a Browns cap and an Indians hat to start? Maybe something a bit more exotic later on. Keep us informed. Love, Mom and Dad."

I shared my surgery update on a chat bulletin board. My attention had been laser-focused on CI research and the evaluation process, so I was caught off guard when a deaf man emerged from the online shadows and expressed interest. Go figure — sometimes romance blossoms when you aren't even looking.

The time was before Facebook and Instagram. The new guy was a fellow CI candidate and contributed to several online bulletin boards I frequented. His insightful and genuine posts impressed me, so I was flattered when he reached out. I named him "Vertigo Boy," as he suffered from the dizzies and was also a major flirt who apparently sent female hearts a-spinning.

The bulletin board participants were from around the world, but Vertigo Boy lived in my town. He was a month older than me, recently divorced, and had several children. It turned out that my surgery was on his birthday, and his implant activation fell on my birthday. Coincidence or foreshadowing? I thought it established a rom-com "meet cute" factor between us.

I found myself drawn to Vertigo Boy's charm and conversational skills, and it was easy to see why he remained friends with his exes. He wasted no time sending me his photograph, and he had the confident good looks of someone who mated easily and frequently. I knew he was popular on the online boards and had a friendly smile.

Vertigo Boy said he wanted to visit me in the hospital and drive me home after my surgery. That was a quandary. He was a complete stranger. Vanity prevailed; I didn't want him to see me in person for the first time with a swollen face, black eyes, and various post-surgery marks. In an attempt to turn the tables, I offered to stop by and see him after his surgery, which was scheduled a week before mine.

He seemed laid-back, but my risk radar beeped *red flag*. He could have been an axe murderer or a con artist. Maybe he stalked cochlear implantees, killed them in a back alley, ripped out their electrodes, and sold the parts on eBay. (Just kidding; there was no resale market for internal cochlear implant parts.) However, he was friends with Doris, an older member of the online bulletin board who was kind and trustworthy, so he was probably all right.

My guarded reaction to Vertigo Boy paralleled my concern about the easy acquaintances I had formed online, an artificial sense of intimacy created from our shared experience, similar to Antarctic penguins instinctively clustered together against the cold. Eventually, the weather would change, and we would no longer need each other. For now, though, we huddled close.

* * *

M y clinic provided some helpful information about the surgical procedure. They were clear that the operation would permanently destroy my natural hearing on the implanted side. They disclosed other potential complications:

- Facial paralysis.
- Infection.
- Pain.
- Sound disturbances such as tinnitus or roaring.
- Taste disturbances.

Taste disturbances after cochlear implant surgery were common. Crucial nerves near the implant location controlled facial movement and sent impulses to the taste buds and tongue. Because of the risk of damaging the facial nerves and/or causing paralysis during surgery, the procedure purposely steered away from those risk areas and toward the nerves controlling taste. While the bad taste after CI surgery was usually temporary, a couple of implantees complained it had been years. So, that was another potential risk to ponder since I liked my palate and hoped to avoid this side effect.

Wrapping up appointment obligations, I had my last visit with the psychologist at my family practice as a condition of getting my medical referral. She imparted some helpful advice:

- Instead of offering a lengthy explanation when strangers pointed at my cochlear implant processor, say, "This is how I hear," and leave it at that. They could ask additional questions if they wanted.

- When experiencing communication difficulties after the operation with my now completely dead ear, offer a pen and paper and say, "I just had surgery. Write it down." No apology. Do this consistently. It would get easier.

- If I had a bad day, say, "I'm having a bad day" and accept that whatever emotions I felt were temporary. There were no invalid feelings. Allowing myself to feel and express them would help in the long run.

Back home, I quickly checked my email and found a second message from my mother waiting for me. She wrote:

> "So, your sneaky sisters jumped the gun and invited themselves up to your town before Dad and I had a chance to get into the flow. By virtue of my seniority, I overrode them. So we propose to drive up when the time comes and spend a few days playing Clara Barton. This plan is a great one. We can travel at our leisure, probably taking a few days to do it. We are very flexible as to the date, etc. WE REALLY WANT TO DO THIS. Love, Mom."

As I read the note from my mother, a feeling of dread washed over me. "Oh, no, no, no, no," I groaned inwardly and even smacked my head in frustration as the psychologist's exercise flashed in my mind. "If I tell people ... my mother will get involved."

I knew that my mother genuinely believed her plan was doable and heroic. However, I could not see the bright spot on the horizon. Despite her generous and hard-working qualities, my mother tended to impose her will on a given situation. If the process deviated from her plan, she would get mad. I knew she cared for me deeply but was set in her ways, particularly when it came to hearing.

Growing up, I never felt brave enough to suggest that my mother try alternative approaches, such as flicking the hall light switch — right where she was standing — to get my attention visually instead of hollering in vain from the bottom of the stairs. Meanwhile, my sister Barbara figured out the overhead light signal in our bedroom before she was ten.

I mentioned earlier that my mother was my Girl Scout troop leader for a short time. Once, during a camping trip, she furiously dumped a plate of spaghetti on another scout's head, which you might think would be a disqualifying offense. *Please.* The troop was run by a Catholic parish during the heyday of corporal punishment. No, I was the one who got kicked out. I was playing with a ball at a meeting and didn't hear my mother telling me to stop. She sent me home and expelled me from the troop altogether.

In regards to my surgery, I knew my mother would propose to come, never mind her disastrous last visit, because she was a giving person. She liked the idea of playing nurse. I was also sure she mistakenly thought (as most people did) that a cochlear implant would instantly restore my hearing upon waking from surgery. However, implant activation would not happen for another three weeks. I'd have even *less* sound during her proposed visit because the surgical procedure would destroy my natural hearing. Was she going to pull a rabbit from a hat and suddenly start signing? No, the burden would be on me to lipread and do all the work to communicate.

Since my mother predictably got angry when I didn't understand what she said and since I never stood up to her, I couldn't see the benefit behind her generous proposal, only additional stress. I lived in a small condo. I wouldn't hear the lobby intercom or a door knock. I did not want to give them keys to walk in any time.

Perhaps my thought process had crossed the line into being ungracious. Returning to Minneapolis after visiting my hometown was always such sweet relief, and I felt like I could breathe again. I didn't want the work of having to be hearing while recovering nor endure annoyance at my refusal to conform. *Maybe it was me who was controlling. Maybe I was even more like her than I thought.*

My mother had usurped my siblings' offers and cut to the front of the line, so there was no way I could ask one of my sisters to come without causing an international diplomacy incident. Therefore, I politely declined my mother's kind offer in a note, explaining that having people here twenty-four/seven after surgery would be too challenging and that I needed to recuperate in silence in the days following, which was quite true.

To her credit, she replied that she understood. Vertigo Boy shared that his mother was in town to render post-surgical assistance, and I thought it was sweet. When I mentioned my mother's note to Mark Alan, he looked at me incredulously, saying that he would have loved to have his mother, who always made him feel better when he was sick, come and take care of him.

So, clearly, our mother–daughter relationship was missing a secret ingredient. Maybe the surgeon could fix this, too, while he was at it?

I met up with Linda and commiserated, as her sister also tended to interfere. I felt indebted to Linda because her surgery date was first, and I was drafting in her wind, using her experience as a reference point. It was helpful to follow someone else going through the same thing at the same place with the same people. It helped me understand what to expect. It satisfied my need for predictability.

Linda knew her appointment dates already. Her activation was only three weeks after her surgery, which boded well for me since we had the same surgeon and audiologist. Vertigo Boy had a different timeline: His activation was scheduled six weeks after surgery, yikes, but he was being implanted at a different hospital and with a different equipment brand.

My audiologist had promised to email my activation date and refer me to an aural rehab therapist. As luck would have it, my conference call got canceled that same afternoon, and with Mark Alan interpreting across from me, I called the CI clinic. Surprisingly, the receptionist simply pulled up my appointment details on her computer and informed me of my activation date, July 28, three weeks after my surgery. In addition, she mentioned she had my follow-up appointments.

"I don't know if I'm supposed to give this out," she said hesitantly. I quickly reassured her it was fine, *it was fine,* that the audiologist was going to email them today anyway. She read off the dates rapidly, and Mark Alan didn't even bother to interpret. He lunged for a pen and scribbled them down before she changed her mind.

Now that I had my surgery and activation dates, I finally knew my bionic name (a string of codes representing my equipment, surgery date, software, and hook-up date). "Welcome to Bionic World," Mark Alan said, laughing, as he shook my hand. "We hope you enjoy your stay."

***

Vertigo Boy was implanted a week before my surgery, so I headed to his hospital to meet him in person. He was asleep when I arrived, so I left a care package and note on his bedside table with a trashy tabloid magazine about aliens landing adjacent to his hospital.

As I strolled through Vertigo Boy's ward, I thought about the logistics of my upcoming procedure. Mark Alan and my friend Patrice would be at the hospital on Day One. A former work colleague, Patrice asked great questions without judgment and was as fascinated by the procedure as I was. She insisted on taking the day off work to be there for me at the hospital.

Getting home on Day Two was still a question mark, though. I didn't know when I'd be discharged or the time of the audiologist check-in before I left. Linda offered to pick me up, which was incredibly kind of her. We would both be at the CI clinic that day. But would our schedules align?

Vertigo Boy reiterated he wanted to drive me home, even though he would only be one week post-implant. I knew he had recently experienced a vertigo episode and was nervous about driving. Was I nuts to consider getting in a car in a vulnerable state with someone I'd only recently met online?

The day after Vertigo Boy's surgery, we chatted. He told me his procedure went well and was sorry he missed me in person but loved his care package. He was determined to visit me during my hospital stay and was bringing a book he thought I would like. If I was asleep, he said he would draw a red dot on my forehead (the Hindu cultural mark called a bindi), which I think he mistook as the equivalent of drawing a mustache on my face. So, I had that to look forward to.

18

Surgery

I awoke at 3:59 on the morning of my cochlear implant surgery and intercepted the bed-shaker alarm clock precisely one minute before detonation. The bed-shaker was an early piece of adaptive technology — an alarm clock attached to a small box that simulated a violent earthquake underneath my pillow at the designated time.

The experience of waking up to a bed-shaker alarm clock is the equivalent of lying in a busy street before being run over by a Hummer. If Jimmy Fallon were to write a "Friday Night Thank You Note" for bed-shakers, it might read something like this: "Thank you, bed-shaker alarm clock, for making sure I am wide awake when I die from a coronary out of fright." Nothing trains your mind better to wake up on its own — at any time desired — than using a shake-awake.

I started to check my email and got an unexpected instant message from Vertigo Boy. He couldn't sleep, he said, so he logged on. We ended up chatting for an enjoyable twenty minutes. To my amazement, our mutual friend Doris logged on. The odds of all three of us being online at four o'clock in the morning on the day of my surgery seemed astronomical, so I took it as a positive sign.

I arrived at the hospital early and saw Mark Alan outside, flagging me down. He was nervous enough for us both and had been aimlessly walking around in the dark. Mark Alan was there as my friend but also as my official interpreter.

The registration area was bustling with activity. I mentioned to the intake nurse that the visitation pastor from my church might be stopping by, and she promised to send him through. I nodded and took a seat in the waiting room, distracted by the thought: *What if the visitation pastor tried to shake my hand or hug me?* Typically, these gestures were comforting, but not today. As per hospital protocol, I had just spent the last two days scrubbing my head and every inch of my body with a stinky, sterile solution estimated to cut the risk of infection by 70 percent. I really, really didn't want anyone transferring germs.

I was aware that my mind had taken an irrational U-turn. Logically, just stepping foot into a hospital unleashed a tidal wave of bacteria swarming my body. But in a spectacular display of stress-induced insanity, my germaphobe tendencies went turbo, and I imposed a ridiculous, no-contact zone for myself before surgery. Even Mark Alan got caught in my obsessive snare.

"Don't touch me!" I screeched when Mark Alan reached to hug me upon arrival. He jerked back, his hands raised in the air as if I had barked "Clear!" with a defibrillator. I felt silly for reacting so strongly. I could only imagine what the visitation pastor would think, alarmed, if I shrieked and pulled away as he reached to pat my arm in comfort.

Touching in the name of faith tended to get awkward, anyway. A few years earlier, during the opening night of one of my plays at church, a pastor's wife hugged me a bit too enthusiastically, inadvertently placing her hand smack-dab on my hearing aid, which triggered a loud squeal of feedback. Instinctively, I turned my face away to stop the sound. She probably thought I was a pathetic soul who must have needed hugs because she then doubled down, clutching me even tighter. Her embrace evolved into an unfortunate tussle of wills, her determinedly gripping my head and me trying to pull away to stop the loud feedback blasting in my ear — my good ear. It was such an inelegant moment. I should have gently said something like, "No harm done, just my hearing aid beeping," but I didn't want to embarrass her for not knowing that touching electronics caused feedback. (Although you'd think the noise might have tipped her off.)

It was a déjà vu flashback. A decade earlier, I had attended a tent revival as a friend's guest, not knowing what I was getting into. The preacher, a Tammy Faye Bakker look-alike, began wading into the audience and casting out demons without consent, using both hands to box people's ears. Instantly, she zeroed in, startling me by clapping her hands around my head. I pulled back, my hearing aids squealing loudly. Until then, she had been muttering in a trance-like state, but the unexpected sound shattered her concentration. Our eyes met. She froze, her face a picture of shock. I suppose she could have exploited the situation further for dramatics, but after a momentary paralysis, she simply moved on to the next dark soul. While relieved she changed course, I had questions about her methodology.

First, I was reasonably sure I wasn't demon-possessed. I firmly believe it's my responsibility to be accountable for my own sins instead of blaming third-party influencers. Second, any uncontrollable behavior in others evocative of stereotypical demonic possession is likely caused by a physical or cognitive condition. It's quite the ableist slippery slope to conflate disability and demonic possession, although people do all the time.

But my thought process went like this: She didn't know I was deaf. She didn't see my hearing aids underneath my hair before they announced themselves with a shrill whistle. If she truly believed I was demon-possessed, did she knowingly leave me to rot in eternity by moving on to the next soul? Or was she merely an actor who broke character as soon as the activity went off script, choosing to skip ahead to the next scene?

"What are you thinking?" asked Mark Alan, passing the time. I sighed and replied that I was worried the visitation pastor would try to touch my head when he prayed and that I didn't want anyone contaminating my pre-scrub. But if I tried to stop him, I said, it would seem rude. Should I head him off right when he came in? Was that presumptuous?

Mark Alan looked at me, astounded, and roared with laughter.

"Rebecca," he said once he regained his composure. "This is what you're worried about? That some guy will be offended if you tell him not to wipe his snotty hands on your head?" He covered his eyes with his hands and convulsed with laughter. "They're cutting your head open in two hours!" he stated emphatically, gesturing with his hands. "Aren't you afraid?"

"No," I shrugged. And I wasn't. My worries were channeled into things like having to hear my name called in a doctor's waiting room or the possibility of the visitation pastor sending word back to the church, questioning my emotional stability, and suggesting I might need professional counseling.

My frowny-faced surgeon stopped by. It was only the second time I'd ever seen him, but now he felt like an old friend. He said he liked my haircut, as I had cut off most of it in anticipation of the surgery. Jokingly, I told him he could shave as much as he needed. However, he grimaced and said, "I'm afraid I'm going to have to."

I chose not to read anything ominous into that comment. By comparison, Linda had undergone surgery a week prior and had only a tiny patch shaved behind her ear. However, she got the side effect of the bad taste in her mouth. What was a little baldness in case there was a correlation? The hair would grow back.

The nurse announced the arrival of the visitation pastor.

"Do you want me to leave when he starts to pray?" signed Mark Alan.

"No," I signed back. "Interpret, please."

The visitation pastor entered and uttered the most cringe-worthy question possible: He asked if Mark Alan was my *father*. (Mark Alan is only six weeks older than me.) Two decades later, Mark Alan still recoils at the memory of this indignity. To make matters worse, since the visitation pastor was speaking to Mark Alan and not to me, I missed both the comment and the signed interpretation. Meanwhile, Mark Alan was waiting for me to respond, to defend the honor of his perpetual youth, and I obliviously remained silent. *Ouch.*

The visitation pastor sat down and chatted. He did not shake my hand or touch me. He was far enough away that we were probably not even breathing the same air. Mark Alan winked at me and snickered, reading my mind.

During our conversation, the visitation pastor mentioned the last time he'd seen me in the hospital was four years earlier when I had pneumonia. His comment made me realize that the church obviously kept notes of each visit, leaving me to wonder what he would write this time and how close it might have come to "screams when touched."

It was a lovely visit. I was glad I'd asked the church for prayers. I believe in God, I do, and I pray regularly. I just hadn't realized that checking the box for prayers from the church on the preregistration forms would result in an in-person visit. When the visitation pastor left a message saying he planned to come to the hospital to pray with me on the morning of the surgery, I felt myself starting to balk. Would it be bad form to decline?

"Well," I imagined myself responding, "I did ask for prayers, but I meant only on my terms, from the privacy of everyone's home."

True to his word, the pastor prayed. But what was more astonishing was Mark Alan's interpretation. His rendition was so breathtakingly beautiful that I wanted to interrupt the pastor, for goodness sake, and urge him to witness the stunning visual representation of his words. Nevertheless, I quietly joined in prayer until the pastor finished.

Key surgical team members began to arrive. I named the surgical resident "the Deadhead" because he looked like early Jerry Garcia with a ponytail. I liked him immediately. *Bet you anything, he blasted Grateful Dead in the operating room.* The anesthesiologist was fabulous, flirty, and full of wit. Even Mark Alan — a total needlephobe — asked for her business card in case he needed medical attention someday. I laughed and rolled my eyes.

I asked the anesthesiologist to tell me before she started pre-sedation, as Linda told me she didn't remember anything after, and I needed to remove and store my hearing aids while I was still lucid. "I will never hear natural sound through this ear again," I signed a tad dramatically to Mark Alan as I placed them in a plastic bag, before thinking that I couldn't hear out of it now either, so I mean, really? *Good riddance.*

The anesthesiologist was prepared to start. I handed the plastic bag to Mark Alan and signed, "Ready," with my free hand. I asked her how soon it would take effect, enunciating carefully since I was without devices, and she replied, "About fifteen seconds," which Mark Alan interpreted.

Incidentally, the sign for "fifteen" resembled a "bye-bye" gesture. I was struck by how forlorn Mark Alan looked, his hand folded downward in a sad wave, his palm turned toward his chest. By the time he finished, *whoosh!*

The sedative was not what I expected. I thought it would be warm, relaxing, and pleasurable, like floating on gentle waves in the ocean, but it hit me like a stun gun followed by a steamroller. *I am Flat Stanley,* I thought, aware that my tongue was touching my lips, but I couldn't close my mouth in my paralyzed stupor. I wondered if I was drooling.

The next thing I knew, I was in the recovery room, and Mark Alan was signing that the surgery was over. "Surgery. Finish. Finish."

He interpreted: "Pain, question mark."

I replied in sign language: "None."

"Nausea, question mark."

"None."

At that time, overnight hospital stays were common for cochlear implant procedures, although today they are typically outpatient. Linda had told me that after her surgery, a giant foam doughnut was placed over her implanted ear and wrapped to her head with gauze and an elastic bandage, then taped to her forehead. Because the taping was too low, it pushed her brows down into her eyes, making it difficult to see. This was particularly distressing to someone deaf who had just lost her residual hearing. The turban bothered her all night until she was crying. She regretted not being alert enough to say something.

Remembering Linda's distress, I wasted no time and asked the nurse to trim my turban as soon as I settled into bed. I thought I asked nicely. I even joked, like, "Please leave the eyebrows." Meanwhile, Mark Alan was laughing hysterically.

I asked him later why that was so funny. Apparently, Linda's turban trauma was foremost on my mind when I came out of anesthesia. (I have no memory of this.) But Mark Alan, who interpreted in the recovery room, said I woke up and, in my deafened state, complained about the turban at maximum volume, prompting the post-op nurse to comment, wide-eyed, "Boy, she's not going to need speech therapy."

According to Mark Alan, the post-op nurse actually *faked* trimming the turban to humor me because she feared the surgeon would get upset if she called to ask permission. Later, when I asked again for turban trimming in my room, Mark Alan couldn't help but laugh at my single-minded obsession.

Strange things happen under the influence of narcotics. I have a hazy memory of an older woman in my hospital room being taken away in a body bag shortly after I arrived. While it was most likely a drug-induced hallucination, the second bed remained unoccupied for the remainder of my stay. I'm just saying.

When I awoke, Vertigo Boy was lurking in the doorway. His head was shaved, which looked fabulous, and his incision was still bandaged. He must have already visited my room as a flower bouquet and a book were lying on the bedside table. In my disorientation, I couldn't remember if my hearing aids were plugged in, but I thanked him and mumbled that I needed to sleep, that I just had a shot of morphine and was drugged out of my mind. He departed. I passed out for an hour.

I woke, sensing something amiss. A wave of nausea suddenly gripped me, and before I could grab the plastic basin at my fingertips, I projectile-vomited on my bed, the dead roommate's bed, my gown, the wall, the chair, *everywhere*. It was the scene from *The Exorcist*, minus the head swiveling.

But vomit was not the point. Rather, a high-pitched ringing had started inside my head, and it seemed inevitable that my violent upheaval had either broken the implant or somehow shaken it out of place. I envisioned a gaping dent in my skull, with the electrodes and magnets in disarray, like when the interstate buckled last summer from the heat into a heap of debris and exposed electrical wires. My body dripped with cold sweat. I wondered if my Accidental Death and Dismemberment Insurance policy covered this kind of thing.

I hesitated to ring the buzzer for the nurse, remembering Bill, who rang and rang, not realizing the nurses had been speaking to him through the intercom. However, the floor station was right outside my room, and someone had already come running.

The nurse was unfazed. She hauled me out of bed, pulling my arm across her shoulder like a drunk's to ensure I didn't pitch forward as I was already tipping precariously. The hospital room was splattered and spiraling around me, but she remained composed. She whipped off my gown and stripped the bed while propping me up. It was like watching someone make scrambled eggs with one hand. I wanted to applaud her multitasking skills, but the room was spinning in circles.

Suddenly, everything changed. The nausea vanished, the shrieking subsided, and my head was intact. Nothing was broken. I felt elated as I realized everything was back on track.

My friend Patrice had been at the hospital all day. She popped into my room mid-afternoon and told me she had talked with the surgeon after the procedure. He told her everything went well, confiding that I had "such a nice cranial opening." She said she nodded solemnly and tried hard not to laugh at the odd compliment.

By way of explanation, some implantees have bones or cochleas that are too brittle to work with, forcing the surgeon to abort the procedure. However, my skull crumbled under the drill like a perfect building demolition implosion, and it apparently was spectacular enough to warrant multiple shout-outs. I had no idea.

I declined additional morphine because I thought it was causing my nausea, plus I didn't want the dead roommate coming back in the middle of the night. It was the right call. I gave myself a pep talk. The experience had been positive, with just minor hiccups. Everyone had been highly professional and caring. Having Mark Alan and Patrice there meant a great deal to me. Despite my fears, the inside of my head was not broken. The worst was over.

Plus, I learned how to projectile vomit, which I'd never done before. Continuing to learn new skills was essential for personal growth and self-development.

* * *

The dawn rose on Day Two, and the Deadhead resident came by to remove the turban. To my surprise, he didn't replace the bandage. The head wound was visible and open to the wind, which alarmed me initially, but he said it was intentional, plus it allowed me to get a good look. As soon as he departed, I wobbled into the bathroom to check out the incision in the mirror.

When the surgeon said he'd need to shave a lot, he wasn't kidding. I looked like Frankenstein's monster: a dramatic incision ran from the top of my head to the bottom of my ear. I counted no fewer than seven heavy-duty staples and seventeen stitches holding my head together. (Note: CI incisions now are usually just a slight curve behind the ear and even sealed with glue.)

My inflated ear stuck straight out, Dumbo-style. The swelling also distorted my face, with one cheek puffed up and my features lopsided, like botched cosmetic surgery. *This is so ugly that it's fierce,* I marveled, yet I felt no pain for such an impressive wound, only a strange numbness as if I were tapping a wooden crate instead of my own skin.

My frowny-faced surgeon stopped by, and it was lovely to see him now that it was over, now that the deed was done. He assured me the operation went well and waxed poetic about my "beautiful mastoid." Although I like a compliment as much as the next girl, I wasn't quite sure how to process that information.

Upon discharge, I was taken to the CI clinic next door. I met with the audiologist, who mentioned that the surgeon raved to her about the crumbliness of my skull. This was becoming a thing, my claim to fame. *Would they hang my picture in the hall?*

The audiologist turned on my cochlear implant processor for a few seconds as a test. The magnetic headpiece didn't even stick due to the incision swelling, so I held it against my skull with my hand. The audiologist pinged the electrodes from her computer. I heard muffled sounds, like being underwater, consisting of static and beeps. It was not an official activation, just a quick test to prove that the internal components were functional. It didn't sound anything remotely like speech.

Linda was also at the clinic getting her staples removed, so we had a joint session as the audiologist explained our external equipment choices. Despite my best efforts to stay awake, my eyes began crossing independently, and all I could think about was wanting to sleep. Linda's husband drove us both home, and I finally crawled into bed for the rest of the afternoon.

I appreciated the silence in the days following the surgery. The recuperation process wasn't particularly gruesome, but I felt tired and unsteady. Lying still was quite comfortable, however. Midmorning, I stepped into the hallway outside my condo to grab my newspaper and discovered an overnight care package waiting for me. The technical team on the East Coast had sent cookies, a teapot, and

State of Maryland magnets (as a joke, to affix to the magnets in my head). This made me laugh out loud, and I sent a mental thanks for the boost.

I was allowed to bathe immediately. Frankly, I was afraid to even touch it. I imagined snagging a washcloth on a staple and sheepishly returning to the surgeon's office with a white terrycloth square dangling from the side of my head. I didn't trust my balance either, so I waited two days after returning home before trying. I cautiously knelt in the bathtub and gripped the safety bar tightly as I gently dabbed at the incision with baby shampoo and a washcloth. With the bloody-looking iodine stains gone, my head looked significantly less frightening.

Time passed slowly as I recovered, still dizzy and with not much to do. One of my sisters happened to be on medical leave while I was recovering, so we emailed daily. She mentioned that during her time off, she assigned roles to each sibling within our family hierarchy.

"Well, which one am I?" I asked.

"You're the 'fuck it, I'm gone' child," she replied. "You take off and never look back."

I reclined in bed with an icepack under my neck and initially disagreed with my sister's lay diagnosis. After all, my top competency on leadership assessment tests was "responsibility." Nothing resonated with me more than the story of a young boy in China who dug through dangerous rubble immediately after an earthquake demolished his school because he was the assigned crossing guard that day. I totally understood. Once, I drove through an F3 tornado because I had promised to babysit someone's cat.

As much as the Cult taught me to honor responsibility, however, my sister's description was spot on. I cut ties quickly when I felt betrayed. Walking away from my law firm job had been a moral imperative. Moving out of state created a necessary distance from my mother. Admittedly, I could have navigated those situations more adeptly, but they were lessons learned for the future: I needed better skills in sticking things out, practicing confrontation, and validating assumptions instead of just walking away. I needed to become a more effective self-advocate.

A few days after surgery, I started to feel like myself. Neighbors left food at my door, and pals emailed to make sure I hadn't electrocuted myself with the new hardware inside my head. People brought lunch, and my friend Heidi drove me around a nearby lake in her convertible. Mark Alan and his husband Tom stopped by with smoothies and a package of anti-bacterial wipes (as a joke because of the earlier incident with the surgical scrub) to give me germ-free hugs. They mentioned they had visited my hospital room earlier but found it empty, with the bed neatly made.

"Where's Rebecca?" they asked the nurse, and she replied, "I'm sorry, she's gone."

She meant that I had already checked out. Poor Mark Alan was sure I was staying another night and said he had a moment of panic, thinking I was dead. Sad.

My clinic was clear that the surgery would permanently destroy my natural hearing on the implanted side. Until then, I'd been afraid even to try. I tentatively put my old hearing aid in my implanted ear, turned it up, then yanked it out quickly and shuddered. It was a gross sensation, like touching a lifeless body in a coffin. No sound whatsoever.

Dead as a doornail.

19

Interim

I returned to work a week after my cochlear implant surgery, wearing a sports headwrap to cover the jaw-dropping incision running down the side of my head. Mark Alan continued to interpret for meetings at work, but socially, I felt it was fair just to let people deal with my lack of hearing. I don't remember the transition being terribly difficult, but I also declined most hearing-specific social activities during that period. After all, I had a really good excuse.

Vertigo Boy asked me to attend a weekly online CI gathering while he was out of town. When I logged in, I quickly realized why. He was certainly popular with the ladies. The moderator introduced me as VB's "special friend" without my saying anything. I felt I had wandered into a reality television show. One attendee I'll call B told me she was not speaking to him because she heard he brought me flowers at the hospital. Despite the cattiness, I enjoyed learning more about Vertigo Boy from his online admirers. He was clearly a fan favorite.

The next day, he asked if I had attended the online chat. I told him B wasn't speaking to him because he brought me flowers. He said B was interested in more than just chatting. He said she had been reprimanded by the group for making inappropriate sexual advances, and I had to laugh. Even cochlear implant networking sites were not immune to relationship drama.

We talked about college basketball, and he asked me to attend the games with him. It occurred to me that this would be our first date as well as the first time we were both conscious, in person, together.

Twelve days after surgery, my staples and stitches were removed. The relief was immediate, as they had been pulling uncomfortably. I went home and looked at the incision in the bathroom mirror, impressed by the gash in my temple. Who would have thought to open someone's skull and insert things inside — like a turducken, stuffing a chicken inside a duck inside a turkey, except with my head as the carcass?

The big decision now was when to stop wearing my head covering at work. Mark Alan and I devised a system to measure progress:

Rebecca and Mark Alan's Scary Scar Rating Scale.

9–10: blindingly grotesque.
7–8: hideous and disgusting.
5–6: noticeable but not offensive.
3–4: unfortunate but excusable.
1–2: invisible scar and full follicle distribution.

Every day, I lifted my head wrap to show Mark Alan my incision, and we rated it independently. Our first vote was unanimous: seven out of ten.

Driving home, I ran into Linda and her husband strolling with their kids. I stopped my car in the middle of the empty street to chat. Linda's CI had been activated recently, and her reaction was less than enthusiastic. She said speech was robotic for her, and her implant was not yet giving her better sound than her previous hearing aid. While she seemed concerned, she was also scheduled for adjustments in a week. We both knew the drill: CI success required more than a few days. Still, her anxiety was real.

I was thrilled not to get the side effect of the bad taste in my mouth, although both Vertigo Boy and Linda did. This surprised me since my ears were a lot smaller than theirs. If anyone were going to have space constraints between the surgical site and the facial nerve, you would think it would be me. Ha, it was not! VB described the taste disturbance as "metallic onions." Linda compared it to "burnt coffee with grapefruit." At least their misery was temporary and only lasted a couple of weeks.

While I didn't get the taste-related side effect, I did encounter an unexpected one that maybe wasn't temporary: an intermittent thunder in my head that resembled a lion's roar. Though my clinic had mentioned roaring as a possible side effect, nobody online had encountered it themselves.

It was not tinnitus (ringing in my ears). Instead, the roaring was a wailing howl that rumbled through my head every half hour with all the subtlety of a freight train carrying elephants in heat. Also, contrary to what I was told, the roaring didn't fade away within a few days. It had been *weeks*. As each day went by, I became more concerned that the roaring had taken up residence for good.

The roaring drowned out everything. It seemed impossible that no one else could hear it. My friend Jesse, a glass-half-full guy, tried to console me by saying that the sheer volume of the noise could be taken as a sign of progress, as it meant I was capable of experiencing sound. I looked at him like he was nuts.

Roaring apparently was my inner ear's passive-aggressive response to being fired from its job, and the bellow came from fluid disruption. Like standing under the "L" train in Chicago, its horrific, ear-splitting scream rattled my teeth and shook my entire body, usually after stair climbing or other physical activity. Sometimes, it even hit unexpectedly while I sat quietly at my desk, a ten-second blast of jet plane exhaust that seemed capable of ratting my hair into a beehive.

When my head roared, I could only hold my breath and grab onto the closest object until it passed. Once, I was in the stairwell at work when it struck, and I sat down abruptly on the steps. One of the executives was heading to the next floor and saw me clinging to the railing.

"Head roaring?" he asked, cocking his head sympathetically. I nodded, lipreading, the thunder filling the stairwell like a building implosion. "I hear it, too," he said, his blue eyes twinkling. "Like birds attacking."

He waved his arms and fake-screamed, fending off an imaginary assault in his fantasy Hitchcock tribute. I held on to the railing and laughed, thinking how lucky I was to work with people who found my medical condition entertaining.

Every night, I continued to say my standard rotation of prayers for each family member, my co-workers, my church, and my friends. Until now, I had not invoked any specific requests to God about the outcome of the implant procedure because I felt what was intended would be. But today, I prayed: *I don't care if the implant works. Please turn off the roaring.*

20

Anticipation

"**S**o, what do you want to hear most with the cochlear implant?" asked Mark Alan. We were at work, between meetings, patiently waiting for the leader to connect our next conference call. I'd gotten this question before. I'd always heard some level of sound, speech, and music — of course, mega amplified — so nothing was particularly mysterious. But my CI activation day was approaching, and I was in a hopeful mood. Mark Alan and I made the following list:

Four Things Rebecca Wants to Hear

1. **Tom Linker's CD, *Time Was*.** The CD was a beautiful collection of classical piano solos (according to Mark Alan English, Tom's husband, who might have been biased). I had enjoyed most of Tom's compositions in person but felt a twinge of sadness that I couldn't identify the songs I knew. Wouldn't it be cool to experience my friend Tom's CD as it really sounded?

2. *A Prairie Home Companion* **radio show.** I admired the writing of host Garrison Keillor. I enjoyed the music on the weekly show but wanted to understand the monologue (as online transcripts were still several years away).

3. **Fast-food drive-through.** This one was just a matter of convenience. Pre-implant, I often traveled to Des Moines for work and typically got a soda at the freeway exit before driving home to Minneapolis. But using the fast-food drive-through had never been an option for me, even in the pouring rain. Instead, I walked inside. I vowed that someday I would order from my car.

4. **Parking ramp warning.** A parking ramp in my neighborhood with an abrupt exit blared an alert whenever I walked past. It sounded like, "A Somalian-ite is approaching," which was ridiculous because (1) "Somalian-ite" wasn't even a real word, and (2) Why would a parking ramp profile pedestrians by ethnic group? It confounded me every time I crossed it, but there was never anyone around to ask.

Mark Alan and I reviewed the list. Except for Tom's music, none of the items were sounds I desperately longed to hear. Rather, they represented accessibility barriers for which captions or transcripts would have sufficed. Frustrated, I grumbled, "I bet when hipster software developers start losing their hearing, they'll finally figure out the end-to-end user experience. Why isn't accessible design on anyone's radar?"

Compiling the list with Mark Alan was a momentary wander into wishful thinking. Otherwise, I tried to keep my expectations low. Gaining a bit of cyborg capability would be an efficiency, I thought, not a transformation. My ears were a function of my body, not a measurement of my worth.

Before surgery, my feelings toward cochlear implantation were, at best, lukewarm. As I awaited activation, however, I began inching toward the hope that I might come out ahead statistically — *it had to be somebody, so why not me?* — and speech comprehension (without lipreading) might be a possible outcome. During the brief moment that the audiologist spot-tested the implant the day after surgery, I heard *stuff*. That momentary gush of garbled static helped me imagine success as a possibility rather than ill-fated foolishness.

I intentionally dialed down my emotions. I hated advertisements that featured weepy individuals hearing their grandchild's voice again after getting hearing aids. Yes, regaining sound was gratifying, but I found videos of amped-up waterworks manipulative and only served to perpetuate the stigma, amplify the shame. The ads targeted seniors, a demographic with a statistical probability of hearing loss in the high frequencies of children's voices. But the grandchild hadn't *died*. It felt wrong to insinuate that hearing their voice was exponentially more meaningful than simply seeing or hugging the child or using sign language. Worse, it implied that a hearing grandparent loved their grandchild more than a deaf grandparent.

Similarly, I felt sad when I encountered exultations posted on the bulletin boards, such as "CI gave me my life back!" At face value, this statement sounded optimistic. It seemed like the individuals had found success with their CIs and felt their lives had improved. Wasn't that what everyone wanted? They wanted back what they had.

But, regaining one's life implied that it was lost somewhere along the way. Ergo, hearing loss had robbed their existence of joy and meaning, likely due to a lack of accessibility and people's unwillingness to accommodate. While the implantees had made a decision to change their circumstances — which was their right and good for them for taking charge of their happiness — the public mindset remained the same. Society (including decision-makers for inaccessible product design) learned no meaningful lesson about the role it played in making that person's life miserable. The scenario reminded me of the ugly-duckling-slasher movies on Lifetime Channel, where women, once rejected for their looks, underwent plastic surgery only to seek retribution toward those who now showed interest. Though I am not aware of any CI-related revenge homicides to date, the moral of those stories still applies here — true love should have embraced them in any form.

The online CI bulletin boards in the early 2000s could be uncomfortable despite the wealth of information provided by helpful peers. I didn't expect participants to wholeheartedly embrace Deaf culture since the groups catered to hopeful implantees. Yet, so much of the content was ableist, with deafness painted as an unacceptable blight. Not only was cochlear implantation held up as the only solution, but those who were not so inclined were attacked and ridiculed. As I was still questioning my own path, I found my posts hit with censored status almost immediately, requiring moderator approval before being shared.

Was the universe designed so rigidly to favor the hearing that humans actually became incapable of listening to each other? That prospect seemed immeasurably depressing and made me less hopeful about my direction. Even if I could hear better, it still wouldn't overcome the stigma and resistance from other people over which I had no control.

Or did I?

Part II: AFTER

21

Proactive Communication

The sad truth about hearing loss is that the people who love you the most often treat you the worst. Imagine having a broken hip or lousy back and your spouse criticizing you because you can't climb steps. Who would do that? Yet it's common for family, friends, and even strangers to marginalize, mock, scold, or throw a fit of rage because they believe your hearing difficulty disproportionately inconveniences them. In online forums dedicated to hearing loss, no one talks about missing the sounds of birds singing. No, they bemoan how their loved ones disparage or overlook them, failing to lend support.

Even with sophisticated hearing devices, understanding speech still relies on the mindful behavior of others. Yet acquaintances routinely ignore the techniques they know will make communication easier. At the same time, those with hearing loss would rather eat worms than restate their accommodation needs. A vicious circle ensues.

Growing up, I was a terrible communicator. I rarely said what I wanted, lied easily, stomped around angrily, and avoided confrontation. Interestingly, my involvement in the Cult improved this aspect of my life. The Cult's insistence on keeping one's word — doing what we said we would do — and demonstrating integrity in communication cultivated a strong sense of accountability. Every year, our New Year's Eve gathering involved a commitment ceremony where members asked for forgiveness from each person present. It was the first time I'd ever spoken directly. With each passing year, it became progressively easier to set aside my teenage angst and verbalize my thoughts calmly. Even so, it took until my thirties before I began to tackle self-advocacy. I wasn't particularly shy, but I lacked the tenacity to follow up in debate,

My twenties weren't entirely a wash. My first attempt at real confrontation occurred a few years after I moved to Minneapolis. I was leaving a social function with hearing acquaintances I'll call Daniel (a man I wanted to date) and Penny (a good friend). As we walked to our cars on a dark street, my hearing aid squealed a few times, as it often did, the powerful microphone reacting to my habit of setting the volume too high.

"What is that noise?" Penny asked impatiently. "What is that beeping sound?"

I hesitated. Other than my co-workers at the law firm, I didn't tell anyone I was deaf back then or even that I wore hearing aids. I was attracted to Daniel, who seemed interested and intensely flirtatious. *Don't say anything,* my ableist mindset warned. I thought he was on the verge of asking me out.

"That! There it is again!" Penny exclaimed.

"It's my hearing aid," I finally admitted. Daniel and Penny laughed like I was joking.

"It's my hearing aid," I repeated. "Why is that funny?"

They laughed again, harder.

Annoyed, I grabbed Penny's hand and stuck her finger in my ear so she could feel the rubber mold, which gave another squeal of feedback when nudged.

"Oh my God, she does have a hearing aid!" Penny exclaimed to Daniel in amazement.

We got into our cars and drove home. I was irritated that Penny had inadvertently outed me to Daniel but more so that she spoke about me in the third person. I hated the stunned looks on their faces, as if I had just admitted to having penguin DNA. I resolved it wouldn't happen that way again. *I need to tell people about my hearing proactively,* I vowed. *I need to control my narrative.*

It was a turning point. Shortly after that, Penny hooked up with Daniel. I felt completely blindsided when I saw his arm around her at a party. I pulled her into the kitchen and confronted her. She was a close friend! Given the numerous times I had confided my feelings about Daniel to her, I expected at least a girl code heads-up. She wailed that she didn't know how to tell me, so she waited for me to bring it up. To my dismay, they had already been dating for weeks.

"What a terrible way to communicate!" I protested in dismay. "You owed me that courtesy as a friend."

She said she was sorry, but the damage was done. If she had been upfront, I could have stepped back to recalibrate. Now, I had to deal with hindsight: that Penny had let me go on about Daniel even after they were already dating, that she revealed my feelings to him by discussing her secret dilemma, and that everyone in our group knew but didn't tell me. I had to retrofit everything now that the truth had changed.

Meanwhile, Penny, who had shared with me her history of mental health struggles when she stopped taking her medication, was admitted to a psychiatric facility from which she ran away. When I next saw Daniel, he informed me they were no longer together.

Surprisingly, he began to cry and sobbed into my shoulder as we sat on the floor. It was a strange twist of events. He asked me if I still liked him, not because he had feelings for me, but because he wanted to use that information as proof that Penny had betrayed us both. However, my feelings toward Daniel had cooled since my confrontation with Penny — a switch had flipped, and I viewed him differently.

It was a milestone moment: I calmly told Daniel the truth, that I felt he had led me on, and the one positive I gained from his coupling with Penny was realizing he never intended to date me. He just liked seeing his desirability mirrored back in my eyes. I resented his calculated touching and was annoyed he threw Penny under the bus now that he knew she was ill. Expressing my thoughts clearly and bluntly was empowering, and Daniel was stunned into silence.

The group drifted apart. I lost touch with Daniel and never heard from Penny again. However, I remember everything about that discussion, a vivid snapshot of my first attempt at proactive communication, a pivotal moment of personal growth.

As I began assembling my hearing loss narrative, I realized that while facing it was difficult, asking people to change their behavior for me was even tougher. The persistent fear of being seen as a burden played out repeatedly in my thoughts. I also recognized it as a caution. For example, I had seen friends hone self-criticism to an unfortunate art form, telegraphing anxieties about their own perceived bothersomeness onto others until their prophecies actually came true. They had become a burden!

One of my most vivid lessons on asking for help came from my late neighbor, Ruth — the same Ruth who frequently lost her credit cards and keys. She was the last surviving member of her generation, with numerous nieces and nephews but no spouse or children. Ruth despised feeling like an obligation. If an invitation to a family gathering arrived with less than two weeks' notice, Ruth declared herself an afterthought and declined without saying why. She fumed about her kin and their perceived thoughtlessness every Fourth of July, Thanksgiving, Christmas, and New Year's. Even if the invitation was timely, Ruth still refused it because she no longer drove and was unwilling to ask for a ride. I offered to drive her, but she insisted it was her family's obligation. Yet, on several occasions, a nephew offered to pick her up, and Ruth said no because she felt he lived too far away. A niece wanted to send a car service, but Ruth turned her down without providing feedback or alternative suggestions, worried others would gossip about the cost.

Ruth frequently told me that when she was younger, she had devotedly cared for her own elderly aunt. Based on this, Ruth felt her nieces and nephews had no valid excuse for neglecting her. From where I sat, I didn't believe Ruth was overlooked. Instead, her mixed messages created confusion. Eventually, the relatives stopped reaching out, assuming Ruth wasn't interested in their company.

"Why don't you just tell them?" I asked her repeatedly. "They can't read your mind." Ruth steadfastly refused. They knew, she bristled, and she went to her grave resenting them bitterly. She had even composed a scathing letter outlining her grievances to be delivered upon her death, which she shredded in a panic the year before she passed.

Ruth was as stubborn as she was endlessly curious. Her love for reading showcased her sharp mind, perhaps influenced by her late father's career as an encyclopedia salesman. Upon retiring from teaching, she vowed to say "yes" to every opportunity, igniting a newfound appreciation for spontaneity within me also. However, observing her reluctance to communicate her needs convinced me — in reverse — to adopt a different approach in my own life.

At the time, I had a serious boyfriend who challenged my view of hearing loss as a private compartment to which no one else had access. The night he introduced me to his parents, he asked which ear was better, and as we were leaving, he attempted to move to that side. It was an awkward transition, the dance of two people not knowing where the other was going until we finally collided head-on and laughed. He told me he was trying to stay on my stronger side. I was surprised, as it wasn't something I had asked him to do and hadn't even occurred to me. It was my problem, I said, based on a lifetime of figuring out my own accommodations, but he insisted that he wanted to help. I thanked him, and his kindness changed my perspective. It was a subtle shift, but he opened a door for me to ask — even expect — others to adapt.

I hoped that generosity would carry over to other aspects of our union. My previous suitors had been bookish math nerds thrilled to be in the presence of a woman, so I had no experience in having to assert my worth in a relationship. I found that, while the boyfriend was always lovely to me when we were face-to-face, he didn't necessarily pick me first if I wasn't standing right in front of him. The examples were minor, but they gave me pause: canceling dates for something better, forgetting me for various reasons, or repurposing plans to benefit other friends.

We never fought. We had thoughtful conversations, and multiple times, I calmly remarked to his face, "I don't think I'm a priority for you unless it's convenient." By freakish coincidence, I was platonic friends with a man (engaged to someone I knew) who consistently picked me every single time for the exact same things during the same period. The universe could not have slapped my face harder to force me to compare and contrast.

Despite the boyfriend's intermittent attention, I liked him a lot. In front of a crowd, he could be charming as all get out, extroverted to the hilt: He once convinced an entire block party to serenade me on my birthday. Yet, other times, I didn't get the sense he valued me the way that even a friend would, and I didn't want to have to keep pointing it out. Eventually, we parted ways.

While my deafness was not a factor in the on-off-on nature of our dating progression, that relationship nevertheless changed my perspective on hearing loss. I evolved from constantly fearing I'd be perceived as a burden (for any reason) to realizing I needed people to prioritize me in the present, and moreover, I needed to be prepared to assert that. My deafness *was* an inconvenience, and so was I! Anyone legitimately in my orbit had to be willing to embrace and accommodate those challenges. Why did I think my hearing loss made me less worthy of consideration?

Hearing devices always worked well for me, but they were never enough. Communication was always my problem to solve, my burden. Yet, thanks to the boyfriend, I discovered that if I asked other people to make small behavioral changes, the load on my end lightened.

Wasn't that the epitome of human kindness?

22

Self-Advocacy

earning to communicate effectively is a cornerstone of both project management and leadership development. A critical principle I learned at work was the importance of managing other people's expectations. I encountered this concept early on when an executive sponsor ended up with a completely different impression of what her initiative would deliver than the rest of the project team. I thought the sponsor was at fault, yet my boss at the time dinged me on my performance review for not managing the sponsor's expectations.

"How can I possibly manage what someone else thinks?" I asked my boss dubiously. "Sixteen other people on the team arrived at the same conclusion as me."

"You needed to step up and steer," he explained. "It didn't matter that you weren't the project leader or how many others dropped the ball. Managing expectations is a leadership competency."

It took some time to absorb this philosophy, but managing expectations was a mantra I also passed along to those who worked for me. It required communicating proactively about limitations and challenges, listening and repeating, validating assumptions, using objective data for measurement, and never, ever presuming to know how someone else thought.

Managing expectations around hearing loss is pretty similar. I own the setting and enforcing of my expectations for how others should behave. Not speaking up or continually apologizing for myself is the equivalent of saying, "Don't mind me; I don't matter." Telling others how to modify their behavior to accommodate me without apology and then reinforcing those expectations establishes that they need to respect my point of view, even if they disagree. While I don't win every battle, I've at least set boundaries.

Managing expectations is a key component of self-advocacy. Self-advocacy means speaking up for myself and my interests proactively. I think it should be taught in schools, like home economics or driver's ed, to learn how to navigate life. Self-advocacy was a skill I didn't have, didn't know was essential, and frankly, I'm still a work in progress. Some days, I'm a mess. All I can do is wipe the slate clean and start over.

Self-advocacy is learned; we are not born with it. It's selective, too. For example, I can battle fiercely for a loved one or even a pet yet still be paralyzed with anxiety when sticking up for myself. Where self-advocacy stalled for me was not being able to reinforce what I needed. Like virtually everyone with hearing loss, stigma was the anchor of doom that silenced me.

For those reading this on behalf of a loved one, I can't emphasize strongly enough how often people, even random strangers, perpetuate shame over hearing loss because it has become normalized behavior. It's probably not even on your radar, but if you take away one realization from this book, it would be to understand and acknowledge how negativity about hearing loss accrues and erodes confidence. Being considered "lesser than" is everywhere and in everything. Overcoming self-reproach is the single biggest obstacle to self-advocacy.

Courtesy of the ex-boyfriend, I learned the importance of sticking to my guns when communicating my concerns (and, in hindsight, realized my shortcomings in that area). Even though I made calm statements setting forth my position, I never persisted because I had no confrontation skills when it pertained to standing up for myself. I was lucky he was such a mellow fellow, and it ended amicably. We both learned and grew from our time together.

Strangely, I had no trouble confronting people when addressing work-related matters. In fact, my nickname was "Rebecca Kill" because I pounced on ill-advised requests with all the subtlety of St. Patrick driving the snakes out of Ireland, fiercely protective of systems changes. I was also known to summon blunt honesty when writing performance reviews for direct reports. However, this ability to champion others didn't extend to advocating for my own needs. I told myself I was taking the higher road, but really, I was just avoiding debate.

I needed to develop some self-protection strategies. I recalled the advice from the therapist I originally consulted when I gave up the voice telephone, who had stressed the importance of detaching from emotion to defuse shame. I compared my hearing loss situation to less-charged interventions I had previously tackled, like the co-worker who left her empty food trash on the floor of my car or the friend who repeatedly canceled outings at the last minute. I granted them a grace period, established guidelines, and held them accountable. No one threatened revenge; they changed their approach. They even thanked me later. So, why wasn't I setting myself up for the same success with my hearing loss?

The Baseline Conversation

Expecting others to accommodate my hearing loss without telling them how was not fair. Like Ruth's kin, they were not mind readers. My next step was to communicate a consistent message to establish a baseline measurement. I drafted an outline:

BASELINE CONVERSATION

"Even with devices, my hearing has limits. You can avoid having to repeat yourself if you follow some basic guidelines:

- Wait until I'm looking at you (and you're facing me) before you start speaking. Otherwise, I will miss the context of the conversation.

- Mute the music, radio, or television when you're speaking. Background noise makes it harder to hear.

- Get within five feet of me before you speak. Speech deteriorates across distance.

- Don't cover your mouth or chew when you speak. It helps to see the shape of your mouth when you form words, even if I'm not lipreading.

- Don't talk over other people. I can't understand multiple voices at the same time."

That was it, my stab at self-advocacy! Ha, if only it were that simple!

Forgetfulness

Most people forgot my baseline conversation immediately. For example, I visited my hometown and had lunch with several sisters and a friend. I politely asked someone to move her hand away from her mouth. She did willingly, but literally two minutes later, the hand covered her face again. I pointed it out a second, then a third time. She got mad. I thought it was absurd — two minutes! — but she only saw me once a year and didn't think of me as deaf. I needed to get comfortable tacking on reminders when asking for repeats:

"Move your hand, then repeat what you said."

"Say it again. I need you to look at me when you talk."

"Please mute the sound. I can't hear over the background noise."

"Wait until I'm closer. I can't hear from a distance."

It's tough for people to adjust on the fly. Baby shower games — where guests receive a diaper pin, are told not to cross their legs, and forfeit the pin when they instantly forget — prove this point. Similarly, when it came to my baseline discussion, most people demonstrated a low recall on the first try, which exasperated me. I felt I shouldn't have to remind them. The guidelines were important to me. Why weren't they for them?

Kudos to the friends who immediately embraced and followed the guidelines. They were my self-advocacy "happy path" folks who immediately committed without reminders. Rather than holler from his bathroom for toilet paper, my friend Jon paged me instead, which was hilarious and much appreciated. Kevin looked at me when he talked and made sure the light was on his face, not behind him. Gina waved her hand to get my attention before she began speaking. Jenna enunciated a little too exaggeratedly, to the point that it actually became harder to understand her, but she still got points for trying!

I made a deliberate effort to applaud my happy-path friends, and they remained eager to keep at it. I also recognized those who initially forgot but self-corrected mid-conversation. That counted also! High five!

Unfortunately, most people were not happy-path material. I had to remind myself that their forgetfulness was not personal. They hadn't yet established a habit, so extra reminders were required. It was tempting to give up when people forgot. However, doing so would imply a lack of commitment to my mission. If I genuinely wanted to train them to face me, I needed to remind them. *A lot.* Twenty-one days make a habit, the saying goes, and it sometimes took that many nudges to implement change (or achieve spotty adherence at best). Grace was reserved for those who truly wanted to help but didn't always register. The guidelines simply fell off their radar. It happens.

After listening to me vent, my friend Lee gifted me one of the most powerful tools for managing and reinforcing behavior changes: the finger point (index finger, not the middle one). Pointing an index finger to my ear with a slightly puzzled facial expression and shaking my head is the universal, age-old gesture for "I can't hear you." As Lee explained, this nonconfrontational motion serves as a gentle reminder without putting people on the defensive. It jogs their memory about the baseline conversation, and, most importantly, it puts the ball back in their court to try again.

The beauty of a finger point is that it practically shines a neon sign of "HEARING LOSS" next to one's head and pricks the recipient's balloon of forgetfulness. The light bulb clicks on. The finger point is excellent from a distance or at a stalemate on the third repeat. The finger point can also segue into a "one moment" gesture to pull up a speech-to-text captioning app as a backup. While the finger point doesn't solve all accommodation needs overnight, it's a good conditioning exercise that gradually influences desired behavior over time. And because it's a visual gesture, it's on brand with deafness.

I recently used the finger point for a reply. My friend Danica asked whether the noise from my air conditioner interfered with sleeping in the summer. I silently pointed to my ear. She took a beat, then burst into laughter, remembering that I hear no sound without my devices. If I had replied flatly with, "No, I'm deaf," it might have come across as a snarky putdown, but the gesture on its own softened it to a humorous moment, no judgment. She even retold the story a month later, still laughing. The finger point resonated.

Another tip from Lee was that my follow-up sometimes gave mixed signals. For example, I coached people not to talk to my back, but only if I hadn't heard them. Since I sometimes could hear people talking to my back (but sometimes not), I decided to say, "Oh, I can't hear behind my back," even when I understood them. It was tempting to skip the reinforcement, one less thing to nag about, but the point was to set others up for success. Since the other person had no way of knowing if the next instance behind the back would be understood, I needed to disallow it. It was a pain but helped remove ambiguity in the long run. With consistent coaching and reinforcement, most people got better at establishing a habit, bless them.

Escalation

For some people, simple reminders were not sufficient to change their behavior. A follow-up discussion was warranted. Additionally, a distinct subset of folks needed drama to alter their approach successfully. While they seemed to understand and even verbally agreed to my baseline discussion, they instinctively gamed the process, figuring they always had a few more passes to plead ignorance. Still others displayed anger even despite finger-point reminders. All were different from those who simply forgot. They needed escalation to spark action. When they continued to profess amnesia despite repeated requests, I turned to a friend (I'll call her Caroline) for advice.

Caroline possessed an incredible talent for lasering through difficult situations with her bluntness. She had multiple sclerosis and zipped around in an electric wheelchair for mobility. She was also moderately deaf and wore hearing aids. Caroline often said having multiple disabilities gave her permission to speak uncensored, a direct conversation style that cut through the games. Caroline talked me through the strategies she routinely used to educate others.

For people used to hiding their hearing loss, honesty can seem like a foreign concept, but it's actually the best first approach when it comes to self-advocacy. The first few attempts at being truthful can be uncomfortable for those not used to transparency. Admitting you haven't understood something can be embarrassing, particularly if you've been faking all along.

People with hearing loss shy away from honesty for good reason. First, truth isn't always appreciated by those who are predisposed to view you or your hearing loss negatively. During my mother's last visit to Minneapolis, for example, when I tried to tell her what I needed for communication, she took offense at my requests — that

I had the audacity to tell her what to do — and just got angrier with each exchange.

Second, as much as people say they want you to tell them when you don't hear something, they aren't necessarily prepared for you to actually do so or change their behavior to help you out. But your commitment to honesty brings liberation from shame, and in the long run, it's worth it just to swallow hard and go for it. If you commit to honesty, you might as well hold firm and also get what you need.

I remember a situation at work when I brutally bungled a casual conversation with a colleague to the point that I created a misunderstanding over whether Mark Alan and Tom's son was my own. The co-worker was a great business partner to me, and I valued our working relationship. It bothered me tremendously, so I sought him out the next day, took a deep breath, and explained that I hadn't heard part of what he had said earlier and was too flustered to correct the situation then. He was quite gracious, although I'm sure he thought how I handled it was peculiar. I had made the situation more embarrassing than it needed to be by not speaking honestly at the time.

Caroline chose to master total honesty as her first step. When she didn't hear something, she decided that saying "What?" or "Excuse me?" was not sufficiently memorable to encourage habit-forming behavior and that more explanation was required. She taped the following phrases to her bathroom mirror and recited them aloud each morning:

"I can't hear what you're saying."

"I didn't understand what you said."

Once she began replacing "Pardon me?" phrases with more specific reminders about her hearing loss, Caroline said the change was noticeable immediately. Like the finger point, Caroline's spelling out the situation for people counteracted their kneejerk response to feel annoyed. Caroline said it was a surprisingly simple adjustment to make, and it nipped their false assumption in the bud, remarking, "I had no idea how easily people forgot that I was deaf."

Caroline also learned to get comfortable proactively backing out of a conversation after multiple repeats. That's another side of speaking the truth, to screw up the courage to admit, "I'm getting less than 5 percent of what you're saying. I'm going to bow out of this conversation right now, thanks."

Anger

As I mentioned above, one of the most common reasons why people with hearing loss aren't forthcoming about when they can't hear is because recipients either exhibit anger at having to repeat themselves or have a history of doing so. I asked Caroline about her experience. When people showed annoyance at Caroline for not understanding something they said, particularly if they had to repeat it multiple times, Caroline felt she had two options: let it go or confront them directly.

Letting it go meant letting it slide down her back, filing it away for historical reference, but otherwise deciding the situation (or person) was not worth the time and energy to pursue. When faced with anger from strangers, for example, Caroline often ignored it because she didn't know if the person was capable of a road-rage reaction, plus she doubted she'd ever see them again. She'd make a judgment call on whether to leave a parting comment for educational purposes, a gentle "no need to get angry" (or a saltier version, depending on the situation), followed by a quick exit.

Passively swallowing hurt and then complaining to others instead of confronting the source was not letting it go, said Caroline. That was just venting behind their back. It did nothing to move the needle closer to a solution.

Carolyn agreed that letting it go was not an ideal communication strategy for regular acquaintances. For example, my relationship with my mother was an excellent illustration of what *not* to do. I chose not to deal with it and rationalized it wasn't worth the effort for a few hours of contact per year, even though the significance of the relationship strongly suggested otherwise. (For what it's worth, I regret it now.)

Wading into a confrontation when someone expressed irritation was scary, said Caroline, but remaining silent gave the squabbler permission to continue. The finger point was an excellent first step for anger situations. Most disgruntled people backed down immediately after a finger point and even apologized because their anger was based on a misunderstanding: They assumed she wasn't listening.

Case in point: I was talking with someone I knew in a super noisy environment. He wasn't looking at me, and I needed to ask for repeats. He said it a third time, spitting his words in a hissy fit. I experienced a moment of anxiety. He was livid, apparently, at me! I took a beat, shot him a puzzled "what is wrong with you?" look, and silently pointed to my ear. Instantly, his demeanor changed. "I didn't realize you didn't hear me," he said sheepishly after a pause.

Second example: I got my hair cut at a walk-in salon. The stylist called my name and said something I missed (which turned out to be, "Come on back"). I asked him to repeat himself, which he did, but then he said sarcastically, "I must not have been speaking loud enough." Which on paper seems respectful, but his tone told a different story. (He was scolding me for the repeat, even though he didn't raise his voice.)

I pointed to my ear and said, "I'm deaf."

"Oh! I'm sorry!" he exclaimed, dropping the sarcastic edge.

"Okay," I replied, recognizing that he was apologizing for the snarky judgment and not my hearing loss.

In both examples, the tone of our interaction improved noticeably by not letting it go. In the past, when random people got snippy because I heard incorrectly, I hesitated to pull out the big guns of saying I was deaf because it was like squashing a bug; a conversation couldn't recover from that exchange without them feeling embarrassed. My perspective has since changed. If someone continues to scold me now after a finger point, I no longer worry whether they feel foolish.

Confrontation did not mean picking a fight, said Caroline. It simply meant bringing the matter to the other party's attention in the most comfortable manner. For example:

"Hey, I need you to look at me when you talk."

Most people acknowledged and apologized to Caroline, but occasionally, someone carried over their irritation by shouting their response or snapping, "Would you just listen?" to ratchet up the shame. They continued to air their frustration, assuming that embarrassment would render Caroline silent. However, Caroline insisted that resisting the urge to back down was essential to standing up for yourself. We role played:

Me: "Why are you shouting?"

Caroline: "BECAUSE YOU CAN'T HEAR ME!"

Me: "Why does that make you so angry?"

Caroline: "I'M NOT ANGRY!"

Caroline coached me not to get sidetracked into debating whether they were or weren't angry and to focus on the original issue:

Me: "It doesn't seem like you've been able to look at me when you talk. What's going on?"

The most important lesson I learned from Caroline was this: I did not need to win the debate. The questions merely served to encourage the dialogue, get them to open up, and unmask what hadn't yet been said. Anger is a symptom with many nuances; we rarely articulate what we're really angry about on the first try. A variety of questions worked for this purpose:

"Can you help me understand your perspective?"

"It seems like you're saying that [X]. Is that what you think?"

"Can you explain what you meant by [X]?"

People who show a pattern of expressing anger toward you over hearing loss instinctively bank on stigma to mute your follow-up and often don't realize it. Unfortunately, they aren't wrong. Your determination to pursue the conversation further can counteract that impulse.

Anger could be unpredictable, warned Caroline. It could escalate unexpectedly, even from a typically mild-tempered person. In that case, a second gesture came in handy: the traditional "time out" sign of a vertical hand touching a horizontal hand, forming the letter "T," the customary signal to take a moment to pause. Caroline thought the following responses were also helpful:

"Can we talk about this when you're not angry?"

"Are you just venting, or do you want to talk about this?"

Her last question reminded me of one of my previous supervisors, who would routinely ask, "Are you just venting right now, or do you have a solution to propose?" which was a genius response. The questions are intended to gently nudge the other person to refocus their comments toward a productive resolution (or back down).

In some situations, Caroline warned, persistent anger could indicate bullying. (A bully could be anyone: spouse, friend, family, or colleague.) Bully anger wasn't temporary, said Caroline, and bullies didn't apologize later. Bullying was a pattern of full-frontal disdain compressed into a complete absence of respect. Stopping a bully required confrontation, not the polite kind, because bullies kept returning when left unaddressed. Generally, conquering bullies meant having to put up a fight.

According to Caroline, the "bully communications strategy" was not intended for acquaintances who were genuinely forgetful or had a one-time flare-up. She also cautioned to walk away from situations where physical or mental harm was a real possibility. What worked for Caroline was mirroring back whatever the bully dished out, peppering her responses with expletives. Her intention was to shock the other person from their rhythm and even cause them to question themselves. It slammed the brakes on the interaction, changed the subject, and pointed the finger back at them. They were counting on her to cower or retreat meekly, and ultimately, she made them so uncomfortable in return that they dismissed her as a target.

The good news is that most situations requiring self-advocacy occur due to forgetfulness or a lack of awareness. The key is consistent reinforcement until it becomes second nature. It's not a hopeless endeavor to communicate needs and reinforce expectations so that others honor them out of respect.

23

Undesirable

I had time on my hands as I awaited CI activation, so I spent most of my evenings reading. I knew some of the backstory of disability, the disproportionately negative way it has been perceived throughout history, and I felt compelled to understand why.

For example, in Biblical times, individuals who were deaf, blind, or with mobility disabilities were frequently relegated to the lower rungs of the social hierarchy and consistently singled out as the first needing to be healed. Disability likely was a bleak prospect in an era with no concept of accessibility or diversity awareness, yet few other medical concerns seemed to have been deemed equally urgent. The cultural predisposition to perceive deafness as in more dire need of miraculous intervention than, say, chronic migraines or endometriosis can be traced back at least to the Old Testament.

The first time I saw Deaf culture intersect with religion in art was reading the script of *Children of a Lesser God,*[26] a Tony Award-winning play by the late Mark Medoff. The story was a romantic drama between a Deaf custodian and a zealous speech teacher who wanted her to read lips and voice aloud. She educated him eloquently, saying: "Deafness isn't the opposite of hearing, as you think. It's a silence full of sounds."

Medoff's play derived its title from a poem set in the Dark Ages called "Idylls of the King: The Passing of Arthur"[27] by Alfred Tennyson. Sir Bedivere overheard King Arthur as he lay dying. In his final moments, Arthur expressed his belief that God had forgotten those perceived as weaker, crying:

> "O me! for why is all around us here
> As if some lesser god had made the world,
> But had not force to shape it as he would,
> Till the High God behold it from beyond,
> And enter it, and make it beautiful?"

Tennyson's poem was not about hearing loss. Rather, King Arthur's men were surrounded by fog and blinded. Even though Medoff clarified in interviews that the title of his play was not referring to people with disabilities (he saw the romantic leads as the lesser gods), most online commentary interprets the Deaf characters as the namesake children, given the play's exploration of ableism and religious persecution.

God created individuals who happen to be d/Deaf, so why do humans perceive them as lesser beings? How do people of faith reconcile their belief in an all-powerful God, who bestows beauty and perfection, with the existence of disability?

They don't. They blame the lesser god.

P.S. And in case it isn't clear, the lesser god is Satan.

* * *

Flashback: I am at a Deaf friend's birthday party. I see the two strangers coming from the distance, trudging up the hill to our picnic spot in their white collared shirts and black trousers, dressed much too formally for a picnic, carrying well-worn, leather-bound Bibles with determined expressions on their faces. They are on a mission.

As the strangers approach, their faces display a mixture of confusion and judgment. Apprehensively, they observe the lively gathering of Deaf individuals enjoying the outdoors, laughing and signing animatedly. The strangers attempt to engage in verbal conversation with Deaf people playing Frisbee, who gesture they can't hear, and redirect them toward me. I watch the strangers stride purposefully, hugging their Bibles like protective armor. For a minute, I am tempted to play Deaf to avoid engagement.

"Hello," I say to the strangers, aware that everyone at the picnic is watching. The fact that I regularly go to church — a hearing church, no less — is common knowledge, and the group constantly needles me during weekend camping trips about missing services.

"Jesus can heal you" are the first words out of the woman's mouth. I sigh. "He can heal all of you," she insists.

"He can heal you, too," I agree politely.

She looks at me, puzzled. "I don't need to be healed," she replies.

"Neither do I," I say.

The woman frowns at me long and hard, trying to decide whether further debate is worth the effort. Abruptly, she walks away. The man turns to follow, offers a meek smile, and leans in conspiratorially. "You can't even tell," he whispers exaggeratedly, mostly mouthing. They approach a few others, talking, which elicits blank stares from Deaf People Who Do Not Lipread. I don't offer to translate. I'm relieved when they leave, seeking other picnickers to target.

I feel conflicted. On the one hand, sharing affirmations of God's love and sacrifice is a cornerstone of faith. But this encounter is about turning Jesus into a mascot for judgment and superiority, an exercise that has nothing to do with grace.

"Religious people same-same?" my friends sign to me as the strangers depart. "Did they come looking for you because you missed church?"

"No," I sign. "Lost, confused."

It was a somber encounter, one I've never forgotten. I had been profiled as lesser — by strangers! But didn't everyone reflect God's image? Despite being part of the larger group, I felt targeted and small. I thought about The Sermon on the Mount, which specifically did *not* bless the cherry-pickers who employed selective criteria to promote their personal bias; no, The Sermon on the Mount recognized the pure in heart as those who would see God.

Religion can be an unwitting influencer in pushing ableism, leaning heavily on Bible passages that, within a specific context, appear to link disability with being demonic in origin:

> "When Jesus saw that a crowd was running to the scene, he rebuked the evil spirit. 'You deaf and mute spirit,' he said, 'I command you, come out of him and never enter him again.'" [Mark 9:25 NIV.]

Or as punishment for the wicked:

> "As the enemy came down toward him, Elisha prayed to the Lord, 'Strike this army with blindness.' So he struck them with blindness, as Elisha had asked." [2 Kings 6:18 NIV.]

And, of course, this is from the Old Testament, which indicates people with disabilities cannot serve as priests:

"No man who has any defect may come near: no man who is blind or lame, disfigured or deformed; no man with a crippled foot or hand, or who is a hunchback or a dwarf, or who has any eye defect ... He has a defect; he must not come near to offer the food of his God ... yet because of his defect, he must not go near the curtain or approach the altar, and so desecrate my sanctuary." [Leviticus 21:18 NIV.]

So, the negative portrayal of disability in theology goes way back, while times have changed. The unfortunate takeaway is that disabilities are still considered evil or God's punishment even today, while few other post-Eden challenges exist for which strangers on a street would propose healing. Yet, everyone is broken or damaged somehow; it's just a matter of degree.

For example, no responsible parent would attribute their child's crooked teeth or tonsillitis to Lucifer because those parents know better than to saddle someone with that burden. Yet churchgoers routinely perpetuate the stigma of disability as a product of Satan's paintbrush through outdated hymn lyrics or a disproportionate emphasis on healing. But healing today doesn't necessarily mean an automatic return-to-factory setting. Healing encompasses a wide range of options, including acceptance, accessibility, and alternative ways of doing things.

Churches claim they rebuke the illness/condition and not the person. However, physical and cognitive abilities are intrinsic aspects of one's identity that are part of the whole package. Those with ableist tendencies have no problem shining their flashlight of shame ... so long as it avoids illuminating themselves.

* * *

I had become acquainted with a woman at church. I distinctly remember befriending her when she showed up alone as a visitor. I even got a shout-out from the group leader for being inclusive. She and I socialized in the same circle for more than a year. Unexpectedly, she sent me the following letter [paraphrased]:

> "I feel terrible for writing this letter, but I need to tell you that I can no longer be friends with you. I have prayed for a year that Jesus would heal your hearing because His will makes you perfect and whole. It is just too hard to be around you, knowing that you have been left behind from His perfect plan."

A sigh escaped as I read the letter, although I wasn't surprised. I had just hosted a movie night at the woman's house. When I activated the subtitles for the film, she harrumphed her disapproval. At the same time, she opted to serve unsalted popcorn, saying it was a consideration for an attendee watching his sodium intake! Were accommodations under the disability umbrella somehow different from the everyday kindnesses we typically showed one another?

I couldn't help but feel puzzled. For instance, my friend Nancy hosts me for an annual dinner and Christmas movie night every year. Though she is hearing, she turns on the captions before I even walk in the door. Was a scientific study warranted to distinguish what tripped the disgruntlement wire in the woman from church, while others like Nancy exhibited no similar judgments and, in fact, graciously anticipated?

I read the woman's farewell several times, trying to understand why she needed to make such a dramatic pronouncement. Our paths didn't cross that much, and it would have been simpler to naturally drift apart like anyone else whose friendship wasn't that solid. The fact that someone would openly admit to such toxic thoughts, put them into writing, and mail the letter was beyond belief. I showed it to my friend Geoff, who had come out as gay a few years earlier. In response, he folded the note and skillfully cut origami patterns on it with a pair of scissors.

I asked Geoff if he thought I should respond. "Oh, honey," he sighed. "You don't think I haven't gotten that letter from every person in my family? Good riddance." He opened the note to display a beautiful banner of cut-out shapes, crumpled it into a ball, and casually tossed it toward the trash can.

* * *

Across history, humans have consistently championed a desire to hide disability. A pivotal moment occurred in 1880 during the Second International Congress on Education of the Deaf in Milan, where delegates from seven countries convened. The Congress voted that oral (or spoken) education was superior to manual (or signed) communication for deaf students and prohibited the use of sign language in schools.[28] Consequently, educational institutions in Europe and the United States transitioned to oral methods for teaching the deaf, prioritizing lipreading and speech therapy while sidelining sign language. This approach endured for an astonishing 100 years.

In 1980, the same organization revisited the Milan findings, concluding. "All deaf children have the right to flexible communication in the mode or combination of modes which meet their individual needs." This acknowledgment marked a significant shift in perspective, finally recognizing ASL as a valid language.

However, it wasn't until 2010 that the group issued a formal apology, acknowledging that the ban constituted an act of discrimination infringing upon human and constitutional rights.[29] Their belated apology reminded me of the character Emily Litella, portrayed by Gilda Radner on the *Saturday Night Live* television program, who passionately ranted her opinions based on misunderstandings and, upon correction, sweetly concluded, "Never mind!"

The discriminatory actions of 1880 were not isolated incidents. In 1939, two years before the Nazis began exterminating Jews, Adolf Hitler authorized a "mercy death" program known as T4 Euthanasia.[30] This program systematically executed Germans and Austrians with mental and physical disabilities (including the d/ Deaf), whom Hitler deemed threats to genetic purity and unworthy of life. Healthcare workers were required to report infants and children with disabilities. At the same time, parents were encouraged to unwittingly commit their young children to special wards for care where they actually were subjected to lethal overdose or starvation. Subsequently, the program was deemed a success, expanded to include older youths and adults, and prototyped the gas chambers and ovens used at future extermination camps.

Europeans rightfully revolted when they became aware of the T4 program in 1941. By then, about 70,000 people had been killed, and several death camps were established specifically for people with disabilities. To appease the protesters, Hitler promised the program would end. He lied. Hitler kept the T4 program going in secret. The United States Holocaust Memorial Museum estimates that 250,000 people were murdered via T4 by 1945.[31]

T4 was a pilot program, a test and learn, and a precursor to the mass murder of six million Jews. But targeting the disabled didn't originate with Hitler's quest to create a master race. As early as 1900, long before World War II, the United States developed a program called the eugenics movement,[32] where people deemed "unfit" were involuntarily sterilized. In his book *Mein Kampf*,[33] Hitler credits the U.S. eugenics movement as his inspiration for T4. Laws that allowed this practice were passed and ratified by the U.S. Supreme Court in 1927,[34] well before Hitler's rise to power.

Eugenics did not assess parental fitness. Instead, its purpose was to create a purportedly superior race grounded in prejudice and false assumptions. The eugenics movement unabashedly advocated for eliminating the so-called "undesirables"[35] while encouraging the proliferation of the "desirables," which frankly sums up everything there is to know about stigmatizing disability. I've often thought the phrase "you can't even tell" probably traces back to the eugenics movement. (Because if you could "tell," people were watching.)

More than thirty states passed laws permitting compulsory sterilization of people with physical and mental disabilities. According to The National Women's Law Center, about 70,000 people were forcibly sterilized in the United States.[36] The practice was mostly halted by the '70s. While forced sterilization laws continue to exist in many states,[37] the state of North Carolina officially repealed its eugenics-based statute in 2003.[38]

My first cochlear implant was in 2003. Imagine being admitted to the hospital for the procedure with a big D on your forehead and discovering later you'd been involuntarily sterilized. Because, back then, people weren't dragged into hysterectomies kicking and screaming.

They just didn't tell you.

24

Radio Head Gal

While the term "hook-up" is most commonly associated with random sexual encounters, its meaning differs for cochlear implantees. "Hook-up" is the date after the surgical procedure when the audiologist activates the cochlear implant. Those scheduled for hook-up after two to three weeks are lucky indeed, while those with activation dates four to six weeks out are driven mad with frustration. (Today, some implantees get hooked up as early as a day or two after surgery, depending on the clinic and degree of swelling.)

All implantees secretly hope they will miraculously comprehend speech in its full glory on their hook-up day. Generally, they will not. Worse, their family members firmly believe activation means instant results. It does not.

While a handful of implantees online claim that they understood speech perfectly at hook-up (self-described "rock-star activation"), it doesn't happen often and frankly wins them about the same popularity points amongst their peers as those who boast of losing their baby weight on the birthing table.

Realistically, speech understanding (without visual cues) after implantation differs by individual and can take weeks to months to achieve. But even for those who don't expect to win the hook-up instant lottery, it's still disappointing when perfect sound doesn't materialize on Day One. Lots of new implantees express their bewilderment, lamenting that they cannot hear sufficiently upon activation. Either no one sat them down to set appropriate expectations, or they chose to ignore what they didn't want to believe.

Like most implantees, my activation was underwhelming. Initially, I heard a monotone organ key playing beeps and dashes resembling Morse code, timed with the movements of my audiologist's mouth, then a high-pitched whistle. It did not remotely sound like a voice. It sounded terrible.

I made a horrible, irreversible mistake. What was I thinking?

After the audiologist tinkered a bit with the processor settings, I heard sounds; nothing intelligible, just *wah wah wah* bubbles timed to her mouth movements. "It's Charlie Brown's teacher," I lipread her saying, referencing the famously incomprehensible voice in the background of the Charles Schulz television special. She was right! That was exactly how it sounded! My own voice sounded like a squealing Alvin from the Chipmunks.

For most implantees, that is the typical activation experience that causes their hearts to plunge into their stomachs. It sounds awful at first, which is perfectly normal. It's working. The new electrodes are like drill sergeants, barking orders at the auditory nerve, which is shocked to suddenly report to such precise bosses after perhaps years of quiet-quitter hair cells running the show. In my case, activating my implanted ear felt like rousing a grumpy bear from a three-decades-long hibernation.

Lots of implantees feel panic when they experience the first screeches and static. The misleading *miracle* CI activation videos posted on social media only make the situation worse. People who don't know better share misleading clips (often with sensationalized headlines as clickbait) on YouTube and Facebook, hoping to go viral on someone else's coattails.

Look, most adult implantees have had a previous experience with sound, and the vast majority hear *something* at hook-up. Activation — while emotional — is usually not their first (audio) rodeo. The posters don't consider that sharing out-of-context clips of weepy, newly-activated strangers or wide-eyed babies simply responding to electronic noise falsely implies that they gained instant speech-comprehension-level hearing. The danger in opportunistically sharing videos for clicks and likes is that they create unrealistic expectations for potential implantees, their families, and the general public (none of whom have any idea what the video subject really heard) to erroneously believe that "rock-star" activation is common and also their rightful inheritance.

Activating a cochlear implant is not the hearing equivalent of taking off the goggles the morning after laser eye surgery. It more closely resembles replacing a body part, like a knee, an aortic valve, or a severed finger. Do you see many clickbait videos about instant recoveries from hip replacement on social media? No, you don't, because success generally doesn't happen overnight. It's a gradual journey.

Initial thresholds for volume and pulsing were configured during activation. I could tolerate less than half of the recommended settings. The audiologist suggested that I was "repressing," then grimaced and said, "You have a lot of work ahead of you." She asked if I could come back the next day, even though my next appointment was scheduled for three days out. Apparently, I was tagged as remedial from the get-go.

The audiologist watched me pack up my things. "I hope you're not disappointed," she remarked kindly. I said no since I knew perfectly well understanding speech would take time. Still, I was dismayed by how horrible everything sounded. What if it stayed that way?

As I returned to work with the unpleasant noise screeching and popping around me, I felt my lousy mood expanding. I headed to the computer lab for a scheduled staff meeting. I was late and found my team already seated. I said hello, ready to attack the agenda, when they collectively gasped, eyes lifted heavenward.

I followed their gaze and saw the wall clock directly above me whirling its hands around and spinning forward at breakneck speed. The Firm's campus clocks were synchronized through radio control to adjust for time changes. Coincidentally, my new electronics were also controlled by radio waves. Had my activated implant made the clock go haywire? *No, that's impossible,* I thought.

Was it?

All eyes fixed on the supercharged clock, their gaze shifting momentarily to me before returning to the bizarre spectacle unfolding. Jaws dropped. The clock's hands spun with an absurd velocity, ready to detach from the wall and launch itself out the window. The timing was impeccable.

Laughter erupted and quickly engulfed the room, tears streaming down faces. "How did you do that?" gasped one of my staff, thinking I had pulled off some elaborate prank for which I totally took the credit. "Did you have a remote-controlled timer or what?"

Building maintenance replaced the broken clock the next day.

* * *

It had been a long, unpleasant-sounding day with my newly activated implant, although the static had faded considerably. I drove home from work, aching desperately to take off the processor for the night. As I pulled into the courtyard of my condo building, even before I reached for my clicker, the garage door obediently slid open.

I waited, assuming another car was coming out from the inside. The door went down, then immediately up again. It continued: up, down, up, down. I gunned the accelerator before it could close again and pulled inside. The door finally stayed closed. A neighbor was in the garage watching as I zoomed inside.

"Was that you?" she asked. "Did your head set off the garage door now that you're bionic?"

I sat in my car, dumbfounded. *Was it me?* Was I now a human antenna tuned into a clandestine radio frequency, transmitting signals directly from my mind? Or, on a more paranoid note, was my cochlear implant really a covert microchip or sophisticated GPS tracker buried within me, notifying data trackers of my every move? These ridiculous notions raced through my mind, igniting my imagination with wild, unfounded possibilities. It was a lot to think about. And it was only my first day.

I knew the importance of consistently wearing the cochlear implant processor to train my brain to decode sound, particularly in the early days of activation. However, no specific time frame guaranteed success. While some implantees acted as if disconnecting the processor for even a second during the day was the equivalent of turning off life support, others mistakenly believed that perfect hearing was their right without any effort on their part. The truth lay somewhere in between.

Like training for a sport, I opted for balance. Rest and recovery were crucial for optimal performance, as I didn't have an easy go from the start. I was seasick from the processor pulsing at first and needed time to adjust, so I limited my "on" time to about ten hours a day during the first couple of weeks. Linda wore hers for fourteen hours but enjoyed turning it off a few hours before bedtime. Vertigo Boy wore his every waking minute. There was no universally correct approach. Yes, implant rehabilitation required ongoing stimulation, but rehab was also a long game. I was intentional about listening practice as prescribed by my aural rehab specialist, but I also took a lot of breaks. It was summer, and I relished opening the windows and enjoying the silence.

After a blissful first evening with my processor off, I was ready to start over. Realizing that I needed more time before embracing the technology was an understatement. The next morning, I put the processor on and found my hearing had temporarily regressed to the monotone organ sound. Fifteen minutes later, it was back to the Charlie Brown show.

As I drove to work, I noticed everyday environmental sounds but heightened to an exaggerated degree. My car's turn signal seemed to click right inside my head. The sway of my dangly earring banged like a garbage can lid against the processor, even though it was just a gentle tap each time it touched.

I could hear myself breathing. It was like living inside a perpetual obscene phone call, I told Mark Alan. "I had no idea how much noise my nostrils made." Walking across the work campus was embarrassing, hearing the disproportionate whoosh of my breath, louder than my footsteps or the sound of my voice.

I wore the processor all day, feeling nauseated. Mark Alan told me I was weaving like a drunken sailor. I'd never actually been seasick before. I loved turbulence and tiny airplanes. I loved choppy waters on boats. But something was amiss with my inner ear fluid, and I didn't feel well at all.

Coming home the second day, the garage door again opened automatically via my head. (Or possibly not.) The door opened and closed repeatedly, so our condo board president finally turned it off to reset, scanning the neighborhood for rogue satellite dishes that might have caused interference. She mentioned "radio frequency," and my heart skipped a beat.

It's my radio head, I thought. *Was this my secret superpower?*

I had always wanted a unique skill. However, the thrill of my new gift dwindled quickly once I considered how obsolete it was. For example, my neighbor's SUV already stored her remote garage code as a dashboard feature.

"Not to seem ungrateful," I remarked to Mark Alan, "but opening my garage door with my head is not as glamorous as you might think. It wouldn't even make my Top Ten list."

Mark Alan noodled and came up with my new superhero name: "Radio Head Gal." It seemed appropriate. We compared superpowers. I still wanted the ability to read minds. I wouldn't need to hear at all because I would already know. World traveler Mark Alan opted for teleportation.

On the third day, my supernatural saga ended. As soon as my car approached the garage door range, the red light on my remote blinked without me touching it. Upon further inspection, I saw that the device was jammed and sending continuous signals to the garage door eye. Once I jiggled the button free, the connection broke. Like everyone else, I had to touch the clicker to access the garage. Life resumed on a less magical trajectory.

That first week, I turned off the processor a million times. I felt slight pangs of guilt for missing windows of opportunity, like separating a baby duck from its mother at birth so it bonded with a feral cat instead. But I couldn't bear the stimulation for more than a few hours at a time. Every night, I reached for the Dramamine.

Eventually, I was sure I would get used to it. I'd only had a week to progress from disliking it to merely tolerating it. However, I was inching toward moments of acceptance: I had started replacing the rechargeable battery as soon as it died rather than using it as an excuse to pack it up for the day.

The beeps turned into familiar audio quickly enough. This was particularly impressive, given how long that ear had been nonfunctional. I'd heard voices as amplified by my hearing aids before the surgery, so recognizing environmental sounds was not new. Still, it was a hopeful sign of progress.

Fellow implantee Bill told me he loved all the jingle-jangle. I did not. I considered noise to be unnecessary litter that, unfortunately, was included with the new soundtrack to my life. My condo was in a direct flight path to the airport, and jets roared overhead every five minutes. Power mowers buzzed virtually all day amidst dog yaps. Sputtering buses and honking cars continuously drove the snow emergency route right under my bedroom window. *How did people even think with all that racket?*

A bright spot emerged: I still had the ability to turn off the electronic noise at my discretion, a significant blessing and source of endless joy. Really, I just wanted speech comprehension, but that was still far beyond my implanted ear's grasp. Listening to people talk was whooshy with high-pitched tinkles and robotic chipmunk squeaks. It wasn't pretty. It was not understandable without lip-reading.

My CI had not yet surpassed the little hearing I had before with hearing aids. I knew it was too soon to tell, and thinking about it only made me anxious. It was like being stuck in travel delay limbo, eagerly anticipating a boarding announcement, uncertain of the departure time, but also facing the distinct possibility that the flight could still be canceled.

Around this time, I noticed an odd person who posted frequently on the CI online bulletin boards. From what I gathered, she did not have hearing loss. Yet she obsessively called her clinic, asking to be selected as a CI candidate. She believed that all she needed was a cochlear implant, and once she had a cochlear implant, her life would change. Miraculously, all of her problems would be resolved. Didn't a CI fix everything?

I found her situation fascinating. She fraudulently claimed an oppressed viewpoint to gain attention or maybe even a sense of belonging. Meanwhile, this was what I struggled with most as a deaf person — learning to be myself unapologetically. "Loud and Proud" was a slogan associated with gay pride that I thought summed up perfectly what I needed in my life: the ability to speak up and advocate for myself just as I was — deaf — rather than trying to blur my differences to blend in.

Interestingly, "Loud and Proud" also meant the act of throwing grenades in warfare and running into combat with an automatic weapon. So, perhaps a happy medium?

Amidst the joyful CI success stories, the online bulletin boards spilled over with tales of pressure from loved ones. Reading about the intolerance people faced was depressing, statements like:

> "My family stopped talking to me because they had to repeat everything they said."

> "My husband left because my hearing was too much trouble for him."

> "Once my family convinced me how awful my situation was for them, I couldn't wait to have surgery."

It was one thing to discuss CI as an option and be mutually supportive. Plenty of implantees wanted the CI because of their own desire to hear again. However, a distinct subset of candidates posted about spouses or friends who led them to believe their hearing loss was unacceptable simply because the partner felt inconvenienced, yet there was no indication of any effort to help out. By comparison,

I was grateful that, while my family and friends mentioned CI as an intriguing proposition, no one tried to influence my decision through gaslighting.

Still, the posts rang so painfully true. Everything circled back to the burden of hearing loss and the inconvenience hearing people perceived.

(On themselves.)

25

Rehab

I called the number Bill recommended to schedule my aural re-habilitation appointments. Mark Alan was interpreting, and his eyebrows shot up in recognition. He told me the voice on the an-swering machine for the speech pathology clinic had a distinct lisp.

Mark Alan was an expert at recognizing accents. During the hundreds of conference calls he interpreted for me, he pegged the inflections and accents with astonishing accuracy (like recognizing vintage cars on the road). For example, I had several calls a week with a woman whose voice Mark Alan immediately identified as indicative of cerebral palsy. When we finally met her in person, he was right.

I wondered: If a speech professional had a distinctive accent, would they pass it along to their clients? I began to sketch out a sitcom in which all the deaf children of a small Minnesota town spoke with British accents due to the work of a transplanted speech teacher.

My aural rehab therapist was a blond, ponytailed cheerleader type who spoke in fractured sentence fragments. Not surprisingly, she worked primarily with children and radiated unwavering positivity.

I am calling her Ally (she whose name is definitely not Ally) because it seems like a sunny, twenty-something woman's name, and perhaps also for the double meaning under the equality heading: Being an ally involves leveraging one's privilege and power for someone with less, even if the pronunciation differs.

Ally's zeal was boundless. I couldn't help but smile at her eagerness to please. It didn't matter that her excitement was disproportionate to the task. I felt like an infant with an overly animated parent dangling a shiny object in my face, beaming brightly and clapping.

"Superfantastic, Rebecca!" she squealed when I repeated the months of the year correctly. "Like, really awesome!"

Ally was an essential partner in my CI journey. Not only did she steer me competently through the ten-week rehab program, but she did so with such quirky enthusiasm that I never once felt like the oddball. Our rehab took place in Ally's playroom, where we sat in tiny chairs around a miniature table. She animatedly waved flashcards and toys and spoke in exclamation points, creating an atmosphere brimming with energy and excitement, perfectly tailored for a six-year-old. (I was forty-three at the time.)

Yes, I thought it was weird. Nevertheless, I've been treated like a child most of my life due to the optics of standing under five feet tall. I've had plenty of kids' menus thrust at me in restaurants. The clerks in the children's shoe department remember me unprompted. Sitting in a kid-sized chair felt refreshing simply because it was Ally's standard room setup and, for once, not because of how I looked.

I had fun telling people I was in rehab. I loved the shock on their faces when they misunderstood, assuming it was rehabilitation for substance abuse, alcohol, or even a gambling dependency. It seemed inconceivable to them that someone who looked twelve years old might have a secret sordid side. Anyway, it was not that kind of rehab. Specifically, I was in aural rehabilitation, specialized therapy for people with hearing loss. Without it, I probably would have stumbled into some progress with the CIs; with it, however, I learned how to hear.

It had only been a week since hook-up. I wondered if it was too early for rehab since speech was meaningless to my implanted side. It was not too soon, said Ally. (Her exact words were, "The timing is, like, you know, not too soon, also?")

There were three stages to rehab, in this order:

1. Environmental sounds.
2. Speech recognition with visual prompts.
3. Speech comprehension without visual prompts.

Rehab strategy was important. The CI does not restore natural hearing; it rewires it entirely. (Fun fact: Cyborg hearing leverages the side of the head for hearing, not the ear canal.) Some adults self-rehabbed by jumping into full sentences without addressing fundamental listening skills. As a result, they risked not breaking their habit of guessing based on sentence context instead of learning to master the various components of speech.

Aural rehab was like any other medical treatment for which following an established strategy was better than going it alone, like having physical therapy after a knee replacement. It was also helpful to have an objective third party diagnose weak areas and assign home exercises to strengthen them.

And so we began. With my aided ear turned off and my implanted ear on, we immediately started identifying environmental sounds (that is, random noises that were not speech). We listened to various farm animal bleats — the livestock calls that even toddlers can identify. I got them all wrong. By the next week, however, the moos and the oinks had become recognizable, and we moved on to the following sequence. Progress!

I also met regularly with my audiologist over the first few months and noted how much lighter the atmosphere seemed. In my childhood, visiting the audiologist had been a source of dread. Audiologists were my persecutors, people who made me feel like a failure when, in reality, they probably thought they were being empathetic by sharing their dismay over drops in my hearing.

Anyway, my perspective changed after the implant. Audiologists became my partners, tech support for my radio head, and intrepid scientists who reveled in their quest to discover the precise configurations for impeccable sound quality. I liked to imagine my audiologist as an engineer in a recording studio, expertly adjusting the bass and treble because the electrode and processor settings were not one-size-fits-all and needed to keep pace as my brain adapted.

"Mapping" seemed like a concept straight out of science fiction, literally connecting my head to a computer for a software update to customize electrodes and processor programs to their optimal settings. The audiologist pinged each internal electrode for a response, then tinkered and configured.

Each mapping started with defining thresholds for comfortable stimulation levels. I was beginning to understand why this was important. Voices were muffled and echoed at lower levels, but the sound sharpened into focus when we upped the volume on the program. It was not really "volume," per se; it was power being added to the charge, which was constrained by the limits of what I could tolerate.

Initially, my tolerance was low. My brain had to learn not to react like a skittish pinball machine when the electrodes pulsed harder, so I worked diligently to increase my threshold, a process I called "auditory masochism." It got easier. My tolerance crept higher.

A few weeks in, as I drove home from rehab, I notched a small milestone. I didn't normally listen to the radio, yet I turned it on that day and scanned to a random station. Through the static, I caught two familiar phrases: "The Bible says ..." and "... relationship with God." It wasn't earth-shattering, but still, it marked the first words I had understood (without visual cues) since implant activation.

I told Mark Alan about my progress. Concerned about the subliminal effects of sampling talk radio without actually comprehending it, Mark Alan joked that he was afraid I would show up one day, quit my job, and inexplicably join a conservative think tank. "There must be a Green Party station somewhere," he said worriedly. "Let me find that for you."

My technology peeps in Frederick, Maryland had sent me a generous bookstore gift card in my surgery care package. As part of my rehabilitation practice, listening to audiobooks while following along visually was strongly recommended. I bought a New Testament CD, hoping to simultaneously expand my knowledge for my side job, writing drama scripts to accompany the pastor's sermons at church. I gave listening to the CD a fair shake, but either I couldn't distinguish the components of speech well enough yet, or the narrator legitimately couldn't pronounce his "r's" and "l's."

"It's Elmer Fudd reading the Book of John," I said doubtfully to Mark Alan. "I honestly can't tell if it's him or me."

I got through the audio gospels, barely. After that, my listening practice mutated into lying on my bedroom floor, my implant processor plugged directly into the television's audio jack, watching *Friends* and other sitcoms while reading along with the closed captioning. Sadly, this lowbrow activity was less frustrating than my hours with Elmer. It reminded me of the movie *Splash,* where the mermaid taught herself English by watching television. Entire evenings went by, propped in front of the television with VHS recordings of Monica, Chandler, and Ross.

Most implantees say that music sounds unpleasant at first. I enjoyed music previously with my hearing aids, though I mostly gravitated towards familiar '70s albums for which my brain was probably leveraging my teenage memories of sound. With the implant, I could hear music as well as I had with my old hearing aids within a month. Whether pre- or post-implant sound was an accurate representation of what was real or based on memory, I can't say, but I thought it was good. However, I had no ability to repeat it back accurately. Identifying unfamiliar lyrics still eluded me.

In the first months after the implant, my brain processed melody somewhat unpredictably. For example, the tune of every bouncy hymn at church became the folk ballad "Oh My Darling Clementine."[39] No matter how hard I focused, even tracing my finger across the musical notes in the church hymnal (forcing my eyes to follow the visual expression of the score), my brain stubbornly swapped "Clementine" instead. I knew the first verse from an old Pete Seeger album and decided to look up the rest for context. The remaining lyrics told the tragic tale: a woman drowning, whose lover couldn't swim, and he was unwilling to save her.

Inconvenience. The recurring theme for hearing loss.

* * *

The great thing about rehab was that, though I failed spectacularly in each new task, I could complete the same challenge successfully the following week, showing clear progression. Still, my ability to hear with my eyes complicated things. I thought I had scored 100 percent on my first speech recognition test with visual prompts (where I had to identify spoken words or sentences from a list of choices with Ally's mouth covered). We soon discovered I could accurately predict answers by watching Ally's eyebrows. My skill at guessing also thwarted impromptu rehab with Mark Alan as we practiced while waiting for my conference calls to connect. Picking categories like colors or shapes, I repeated the words Mark Alan thought up while I looked away from him, knocking it out of the park until he introduced unconventional choices.

"Chartreuse," he said as we practiced colors.

"Orange?" I guessed.

"Crescent," he said for shapes.

"What? Rectangle?" I asked.

Infuriating Colors for Rehab Practice
by Mark Alan English
Chamomile ~ Indigo ~ Granite
Teal ~ Saffron ~ Orchid
Khaki ~ Mauve

For the third week of rehab, Ally focused on the Ling Six[40] sounds: *ahh, eee, ooo, mmm, shh,* and *sss.* Developed by auditory habilitation professor Dr. Daniel Ling, the Ling Six represents the spectrum of low, middle, and high-frequency sounds needed to understand spoken language. Mastering those elusive specifics was a critical milestone in learning to hear.

I could identify four of the six consistently, but *eee* sounded like a guitar squeak, and *mmm* was an undefined grunt. Those were the most challenging two, Ally said encouragingly. I remained determined and refused to give up. Ally said I was doing "like, totally awesome, dude!" Word recognition with visual cues was going well, and we had now advanced into more complicated activities, such as identifying words amidst a fan whirring and a radio blaring.

"Snaps to you, Rebecca!" she gushed. "You are, like, so on it!"

We repeated the failed listening exercises to success the following week and charted progression to show improvement. We also added a more challenging activity at which I invariably failed. Two weeks earlier, it was placing the accent mark in multisyllabic words. The previous week, it was identifying questions versus statements. I wiped out completely — couldn't distinguish the pitch change at the end — but remained optimistic for the next attempt.

A few weeks into rehab, I received an email from church, wondering if I could now hear. I explained that cochlear implantation was not like flipping a light switch; it was a gradual process of rehab and listening practice and acclimating to increasingly intense stimulation. I told them I could hear the sounds of speech but still relied on lipreading with visual cues to comprehend words, at least for now, so my situation was not that different from before.

My initial apprehension about destroying my natural hearing had passed. The progression of my bionic hearing was almost to my pre-surgical level (which wasn't saying much, relatively speaking). My latest anxieties had migrated to the potential for inadvertent freak accidents which could only afflict implantees, like my head igniting in a ball of flame if I had a facial mole removed with the wrong kind of cautery tool. Stuff like that.

Indeed, the previous day, Mark Alan had informed me with great excitement that he had just seen an episode of a crime procedural where a man's cochlear implant detonated in the crematorium. "That's how they found the killer," he exclaimed gleefully. "His head exploded!"

While focused on learning listening skills in rehab, I had a conversation with two acquaintances who were the worst — the worst! — at unconsciously covering their mouths while talking.

"Hey," I said. "You always have your hands over your mouths when you talk to me. Let's do some rehab exercises since I need you to cover your mouth anyway, and you can't seem to help yourself." Then, I pulled out a long list of words from my purse and made them practice with me. It worked like a charm: I got a bonus round of rehab practice, and they stopped covering their mouths for good.

They weren't close friends, so it was easy to risk offending them with my snark. In fact, the whole point was to tick them off enough to spur action. How often had I told them, "I need to see your face when you talk." Inwardly, I thought, "If you were my friend, you would remember just one time without me having to ask again." Moments later, when they did it again, I had to reconcile the abject hatred I felt at that moment. *Because if they cared about me, they should have been able to do this without me resorting to trickery.*

Yet, they couldn't.

It was tempting to pass judgment (and I just did). Their belief system was anchored in two fundamental ideas: Being able to hear was the only default their brains could recognize, and to them, hearing loss was not worth the inconvenience of having to change their practices, the perfect storm of inherent bias and human nature.

Hearing people love to see themselves as being accommodating. They believe wholeheartedly that they embrace diversity. They genuinely like the idea of helping out but underestimate the commitment required to learn new habits. Deep down, they just want the problem to go away.

What they really want is for me to be hearing.

26

Cyborg

Rehab continued to advance, but there had been no undisguised, high-five-worthy, praise-be-to-Jesus moment of clarity where I suddenly comprehended speech. Even though I suspected I was maybe hearing better — for sure, sounds were louder, and lipreading seemed like less work — I couldn't tell if people had decided to speak more clearly for a change or whether the implant was slowly turning words into comprehension. Was I still relying on my vision, or had the cyborg started to emerge?

Incidentally, the term "cyborg" is a mash-up of the words "cybernetics" and "organism." Cybernetics is the study of control and communication in machines and living things. And organism, in this case, is a human being ... me!

So, as a cyborg, I have both natural and biomechanical body parts, plus a computer interface that relies on feedback. A diabetic wearing a glucose meter and insulin pump is also a cyborg since those technologies provide feedback to dispense medication. However, someone with an artificial arm would be bionic because they have a mechanical limb but still rely on their own thought processes to move it.

I thought it would be evident if or when the cyborg took over speech comprehension. It wasn't, at least not for me, because there was no perceptible handoff between my vision and the implant. My eyes continued functioning like before the surgery, and my brain still unscrambled words based on expert lipreading.

I had always heard with my eyes. For as long as I could remember, whenever I saw movement, my brain responded with the appropriate sound, regardless of whether I heard or saw it. As soon as closed captions were invented, I switched to watching television on mute with subtitles. My eyes told me the sound of the character's voice, the foreign accent, the smack of the broom falling to the floor, the cat meowing. It was so routine I never thought twice about how I experienced sound with the TV volume off. But with the implant, I needed to know: How much was my brain actually hearing, and how much were my eyes still lending a hand?

Always the diplomat, Mark Alan was my sounding board.

"Were you just talking loudly?" I asked as he finished a dramatic tale about his vomiting dog, Corky.

"No, I was very quiet," he replied.

"Are you sure?" I queried. "You weren't shouting at me about barf out of pity?"

He shook his head and smiled.

It was freaking me out. It started with a few words here and there, but now I was conversing with people I couldn't understand before, like Patrick the Mumbler (an actual name sign created by Mark Alan). I was sure the other individuals had changed, not me. But if it was them, why did they wait until after my surgery?

What was wrong with these people?

* * *

E ight weeks after CI activation, I had met my original, low expectations: Stop the cycle of progressive hearing loss while destroying the remainder of my natural hearing and recreate the minimal ability I had from before.

By now, my cyborg hearing was slightly better than what I had started with, and the sound quality was pretty good. The roaring had gradually subsided, thank God, and the robotic grunts had turned into voices, but I still needed my eyes to understand words. Acoustic music sounded great, despite not understanding lyrics I didn't already know. I could identify familiar songs within the context of the opening notes but couldn't name the tune if I joined midway through.

I clung to my initial benchmark: understanding speech without lipreading. My audiologist measured CI success at 50 percent for speech comprehension of spoken sentences. Plenty of implantees scored higher than 50 percent, but others didn't, which pulled down the average.

With a CI, so much was unknown. Since my life was geared toward forecasting outcomes before they happened, the CI presented an uncomfortable conflict. Beyond the surgical (for example, successful electrode insertion) and mechanical (such as working equipment), no one knew how well an individual's auditory nerve would respond. Preexisting damage or lack of stimulation could render the nerve less effective, and additional medical issues could complicate an outcome.

Personal qualities mattered, too. Being able to articulate what was good or bad during mapping sessions to fine-tune the electronic configurations was essential. Having appropriate expectations for progress at each milestone was a factor, as well as having the grit to stick to relearning how to hear versus giving up at the first obstacle.

I hated the unpredictability. There were no guarantees. Some implantees would eventually comprehend speech well; others would not. I thought there would be some warning if it happened — a brilliant ray of sun bursting through the clouds maybe — but I'm embarrassed to say I wasn't paying close attention. My brain had quietly started to adjust, unscrambling the electronic signals from the auditory nerve into speech without telling me, yet my eyes kept showing up for work. Nothing seemed any different. Nothing even sounded different because I had been hearing with my eyes all along.

I finally noticed it at rehab. Ally said, "Today is going to be, like, totally awesome. I'm going to call you on the phone from, like, next door, and you, like, totally pretend to take my pizza order, and I'll, like, repeat it back wrong, and you, like, tell me off, also? You know? My bad."

I let out a sigh of frustration. Ugh, the telephone. It had been such an ordeal to stop using the voice phone a few years earlier that I had to consult a therapist. I was not looking forward to the exercise.

We started the task. Ally even had props on the table: a green order pad, a plastic pizza cutter, and a pizza pan. I rolled my eyes and reluctantly committed. Only after we finished did I realize a significant hurdle had been crossed: a ten-minute conversation with no visual cues about flat-crust pizza and whether drinking soda pop caused cancer. I was six years old again, still riding my bike with the training wheels, unaware I no longer needed them.

It wasn't a tearful moment. It didn't give my life new meaning. It was a milestone, that's all, but one to which other Microsoft Project dependencies were attached. I wasn't ready to make conference calls without an interpreter. I wasn't about to telephone family or friends (not because I couldn't, but because I didn't want to).

But this milestone completed the first phase of a journey that had begun four years earlier: my bout with pneumonia when I first knew I would lose what was left of my hearing. I was struck by how closely my life mirrored a project management cycle: initiation, planning, executing, monitoring, and closure. There were more phases ahead, but for this first iteration, all that remained were metrics and lessons learned.

I went home and listened to a tape recording of one of my plays. Granted, I had written the script, but it had been a few years, so I didn't know the words by heart. I measured my success: I understood it all. I savored the moment and smiled at the wonder — speech comprehension without lipreading! Like an assumption flipping from false to true, it changed everything.

The cyborg had emerged.

27

Breakups / Breakthroughs

In between dates, Vertigo Boy and I connected almost every day through instant messaging, and we chatted the evening of my breakthrough day. He asked what was new, so I told him about rehab and that I had reached my speech comprehension milestone. He said he was happy for me. I tried to be sensitive since his activation had been later than mine, and his development was further behind. He was heading out, so we said goodnight. I remembered thinking how much I liked him. I thought we might be at a launching point from the post-surgical bubble into the next phase of our relationship. Was Vertigo Boy my next milestone?

I didn't make the connection right away, and it could have been entirely coincidental that it happened right after my cyborg breakthrough, but that was our last conversation. Vertigo Boy stopped responding to my communications — he ghosted me — and that was that. It was still years before cell phone texting, and while we knew where each other lived and worked, I didn't even have his landline number since neither of us was using the voice telephone yet. But also, why would I? Our relationship had been rooted in the realm of Bionic World — had it ever been real? We came to a fork in the road, and our paths diverged.

I never saw him again.

As I mulled over being forsaken by Vertigo Boy, I was nearing the end of rehab. I couldn't help but notice that my aural therapist, Ally, had formed an unhealthy professional attachment to me. As her only adult client following a gaggle of preschool children, she greeted me with far too much relief and, dare I say, clinginess.

We were focused on discerning speech with background noise. The curriculum called for us to find a crowded spot for practice. Ultimately, we ended up at a bar with outdoor seating in the middle of the college campus. Music blared, buses whizzed by, and lively students hoisted beers as it was late in the day.

Ally forgot to bring the written text for the session, so she improvised, turning our rehab session into a therapist's couch by confiding personal details. "I'm, like, finding my family's expectations for when I should, like, get married and have children, like, totally bogus," I repeated back to her as other bar patrons eavesdropped and stared curiously. "I am totally busted, you know?"

The session was a peculiar hour of oversharing, echoing back Ally's angst over her dating life as she covered her mouth with a napkin. I considered finishing early on that high note since we were at week nine of the ten-week rehab plan. However, Ally was so excited about next week's session that I couldn't break it to her.

"It's so great to converse with an adult for a change," she confided to me like a best friend. "Like, it's totally awesome to just talk. I look forward to this all day."

Mark Alan thought my inability to let Ally down gently was hilarious, and he predicted I would never get out. "It's me, not you," he demonstrated, trying to coach me in the fine art of breakups. "It's time to move on. We've gone as far as we can go. I just don't feel I have any more to give."

I vowed that week ten would be my last rehab session. Ally tried her best to get me to book more, but I held firm, telling her that my work schedule was demanding. I praised her for giving me sustainable tools to continue rehab on my own. I said she had taught me to lead myself, pumping her up, and I hoped she was proud of what we achieved together. I found my time in rehab worthwhile and believed it made a difference. I thanked her, and we said goodbye.

It had been a few months since activation, and I had to break up with Mark Alan, too, but only as my work interpreter. I was hearing conference calls well enough on my own, even though Mark Alan was still interpreting simultaneously. It was time. Fortunately, the initiative I was overseeing was also winding down, so our conclusion happened organically. As the project calls dwindled, Mark Alan and I found ourselves penciling in fewer days until we mutually agreed we didn't need to schedule any more.

It was not traumatic. Mark Alan, his husband Tom, and I were good friends by then, so it didn't mean we wouldn't see each other. I went to their house for Sunday brunch, attended Tom's classical concerts, and was in charge of Thanksgiving desserts. We had the surrogate egg talk when they explored becoming parents and a co-parenting discussion when they adopted. I babysat their son when he was a toddler, although, to be honest, I was an anxious babysitter, so that didn't last long. (Luckily, they had other parent–friends on whom they could depend.) I had the privilege of signing their marriage license when same-sex marriage became legal in Minnesota. I was the emergency contact for Tom's parents when the boys spent weekends at the cabin, and I took his mother to the Emergency Room when she hurt her shoulder. They will always be two of the most important people in my life.

That said, I had withdrawal pains on my first day at work without Mark Alan. The moments spent waiting for conference calls to join seemed strangely hollow without our customary catch-up chats. It was the end of a meaningful chapter, and I felt both nostalgic and empowered.

That I could use the voice telephone again was fortunate as my responsibilities for monitoring project teams and my direct reports increased. My conference calls were often double- or triple-booked at the same hour, which required a hopscotch approach of dialing in and out, even wearing my wireless telephone headset into the bathroom on mute. On the days I did have half an hour between calls, I'd take my processor off while catching up on paperwork and bask in silence, a homemade "unplugged" sign hanging from my desk to alert unsuspecting colleagues approaching from behind.

The day the Minneapolis bridge collapsed into the Mississippi River marked a significant moment in my timeline with the voice telephone. Much like the unforgettable events of 9/11, I remember where I was when the tragedy struck. After work, I had driven to a law firm in the suburbs to finalize new estate planning documents. It was a beastly hot day (which might have factored in the bridge's collapse). By the time I returned home, I was already in the shower, trying to cool off. It was then that my phone began to flash, signaling incoming calls. Since I had removed my CI processor, the calls went to voicemail. The flashing light persisted, penetrating the glass of my bathroom door. After a few repetitions, I hastily rinsed off the soap, put on my processor curiously, and listened to the flood of messages from my brother and sisters. A barrage of emails awaited my attention as well.

"A bridge in Minneapolis collapsed. Call me as soon as you get this."

Even though I had been using the voice telephone constantly at work by then, I rarely made personal voice calls. Why? Stubbornness. It had been such an ordeal to stop using the voice telephone when I lost my hearing that I honestly had no desire to go back. My family had phased out voice calls when I first asked, and they had gotten used to email since, which worked just fine. (With the advent of texting a few years later, our communications became even more convenient.) They were trained.

But a major bridge had collapsed into the Mississippi River, and nine people were dead. I worked less than a mile from the bridge. I'd driven across it hundreds of times. One of my work colleagues was *on* the bridge at the time it collapsed and miraculously walked away. Weeks later, I saw a photo of his smashed car dangling between the upper and lower portion of the dissected bridge, another SUV perched on the top of the roof. By the grace of God.

My family was calling to confirm I was safe, so I phoned them all back for the first time since my cochlear implant four years earlier. The collapse had just occurred, and I wasn't yet aware of the news. I thanked them for letting me know.

You probably assume I call them all the time now, but I don't. Just because I can doesn't mean that I want to. My center of reference didn't change. I still prefer visual communication. During the pandemic, we siblings held regular Zoom calls, but apart from that, we keep multiple group text strings going, with just an occasional voice call.

To me, that's perfectly normal.

28

Bilateral

My cyborg hearing steadily improved over the first few years. I ran across the "Four Things Rebecca Wants to Hear" list that Mark Alan and I had made and assessed:

1. I could finally appreciate Mark Alan's husband **Tom's CD** of his classical piano compositions. It was beautiful. I played it nonstop in my car.

2. I regularly listened to *A Prairie Home Companion* radio show and had the opportunity to join their Alaska cruise. It was an incredible trip: a literary escapade spanning an entire week, surrounded by like-minded strangers who quickly became friends. It was the best possible use of the cyborg, and I couldn't have been happier about it.

3. My quest to use the **restaurant drive-through** lane to get a soda for the commute home from Des Moines fizzled out when work travel was halted due to budget cuts, so the issue became moot. Then, two decades later, innovation struck: Restaurants rolled out online ordering apps with curbside

pickup in response to the COVID-19 lockdown, a boon for accessibility, bypassing the dreaded drive-through intercom. A win was a win, even if it was a solution to a different problem.

4. And finally, I had an answer for the verbal **parking ramp warning**, which I had previously thought was, "A Somalianite is approaching." It wasn't the revelation I felt it might be, but I could understand it now. The voice said, "A small child is approaching." I was relieved it wasn't racially motivated but dismayed to realize it was still profiling me … by my height! In this case, understanding speech was not especially welcome.

As technologically proficient as the CI was, I wanted to be careful to distinguish that my life was not *better;* it was more *convenient,* the way being a size two wasn't superior to larger sizes but certainly made shopping easier when stores only stocked sample sizes. I did not want to hang my hat on the ability to hear. I felt I could praise the advancements in hearing technology without putting down deafness and, by extension, myself.

When people disparage hearing loss as being undesirable (and not merely a life circumstance), they reveal a surprisingly deep and often disproportionately vicious prejudice toward a growing slice of the world population for something that can't be cured by assistive devices, not truly, while simultaneously exhaling judgment into the universe. Kudos to those who choose gratitude for the sounds they can hear instead of minimizing others, who praise the device manufacturers and technology instead of sniping about brands, and who kindly accommodate those who ask instead of excluding them.

By now, the cyborg had surpassed my natural hearing ability at any point in my life. It wasn't perfectly perfect, but speech comprehension was pretty darn good. The sound quality was excellent; it wasn't robotic or distorted. It sounded just like my hearing aids had, which was awesome. I could hear my name being called at doctors' offices most of the time, prompting me to switch from my tense general practitioner, who always contradicted me, to a different clinic. The new, randomly assigned internal medicine guy sported a shaggy mullet and purple earrings, made vaguely inappropriate comments, and seemed a bit too eager to prescribe narcotics. Clearly, not everything was an improvement.

It had been six years since the implant. However, life was not much closer to my big-picture wish: end-to-end accessibility, where a visual representation of sound was just another preference to select in a user profile. I held on to hope that alternative technology options were on the horizon, but perhaps I had been born several decades too soon. Meanwhile, the next move was still mine.

I considered implantation for the second ear — going bilateral — but I had it in my mind to wait until the operation no longer destroyed the natural hearing. In the meantime, speech comprehension in my remaining ear (previously my good ear) had nosedived, but it didn't matter much because the implanted side was performing so well. I no longer experienced the cycles of grief with each drop in the natural ear. *I didn't care.* I was a cyborg — indestructible — at least on one side. Progressive hearing loss no longer carried the emotional wallop that it did before.

Deciding to proceed bilaterally had no expiration date. In theory, ongoing auditory nerve stimulation was critical to keeping the brain connections functioning, like having someone run your empty dishwasher back home when going south for the winter. Many people timed the first and second implants close together. Still, I had gone thirty years with only minor stimulation in my first ear before implanting, and the cyborg nevertheless got as good as it gets. Saving residual hearing wasn't yet possible, but I didn't have enough left to benefit anyway. What exactly was I waiting for?

The next generation of technology, that's what. Specifically, magnetic resonance imaging (MRI) compatibility was in the works, and new internal components allowed for a low-level MRI. My original cochlear implant was not MRI-compatible. The lack of MRI compatibility initially didn't worry me much, but decades later, it has mattered. For instance, when I had an arthroscopic procedure on my knee, the surgeon proceeded without imaging, not knowing what and where the injury was. Did I want to do that again? Definitely not. Technically, I could have had an MRI with my older, noncompatible implant, but it would have required surgically removing the CI magnet before imaging, which I wasn't inclined to do.

Going bilateral was anticlimactic because I had a pretty good implanted ear as a fallback. Having gone through the procedure once cut the preparation necessary for the second substantially. No psychological screening or CAT scan was needed, just the pre-surgery physical plus meningitis and pneumococcal vaccinations. I scheduled the second surgery for the same date precisely six years later since I already knew the recovery timetable. I didn't tell many people, not for the same reasons as before, but because the procedure seemed like a non-event. I had a much more hopeful outlook going into it, expecting my ear to respond to the electronic pulses after an appropriate recovery period. The bilateral option would balance things out. It was time.

The morning of my other-ear cochlear implant surgery started with a bang. As I dutifully followed the nurse to the tiny pre-op room, I promptly wiped out on a glassy spot on the floor in front of the family waiting room, like a cartoon character slipping on a banana peel.

What to do? I thought about Radio Head Gal. While she might fall occasionally, she always got back up, her powers intact. I dusted myself off as strangers stared, my hip smarting, embarrassed. The nurse promptly fastened a yellow silicone band around my wrist. I imagined it as Wonder Woman's bracelet (the source of her power) until I noticed the words "High risk for balance issues." I read the band dubiously and asked if it was due to my crash in the hallway. Because I'd never fallen before in my life. (The floor was wet!)

The nurse quickly reassured me it was standard protocol for inner ear surgeries and unrelated to my unfortunate wipeout. I wasn't entirely sure I believed her since the original surgery didn't include a yellow bracelet. However, her drawer was full of them, so she was most likely telling the truth.

I quickly learned that my primary care physician, Dr. Mullet Head, never submitted my pre-surgical documentation. I was annoyed that I had taken time off work for the physical and had to listen to him ramble about his ex, who happened to be short, so I reminded him of her. He clearly had unresolved issues. Not awkward at all! Still, I wasn't surprised about the missing paperwork. He had no-showed twice when I was his first appointment in the day and seemed like a slacker.

Consequently, the hospital had to redo everything from the EKG to the blood tests. My frowny-faced CI surgeon performed a basic physical, which was totally weird since he had only ever looked at my ears. Obviously, he was a *doctor*, but it felt out of place, like having the mailperson administer my pap smear.

The rest of the surgical experience was so unremarkable that all I remember was my hospital roommate. I assumed she too was an implantee because my surgeon's resident covered her on rounds. I felt compassion because she was elderly and, based on the number of times I heard doctors and nurses asking her to state the year and if she knew where she was, had memory constraints.

But her adult kids were there, and they were terrible hospital visitors. Eight of them crowded my side of the separation curtain, shouting at their mother (which I get, but come on, write it down, people!), constantly entering and exiting. It was chaotic and disruptive, so I muted them, a handy perk of being a cyborg. There was also an emergency in the middle of the night involving a man in a suit and tie running into our room at full speed. I felt the pounding vibrations all the way from the end of the hall until he burst inside. (Note: I'm pretty sure I hallucinated the last event under the influence of narcotics.)

Remember my first implant surgery and how I thought my roommate had been removed in a body bag? The middle-of-the-night running made me wonder whether this roommate might also have died. I experienced a moment of paranoia. Would people think I was the common denominator? Because one dead hospital roommate was a fluke, but twice, they convene a grand jury. But the roommate's annoying family trooped in again the following day, bright and early, shouting with gusto, so apparently, she was still with us.

Was the second implant easier or harder? On both an anxiety level and in a nod to streamlined procedures, the second time around was much easier. There were no real surprises and not much worry. On the physical side, however, I had forgotten how it felt after surgery. I did get dizzy and nauseated, and I couldn't turn my neck to the side or sleep on that ear for a week. The stitches felt like a perpetually tight hair weave, sort of a burning/pulling sensation. It wasn't excruciating, but I had forgotten the discomfort.

On the other hand, it was a happy surprise to find that the CI surgical procedure had changed entirely in just a few years! The first surgery had been quite invasive, with staples and head dents.

Fast-forward six years, and the new incision was just a curve behind my ear. There was no bandage (nothing taped to my eyebrows), just a plastic cup over my ear secured by a Velcro headband. And most importantly, the internal parts for the second implant were a newer generation of technology, allowing for an MRI.

A week after surgery, I felt 100 percent, and all dizziness had subsided. Almost nothing was shaved. I wore no head covering at all. The stitches pinched just a little. The ear wasn't numb anymore, not like last time. I was already sleeping on my implanted side. And no roaring, no metallic taste in my mouth. I had beaten the facial nerve odds, dodged all the bullets, and heaved a sigh of relief.

Psychologically, the idea of having destroyed all of my natural hearing in both ears required some adjustment. My residual hearing had been so limited that I was used to silence without amplification anyway. But the fact that it could have been amplified just a smidge gave me a tiny sliver of confidence that was now gone. While those momentary blips of panic never completely go away, the successful result was a fair trade-off.

With the second implant, activation also was easier (perhaps because my brain had already figured it out once). I heard distorted speech sounds right away during activation. Basically, my newly implanted ear had been consistently stimulated by a hearing aid since childhood, and my auditory nerve responded like a pop-up turkey timer. For the bilateral implant, I more aggressively pushed my tolerance threshold until my electronic hearing matched my first. I was two for two.

* * *

After going bilateral, I set a new goal for measuring success. Venturing outside my predictable comfort zone, I volunteered to be a greeter at church, immersing myself in the unpredictable nature of conversing with chatty strangers, something I'd previously avoided. My gig was the Saturday night service, which took place on a different side of the building, so the few people entering via my assigned door were either lost or visiting for the first time. The church scheduler offered to move me to a more densely populated entrance, but I viewed my remote mission like John Dunbar in the movie *Dances With Wolves,* refusing to abandon my desolate outpost.

I stubbornly clung to my role as a beacon of hope to the dazed and disoriented, a messenger of kindness. While the other entrances required repetitively greeting a mass stream of arrivals, my door required troubleshooting. Over the next year, I encountered a tearful bridesmaid searching for a wedding party that had left without her, car problems requiring roadside assistance, loose children running from a parent, a lone bird strolling through the visitor's reception area, and a steady parade of cars looking for the Minnesota State Fair Park & Ride (located in the back parking lot on weekdays).

One Saturday, a woman left the church building after an afternoon music seminar. I saw her walking through the nearby parking lot on foot, lugging an armful of books, as I manned my post. She looped around again ten minutes later, close to tears. She couldn't remember where she had parked her car. My shift was done, so I offered to drive her around to search, as it was a large campus with multiple surface lots.

I flashed back to a subzero day when I couldn't find my own car in our seven-story ramp at work. I usually snagged the same spot every day but arrived later that morning and didn't take a mental snapshot when I parked. It was the afternoon of our annual recognition party at a swanky hotel downtown, and I was leaving work to head to the event. I was carrying my own heavy load: a sloshing glass vase with a dozen long-stemmed roses, a gift from my team. I searched on foot in vain, then flagged down a colleague and asked her to drive me up and down the aisles to find my car. With her motoring determinedly through the ramp, we found it quickly on an exit slope. I couldn't have been more grateful for her kindness on that bitterly cold day, running late.

I remembered that awful feeling of desperation when I pulled up to the church door in my beloved Bug. The woman said her name was Donna. We drove back to the freeway exit, retraced her steps, and pinpointed where she entered the church property. In the meantime, she told me she was a music pastor at a small church up north, that her mother had recently passed, her child had been diagnosed with a chronic illness, and all about the string of unfortunate events that followed. The lost car seemed to be the last straw. When she spotted her vehicle, she started to weep and couldn't speak, mouthing the word goodbye and waving as she started her car and drove off.

The moment resonated. I had fulfilled my greeter's responsibility, solely due to the cyborg's capability. But the woman's pain lingered in my mind. I thought about my own hearing loss journey and wondered if I had a perspective to counterbalance those newly diagnosed. Could my writing help others navigate the disorientation and help tone down the ableist rhetoric? Was the woman's lost car an inadvertent distress call to Radio Head Gal?

I went home and pondered.

29

The Cinderella Bubble

Growing up, I wore my hearing aids for everything except bathing or sleeping. Occasionally, I did homework unplugged (without devices) in the bedroom I shared with my sister Barbara, who was used to me in silent mode at night. Barb also owned the clock radio in our room and, on certain mornings upon request, graciously launched a stuffed animal projectile at my face or, depending on our bedroom configuration, leaned over and shook the wooden slats on my headboard as her patented wake-up call service.

Once I moved away and had my own place, I began prioritizing silence. My hearing aids emerged later and later on weekend mornings. Sometimes, entire days went by unplugged. It was a luxury I felt I'd earned.

In silence, I discovered a sharper clarity and focus as a writer that didn't exist when my devices were on. Eliminating unnecessary sound seemed to expand my creativity and thought processes exponentially, although it was possible that I just sucked at tuning out background noise.

Still today, the absence of sound fosters a sense of inner peace, frees my innermost thoughts, and elevates my writing. I find it highly addictive. I remember the popularity of sensory deprivation tanks in the '80s, a precursor to current-day float spas for relaxation. (People pay money for this!) True silence is the best of profound experiences, a serene euphoria that transcends earthly constraints. While conventional depictions of the afterlife often invoke the sounds of celestial music, my version of heaven is silent, the graceful flight of angels.

Hearing people don't feel this way. I participated in the *Sound and Silence*[41] program on NPR's *TED Radio Hour*. A sound designer also on the program shared his encounter in an anechoic chamber (a professional space intentionally devoid of sound), describing the experience as "more terrifying than anything." Same silence, different perspective. Context matters.

My acquaintances sometimes get prickly when they discover that I don't always wear my cochlear implant processors now that I'm long past the critical rehab window. Imagining a lifestyle where a person enjoys sound on an as-needed basis makes them highly uncomfortable. Yet, once they consider the benefits of silence on demand, they too wish they had it at their disposal.

Often misunderstood, silence can be a source of great freedom. Unplugging is the equivalent of taking off a bra or a tight pair of shoes. Writing or working without distraction makes the task remarkably effortless and more productive. I have fabulous memories of sledding down icy hills on thick plastic book bags when we were kids, flying exuberantly, and silence is just like that, without the bumps and tangles of human limbs. Unplugged, I get a second wind, heightened energy, and a laser-like concentration on achieving my goals, sprinting for the finish line.

The joy derived from unplugging isn't a criticism of hearing devices; it's a means of co-existing. Processing sound is not effortless for those with damaged or rewired hair cells. Hearing fatigue is real. While the average person might get tired, their brains don't experience the same mental shutdown that can occur for implantees, hearing aid wearers, or people who lipread. There's a time limit on how long a deaf attention span can slog. In the context of a non-deaf environment, even mild hearing loss is like constantly walking uphill, swimming against the current, and all the other comparisons that convey the disproportionate amount of work involved. Being hearing is always the default process assumption, even though more and more of the population have experienced loss.

Although my cochlear implants work extremely well — they are an astonishing connection for me to the hearing world — I still want the choice to experience sound in multiple ways beyond hearing. My ultimate goal is to live in a world where information is accessible through diverse avenues, granting me the flexibility to approach tasks according to my sensory preference. Wouldn't that be a stunning reality?

* * *

Cochlear implants are an amazing achievement of science, recreating the human sense of hearing through electronics! However, there's an ableist downside I call the Cinderella Bubble. The process of acquiring hearing through a CI very much mirrors Cinderella's journey, an enchanted conversion from deaf pariah to cyborg princess, but only temporarily. Like Cinderella, society views the d/Deaf as insignificant, and their inclusion at the ball (also known as life) is contingent upon their ability to hear, courtesy of their magical accessories.

Cinderella's midnight expiration is a familiar concept to hearing device users. It's a metaphor for challenges — such as dying batteries, unexpected moisture, or malfunctioning equipment — that return an individual to their undesirable deaf state. For implantees, that list also includes internal implant failure requiring more surgery.

The underlying problem with the Cinderella Bubble is not the broken parts, ticking clock, or even the midnight reversal. The issue is intolerance — society's outdated mindset that insists on hiding disability. Within the Cinderella Bubble, family, friends, and even implantees fixate so rigidly on being hearing as the only valid solution that even temporary visibility of their actual state of deafness becomes unacceptable. After all, the family's disdain for hearing loss didn't magically vanish upon activation. They just recalibrated to viewing the individual as fixed.

While the inconvenience of hearing loss might lessen with the acquisition of hearing devices, it doesn't go away completely. The best CI results can notch top scores in controlled situations but are never perfect in real life. Outside the sterile test booth, hearing difficulties just mutate into different challenges. It's a new normal that isn't always acknowledged.

Implantees often discuss this online: their loved ones' lack of understanding of their post-CI limitations and reluctance to make concessions once activation occurs. To an implantee, transforming from profoundly deaf to maybe even perfect scores on hearing tests is nothing short of miraculous. Yet, remnants of hearing loss still persist. Despite getting their life back, as they say, implantees still experience struggles, just of a different nature. Unfortunately, family and friends consider themselves released from any further obligations.

Recently, I read about a boy who stated that his biggest fear was leaving his CI processors behind in case of a disaster. The father assured him that the processors would be the first thing they would grab.

At face value, I also would probably grab my expensive processors, a credit card, and car keys in an emergency. Yet, out of all the frightening hypotheticals in life, the boy said that going without his CI processors, even temporarily, was his *greatest* fear. His story perfectly encapsulated the terror of shattering the Cinderella Bubble and being forced to expose what lay underneath. The boy's self-worth hinged on his ability to hear. As his personal midnight approached, knowing he would inevitably return to his actual state of deafness, he felt compelled to hide.

I know this fear. Emotionally, it's almost impossible to not buy into society's stigma that hearing loss renders one inexcusably inferior, regardless of assistive devices. But our differences make us who we are. Challenging the shame is not always easy, but it's essential. Speaking out and educating others, welcoming visibility into the Bubble, helps foster a more inclusive and accepting society.

30

Travel

Of my parents' passings, my father's was first after spending his final days in care facilities. Every time I visited, I was sure it was the last time I'd see him alive until, sadly, it was. I took comfort in the fact that he recognized me until the end, even if he couldn't remember the terminology.

"How is your head transplant?" he asked. I knew what he meant.

After my father's funeral, I decided to take a month-long trip to Italy. The journey had been on my bucket list for years, but I held back, fearful of being out of the country when my father died. It was also a year after my bilateral cochlear implant surgery, and I was trying to embrace risk. A milestone birthday was approaching, and I had the most proficient hearing of my entire life. If that wasn't worth recognizing, what was?

I was no stranger to traveling alone. For a third of my career, I flew every week for work, albeit with a lot of unnecessary stress. Despite accommodation laws, virtually every aspect of airport travel required the ability to hear. Gate agents announced boarding instructions over a garbled loudspeaker. Safety announcements were audio; even now, only the larger planes show captioned videos. How I got to my destinations unscathed through inaccessible airport travel was a miracle. It helped that my work trips were a repetitive pattern of familiar airports and direct flights, following a routine so predictable that the Des Moines rental car counter kept my signature on file and tossed my waiting keys as I ran by.

I was quite vocal in expressing disapproval about barriers created by airlines facing deaf travelers. "It's just not that hard to post information visually," I fumed on hundreds of customer surveys. "You already have the technology to do this." (I'm pretty sure the airlines kept a file with my name on it.)

Years before the first implant, I flew to Chicago Midway to meet one of my sisters before driving to our hometown together for Christmas. In the air, my flight was diverted to O'Hare Airport. Upon landing, random passengers were then paired up and shuttled across town via taxi to Midway. All this was announced solely through a loudspeaker, leaving me to navigate the situation through visual cues alone. It was like competing in a Ninja Warrior competition. (Asking busy gate agents for assistance rarely worked; they'd set you aside, forget, and only sometimes realize when you were the last person standing, waiting. It was better to figure things out independently to stay ahead of the situation.)

I'm not sure which was worse: flight cancellations or gate changes. Before smartphone apps, flight cancellations required rebooking on a voice telephone if no one was at the airline counter. Meanwhile, gate changes were announced incomprehensibly over a muddy loudspeaker. If I was lucky, enough passengers rose simultaneously to head to the new gate, and I followed the parade. Still, mindlessly following others didn't always pay off. While boarding a float plane in Alaska once, I inadvertently followed a man in front of me right into the men's bathroom.

The dread of encountering inaccessible travel challenges often torpedoed vacation enjoyment. A few years after I moved out of state, I was waffling about going to my hometown for the holidays due to harsher than usual winter weather. My parents offered a frequent flyer airline ticket as an incentive for me to come. However, that particular airline did not fly directly; I would have had to connect in Pittsburgh each way. I thanked them profusely for the offer but declined and bought a direct ticket on my regular airline.

From my parents' hearing perspective, my reluctance to accept the connecting ticket seemed ungracious and petty. From my deaf perspective, having to fly four inaccessible flights instead of two, with the added threat of getting stranded solo in an unfamiliar city in a winter storm, only quadrupled the stress. The anxiety of the return trip would hang over my head the entire visit. How would that be fun?

Two perspectives, wavelengths apart. Context matters.

Predictability is often key to navigating an inaccessible world. The very best developments of the twenty-first century have been the introduction of smartphones and travel apps providing status information at one's fingertips. Often, the apps have more current data than the airline agents! Today, I get a particular thrill from my phone alerts when gates or flights change. Now, I'm halfway to the new location by the time the other travelers get a verbal announcement.

I'm constantly frustrated by airlines not displaying which boarding zone is called when it's announced verbally. Occasionally, I get the glorious surprise of finding an airport with a few dedicated screens for posting boarding zone info, but it's still rare, even for newly renovated airports. It makes no sense that every gate and airline has a digital board for flight info but can't leverage it for boarding details. Both the ADA and the Air Carrier Access Act were implemented over *thirty* years ago, yet rather than require airports to incorporate accessible design as part of their latest remodel, airlines still advise d/Deaf passengers to open service requests for a red-vested aide to meet them at the gate as their brilliant, *not-absurd-at-all* boarding accommodation because short-sighted process design was exclusively audio. It would be far more practical, intelligent, and embarrassingly low-tech for gate agents to just hold up printed cards with the applicable boarding group name while making the overhead announcement.

Think about it: If 100 passengers are waiting to board a flight, statistically, twenty (or more) probably have some degree of hearing loss in addition to those not listening or hindered by unintelligible microphones. Invariably, most of them privately fume about the discomfort of not knowing when their zone is called. Some will intentionally board in the wrong group, risking a tense confrontation with a gate agent who might pull them out of line and embarrass them. Some might rely on a partner or another passenger to tell them or simply board at the end. It leaves a terrible impression of the airline, as I've complained countless times on customer surveys. Why wasn't the boarding process designed to be accessible from the start?

Perhaps my complaints were heard. I don't know when this feature was rolled out, but during a recent trip, I was shocked senseless when the Delta app notified both my iPhone and Apple Watch that my flight had started to board. Even more amazingly, it tapped me again when my own group began to board (*it knew*). It was both stalkerish and the coolest thing ever.

However, for my return flight, I received no boarding notification from the Delta app, and the audio situation at the gate was impossible to decipher. What happened? The first flight had displayed the boarding information on a dedicated screen at the gate (the return flight did not), so perhaps the app feature relied on this data? But if the boarding info was already displayed at the gate, then the push notification was duplicative. Hmm. Was the app's cool new functionality actually designed to notify hearing travelers who simply weren't in the gate vicinity and not for accessibility purposes? *Seriously?*

* * *

So, Italy was a dream several years in the making. I booked the journey, navigating a series of connecting flights across Europe before meeting up with thirty strangers in a travel group in Sorrento a few days later. The snow in Minneapolis had melted by April, and I boasted to my friend Geoff that the odds of getting stranded overseas seemed low. Geoff knocked on wood and said my comment probably would be considered foreshadowing in a movie script. We both laughed, brushing off any threat of mishap.

My overnight connection was in Paris. I remembered Paris CDG airport vividly from a previous trip, which was helpful as I had to go through customs at three in the morning and connect to Naples. I felt comfortable overseas in general because deafness was basically just a language barrier. Europeans were already accustomed to multilingual exchanges and at ease with gesturing. American tourists, not so much. When faced with an unfamiliar dialect, they often displayed the same indignant impatience they showed toward those with hearing loss.

I had learned a tiny bit of Italian for the trip, and the front desk manager at the hotel in Sorrento seemed to like me for that. In return, he gave me a stunning room on the top floor. It was tucked away in a corner and boasted not one but two balconies that overlooked the breathtaking Bay of Naples, glistening with a vivid shade of blue. Surveying my kingdom, I could see a ferry dock nestled below, a straight drop hundreds of feet down the cliff on which the hotel was perched. I vowed to have an adventure before meeting up with the group for dinner the next day. With a heady mixture of anxiety and excitement, I was ready to embrace the journey.

Embarking into the unknown was quite unlike me. Twice now, my brother has called me the most adventurous person he knows. How I wished I saw myself that way! I was a planful, organized, analytical overthinker who anticipated conversations before they occurred and strategically weighed risks in advance. Yet the following day, my brother's tag sparked within me. On a whim, I bought a ferry ticket to Capri, an island not on the group's itinerary.

I didn't yet own a smartphone or portable GPS, so not knowing where I was going was way out of my comfort zone. However, with half a day to kill, I felt uncharacteristically bold. As I boarded the ferry, a charming man roamed the deck, enthusiastically promoting Capri tour packages, making his pitch in Italian with many expansive gestures. I was too cautious about possibly getting scammed, so I declined his offer. However, since I hadn't planned to be in Capri, I didn't know what I was missing by not taking a guided tour. (The Blue Grotto! The view from Monte Solaro!) With no set agenda, I stayed within walking distance, took a lot of photos, and had a tame but lovely morning.

Capri tourists generally returned on the four o'clock ferry to Sorrento, but a few boats circulated throughout the day, according to the hotel front desk. I knew I needed to be back for our travel group orientation by early afternoon. After exploring the Capri shore, I retraced my steps to the old, horseshoe-shaped pier with no less than fifteen docks. And no signs indicating which one led to Sorrento. Or anywhere, for that matter.

I walked the entire pier nervously. The boat drop-off had been somewhere vaguely in the middle. I spied a small Coast Guard office and entered. Two sweet older Italian men inside, best friends, eventually understood what I asked. However, they only knew about the four o'clock ferry to Sorrento.

I walked the pier again, searching for clues. A crowd of locals had congregated at one dock. I approached the general group and asked, "Sorrento?" for confirmation.

"Naples," they replied. Despite their friendly demeanor, nobody understood my question about where to find the dock schedule. I contemplated boarding the ferry to Naples with an hour-long taxi back to Sorrento or even buying a ticket at the Ischia booth and then taking a third leg to Sorrento.

I found a bench at the farthest end of the pier. An elderly gentleman shuffled by, his weathered face reflecting curiosity. He asked a question in Italian. I was pretty sure he thought I was a lost child and wanted to help.

Despite the lines around my eyes that betray my age, it's my height — that of a gymnast or a jockey — that tricks one into believing I am a minor in need of supervision. Being regularly mistaken for a child is both a blessing and a curse. Mostly, I embrace the kindness it inspires from strangers. Unaccompanied, I stand out, often plucked from crowds for special consideration, like autographed balls at sporting events, rides offered at airports, or assistance from fellow shoppers reaching items on high shelves. Whenever I run into trouble, angels emerge, like celestial Lyft drivers, providing help when I need it most.

Angels have been a recurrent theme in my life. Back during the Cult years, an artist asked me and another teenager to pose for a mural of angels he was painting. I only knew the other girl briefly, but I remember her sole mission in life was to play tuba for God. Her goal was stunningly original and revealed a responsibility-driven superhero within her. It left a strong impression on me, and I knew I would write her story someday.

A few weeks later, she was shot in the head by a stray bullet while riding in a car. She remained in a coma for eleven days before passing. During that time, her story made headlines in the local newspapers, becoming a symbol of hope for the city. Her funeral had to be moved to a larger cathedral to accommodate the thousands of strangers who found inspiration in her story and wanted to pay their respects. Her life had a profound impact, prompting me to reflect on my own. She had fulfilled her purpose. *What if it had been me? Could I have said the same?* That was the year I took charge of my life. That was the year I moved away.

"Sorrento?" I asked the elderly man with a hopeful expression, gesturing to each of the docks, my hands upturned in a questioning manner. He understood but didn't know. He retrieved his wallet and showed me a devotional card featuring Saint Francis of Assisi surrounded by livestock, with an angel child in the background. Holding the card next to my face, he gestured back and forth, indicating a resemblance between myself and the child (which, in fact, there was). And so, in quiet companionship, we sat together.

I was resigned to waiting for the afternoon tourist ferry when suddenly a rumble arose. The crowd at the Naples pier erupted into shouts of "Sorrento! Sorrento!" and waved vigorously to get my attention. Even the old man stood, joining in and pointing to a ferry approaching quickly. I waved to the crowd and thanked him profusely as I hurried along the pier to catch the ferry. I wasn't even sure where it would dock until it suddenly pulled in, greeted by cheers and applause from the excited onlookers.

I had no idea how everyone knew where the boat was headed. "Sorrento?" I confirmed when I boarded the ferry, just to be sure, and the crew nodded, *sì, sì,* and indeed, I was the only passenger on board heading back early.

I was so happy to return to the beautiful hotel and meet my fellow travelers. The tour company had sent a list of names in advance, and I jotted notes to remember conversations after talking to each person. My goal was to memorize their names the first week. I had bilateral cochlear implants now, dammit, and I was going to interact with them all if it killed me.

A few days later, when we stretched our legs at a rest stop, I mentioned the implant to fellow traveler Dale, a retired engineer. He was fascinated and peppered me with questions. Dale had shown paternal attachment since the start of the trip and checked for me every time our coach departed. "Where's Rebecca?" I'd hear him bellow from the back of the bus. I'd raise my arm and wave without turning around, our affectionate departure ritual.

Dale was tall and blond like my father, who had passed only six weeks earlier. Most of the group were retirees, and the genuine warmth and kindness they collectively showed me were evident. But the writer in me was also interested in their lives, their stories, and the lens through which they saw the world, and I think they liked seeing their life refracted through my eyes. Still, they couldn't have been more lovely, and I always had invitations for dinner.

After I shared my implant story with Dale, he joined a retired couple and me for breakfast every morning. We were the early birds, ready to roll at seven. He said his wife took too long to get ready, so he might as well join us rather than pass the time waiting in his room. My cyborg story spread, and as the days passed, I discussed hearing loss openly with my new friends.

One evening in Venice, as our group walked back from dinner amongst the maze of bridges and alleys, one of the retirees, Alex, fell in step with me and confided that he was losing his hearing. He spoke the whole way back, hushed, and told me he had never admitted it before, not even to his wife. It was evident the topic weighed heavily on his mind. Alex revealed he was considering getting hearing aids. He finally said, "I'm so embarrassed. I'm having such a hard time dealing with it."

"I know," I said, linking my arm to his. Hearing loss was an emotional space. I still saw Radio Head Gal as the kind alter ego I wanted to be. In my interactions with Alex, I tried to show compassion, drawing from my own experience of never talking about hearing loss. He had missed information during the tour and asked me about the day's outing. I turned to him when I spoke. It was getting dark, so I made sure the moonlight was on my face. He said he felt better having told me and was no longer scared.

After several days in Venice, big news was on the horizon. A major volcano in Iceland had erupted, disrupting air travel across Europe. Twenty countries closed their airspace to commercial jet traffic just as we neared the end of our journey.

I flashed back to my pre-trip conversation with Geoff: "The odds of getting stranded seem low." Yet, here I was, my worst fear coming true. The thought of being stuck in an unfamiliar place, dependent solely on hearing for rescue, churned my stomach with unease.

We held a group meeting. All flights out of Venice had been grounded. No time frame was given for when air traffic would resume. We would have to rebook via telephone in a foreign land where unfamiliar accents posed a genuine communication challenge. The uncertainty of the situation was growing. My nerves were starting to fray.

I was relieved that I had arranged my original flight through the travel group. Most everyone else had found cheaper fares directly from the airlines and were now on their own. I at least had a sympathetic corporate entity behind me who undoubtedly wanted a perfect score on their customer satisfaction survey.

The tour group leader handed out international calling cards, and I used mine to dial the travel agency in New York. The voice at the other end was friendly and advised they could rebook me once the flights started running again, estimating seven to ten days out due to the backlog impacting numerous countries. However, the agent said she would hold off until I advised otherwise, as I would get the quickest exit by calling the airline locally.

The airline's local phone number rang and rang, likely due to the international incident underway. To further complicate matters, our group was told that even though our flights had been canceled, we needed to go to the Venice airport in person on our original departure day to rebook. Failure to do so would result in forfeiture of our tickets, adding more urgency to the situation.

The women in our group set out together. The Venice airport was packed, and we waited several hours to reach the airline ticket counter. Jean, a woman in my travel group, was ahead of me in line and successfully rebooked her and her husband's flight seven days out, the earliest available option. I intended to ask for the same, as we both were flying through Detroit. To my surprise, when it was my turn, the ticket agent said I'd already been rebooked ... to depart in three days! Puzzled, I asked who rebooked me, but the agent didn't know. I asked Jean if I should still try for their flights so that we could travel together. She looked at me sideways.

"You're getting out with the medical emergencies!" Jean exclaimed. "Don't change your tickets. Someone's watching over you!"

We returned to the hotel and plotted our next moves. Since our organized tour was over and our guide was gone, the core group splintered, switching hotels or taking the train to other parts of Italy. I only needed to entertain myself for a few more days until departure. My breakfast companions invited me on a day trip to Murano, and the day after, I walked the bridges of Venice, exploring. I spent more than an hour trying to find the entrance to a famous museum. Despite a clear view of the waterfront structure from the opposite side of the Grand Canal, I could not find the back alley leading to the museum's main entrance, no matter how many times I returned to the bridge for a visual.

It was incredibly frustrating to see it plainly — the museum was right there! — and still be unable to locate the door. If only the museum had validated assumptions about walking directions and positioned signage more thoughtfully. It was the same exasperation as finding electronics tailored for audio users only. I was always on the canal bridge, standing right in front of the building, without access. I never did find the entrance. Eventually, I gave up and went to a different museum instead.

The morning of my rescheduled departure arrived. It was the first day that flights resumed at the airport, so anything could happen. Luckily, the Venice airport departure board showed other planes leaving, and we took off without delay. To this day, I don't know who rebooked me so quickly (and, a pleasant surprise, upgraded my ticket to first class). Was it my friend in Italy, Marinella, with tourism board connections, who had "liked" my Facebook posts throughout the trip? Did the tour travel agency decide to pull strings but not tell me? Did someone from my work intervene, as the corporate travel department also reported to the same senior leader? Or was it a random fluke because I was traveling alone, and the airline had an unassigned seat? To this day, I don't know.

I have such wonderful memories of my Italian adventure and the lovely travelers I had the pleasure to meet. Most importantly, Italy marked a closing bookend for me, a stark contrast between my life before the implants and where I stood now — a crescendo that mirrored the cyborg's rise. Amidst cobblestone streets and ancient wonders, the trip taught me invaluable lessons; it showed me the power of taking risks and finding solace in the assurance that I was never navigating this path on my own. The unwavering kindness of strangers prevailed. In a twist of fate, my deepest fear of being stranded came true, yet I still found my way home.

Someone was indeed watching over me.

31

Mother 2.0

"I've known you for fifteen years, and that's the first time I've heard you say something positive about your mother," said my friend Danica. We were discussing bagels, and she had mentioned a bakery from which she would be picking up an order, which segued into how to make lox (she needed to ask her mother to show her), which led to my disturbing revelation:

"I don't like cream cheese."

"What?" she exclaimed. "Not even cheesecake?"

"Only my mother's cheesecake. But not any others."

And that's when she made the comment. I didn't typically talk about my mother, but I did with Danica. I realized I needed to recalibrate my portrayal of my mother to make sure I included the positive memories and how I appreciated her, even if it was from a distance.

As my siblings joyfully welcomed their own children, I learned about the strong bonds they shared with Mom. I was glad they sought her guidance, as she was a walking encyclopedia of child-rearing knowledge. Also, their close relationships with her took any pressure off me to be a conduit for fulfilling my mother's desire to be helpful. Yet my conversation with Danica planted the seed within me to forge a deeper connection.

Three months after my trip to Italy, I was given a do-over, an atonement for my life's regret, when I declined my mother's request to stay with her at the hotel during her last visit to Minneapolis. As it turned out, I was given a second chance.

My mother had always wanted to go on a cruise, so my brother and his wife decided to take her and his mother-in-law to the Bahamas. My mother was showing signs of early-stage dementia and moderate hearing loss. She walked with a cane and basically needed some assistance, so they invited me to come and be her roommate aboard the ship. I still felt guilt over having rejected her previously, so I said yes and booked my tickets, hoping a future kindness could undo my regretful past.

We shared a stateroom for seven days. I thought about Mark Alan and his seamless interpretation and tried to be as unobtrusive as possible, serving as my mother's ears without making her feel ignored. (The notion of me playing the listener role for another person was quite ironic.)

It was a lovely trip, with one exception. Early into our cruise, my mother accidentally locked herself inside our cabin's bathroom. With her hearing aids off, she screamed bloody murder the entire time. She repeatedly hollered that I fetch my brother down the hall to come to her rescue. It was a brutal flashback for me, remembering how she would work herself into a state of anger, yelling for me from the bottom of the stairs, and indeed, at this moment, her emotion was not fear or claustrophobia but full-blown rage, which continued for the entire incident. (It was also telling that I was not her preferred rescue choice in the event of an emergency.)

With her hearing loss, I knew better than to yell back, so I pivoted. I grabbed every scrap of paper I could find and diligently slid notes under the bathroom door to let my mother know I was there and keep her updated on the status of her release. Ultimately, I flagged down a maintenance worker in the hallway, who popped the lock in a flash with a simple screwdriver.

I don't know if the lock was temporarily faulty or if my mother simply blanked on how to turn the dial — a large-print knob indicating "occupied" or "available" — but she was absolutely furious when she emerged as if I had shoved her in and locked the door myself. I highly doubt she considered how distressing it was to bear the brunt of her temper; it awakened shaky memories, a flashback that, to me, felt a bit like PTSD. I worried about what the rest of the week would hold.

The boat had scheduled a beach day next, so my mother and I went ashore. Eventually, she remarked she was going to take the tender back to the cruise ship and resume her post on the sundeck. I told her I'd go with.

"You don't need to do that," she said.

I replied firmly, "Actually, I do. I'm responsible for you."

Her expression turned steely, and I braced for an outburst. However, we were distracted by the arrival of the boy band which was performing on the ship. They also were going back on our tiny transport vessel, so my mother and I fangirled like teenage gawkers, spying and taking covert photos.

She seemed to be enjoying herself, so I proposed, "Since everyone else is at the beach, why don't we go to one of the fancy restaurants on the boat for lunch?" Bless her foodie's heart, she was game.

Upon our return to the cruise ship, we discovered that the elegant French restaurant had a special for early-bird diners like us. We were seated at a window table and ordered lobster and profiteroles. It was a beautiful view, a quiet room to talk, and probably the nicest moment we've ever had. My mother mentioned it every time I saw her in the years to come; it was our connection.

We spent a lot of time together that week, more than all of our adult years combined. On the final day, she said she was glad my brother and his wife had organized the trip. She had a wonderful time. It was the best vacation she had ever taken.

It felt like redemption. My penance was complete.

* * *

Like most seniors, my mother gradually lost her hearing as she aged. So, our life circumstances had flipped: I had cyborg hearing now, and she was moderately deaf. During my visits, I did my best to accommodate her by getting her attention before I spoke, always facing her, and speaking slowly. I hoped this life circumstance might forge a deeper bond or even spark a conversation about hearing loss, but I did not initiate these conversations. I let it go.

How do I explain this? Speaking honestly is hard in relationships where a recipient is perceived as not willing to hear the truth and might even respond punitively. The mother of my Paris roommate refused to talk about her hearing loss with her daughter because she didn't feel confident that their emotional space was safe. Likewise, I didn't want to jeopardize our tentative goodwill by introducing unnecessary conflict at this late stage.

After the cruise, my mother's dementia progressed, and she moved to a series of memory care facilities. My siblings bore the brunt of her unpredictable moods, yet my experience was different, living afar. Now, when I visited, my mother was delighted to see me. "Is it Christmas?" she asked during a summer visit and held my hand, enthralled with my presence. I think she thought I visited every day, unaware that six months had passed since my last trip.

I have to admit I liked this version of my mother best. All the difficulties of our previous interactions had vanished from her memory. I mean, we didn't go back in time. The conditional nature of our relationship hadn't erased itself; she just didn't remember that I had hearing loss or cochlear implants. I had an altered identity and presumably a clean slate.

I wish I could say the floodgates opened, and my mother and I said everything unspoken. That didn't happen. But I did gain a sense of peace about the situation. She didn't know what she didn't know. She didn't grow up deaf. We couldn't undo the past, but we seemed to be on good terms now as her days dwindled.

The following spring was our final conversation. By then, her hearing loss had reached profound deafness, and she had stopped wearing her hearing aids. She recognized me and said my name aloud, a minor miracle considering the dementia had limited her ability to speak. She beamed, happy to see me. We communicated by writing on an erasable board, and she read what I wrote about lilacs and spring in Minneapolis. She was still able to respond.

In August, I came to sit vigil. She had been deteriorating fast for a week, probably from a stroke, and was unresponsive. My sister and I sat up overnight with her, knowing she might pass on our watch. Despite her unconscious state, occasional hand squeezes reflected a lingering presence. Surrounded by family, we gathered by her bedside the next morning and said goodbye as she took her final breath.

32

Inspiration

"Inspiration" is a term used often in the disability universe ... by those who don't have a disability. The late Australian disability activist Stella Young coined the term "inspiration porn" in her 2014 TED Talk[42] (*I'm Not Your Inspiration, Thank You Very Much*). Per Young, inspiration porn means "objectifying disabled people for the benefit of non-disabled people" to inspire and motivate.

Inspiration porn often praises individuals as being extraordinary simply because they live life with a disability, which is a pretty low bar for achievement. The usual storylines are about overcoming adversity or a non-disabled person rescuing them. While the narrative might include random acts of kindness that would make you smile in a different context, the point of inspiration porn (like traditional pornography) is to generate an artificial emotional response, specifically, to make you feel superior by comparison. Invariably, the piece includes sensationalized headlines or sad music engineered to make you cry, much like those heartbreaking ASCPA commercials featuring wounded animals.

Inspiration porn plays a significant role in perpetuating the mindset that disability is inferior. I saw a video the other day about a young boy wearing cochlear implant processors, giving his friend a haircut. It was a good haircut; he showed confidence with the scissors for a kid, and it was nice to see CI processors as an everyday accessory. The problem was that the clip splashed a shouty "deaf and mute!" headline as clickbait for people to watch the video, which intentionally changed the narrative from "remarkable for his age" to "remarkable because he's deaf." The comment section was full of "I'm bawling!" remarks. Yet his deafness was irrelevant to the task. He used his hand to tilt his friend's head position (as stylists do). I wished the video simply celebrated a young boy with a talent for hairdressing and left deafness on the cutting room floor (pun intended).

Manufacturing emotion by using one-dimensional stereotypes to make disability a source of pity, apology, and inspiration is my number one pet peeve. It's manipulative and cringey. People who are unaware of the harm then share the content further on social media, and the message is repeated indefinitely.

Marketing campaigns heavily feature inspiration porn, and it's no wonder why. The weepier your reaction, the more likely the ad will stick and be shared. At face value, the haircutting video was cute. If it featured a non-deaf child, you might have liked it on social media but wouldn't have shed tears. Yet as soon as the "deaf and mute!" headline appeared, followed by the camera pan to the cochlear implant processors, your expectations for achievement instantly plummeted. Giving a haircut and providing directions without spoken words became exponentially more miraculous to your unconscious mind.

Contrary to popular belief, inspiration porn isn't simply head-patting, participation-trophy fake compliments. Inspiration porn validates the notion that those with disabilities are *special* — special in the way it makes other people feel grateful that it's not them —

instead of accepting their lifestyle as just another way of getting things done.

When people call me an inspiration, I shut them down fast. I say, be impressed with my writing or my work. Because if you find inspiration in my simply living life as a deaf person, it's because you see my situation as less than yours. (Think about it. You wouldn't be inspired if you thought of me as equal.)

Being an object of inspiration porn is creepy and condescending. The ad that got under my skin was a commercial for a video relay service that interpreted voice calls for d/Deaf customers. The story-line was about a Deaf man whose neighbors conspired to learn a phrase in sign language for him. In theory, this was a nice thing to do, and I am all for communities learning another's language as a means of being inclusive. However, the piece portrayed the Deaf man as an object of pity, and the marketing team felt compelled to engineer an entire community event to rescue him from his perceived isolation.

The commercial focused on the weeks of rehearsal by the non-deaf — hooray for the heroic efforts of the hearing neighbors! They were the stars of the advertisement! It reminded me of a time years ago when friends planned a surprise birthday party for me. They decided to hold a secret pre-party the night prior so that everyone could sign my birthday card. Guests then spent the actual birthday event raving about the earlier get-together, to which I had not been invited (since it related to the surprise). Needless to say, the exclusion felt palpable at the real party, even though the pre-party had been for my benefit.

The video relay commercial likewise prioritized the surprise element of learning sign language at the expense of the Deaf man's inclusion. If he had been invited to the lessons, for example, the Deaf man might not have been relegated to being an observer of someone else's experience. He might have bonded with others as an equal member of the community.

The final reveal was when the Deaf man stepped outside with his sister, and everyone they encountered signed a greeting. In the commercial, everyone cried. People who sent me the video said they cried. Everyone cried because of the implication that the Deaf man led a sad, lonely life simply because he could not hear, and the non-deaf community, in their saintly grace, surprised him by learning a snippet of a foreign language. Yet, no consideration was given to the fact that the Deaf man likely had a Deaf community, Deaf friends, and a family fluent in sign language. There was also no indication that the community intended to keep signing as a courtesy.

A better approach would have been to portray the Deaf man as the hero, given that he was the intended consumer of the product, not the crowd. For more excitement, he could have rescued his hearing neighbors and taught them the corresponding signs for "black ice," "flat tire," or "dog bite." But then it wouldn't have been inspiration porn. And no one would have cried.

By contrast, a Kia commercial featuring d/Deaf race car driver Kris Martin demonstrated the beauty of silence in an electric vehicle (EV) advertisement. "I don't need noise to tell me if something is fast," signed Martin, a National Kart Championship, NASCAR, and Le Mans professional race car driver and d/Deaf advocate. "I've been deaf since I was born. It's taught me one thing: Silence is powerful."

The Kia commercial was blissfully free of inspiration porn. EVs are noiseless, so Kia opted to celebrate silence, not villainize it. I loved that Martin's occupation was presented without footnote or exalted commentary. He's a professional race car driver — why wouldn't he be? It was a fresh perspective on point without lesser-than implications. Well done!

I wish advertising for hearing devices would stop emphasizing the product's invisibility or invoking pity. Just like automobile commercials showcase sleek design and advanced technology, I think hearing devices should celebrate their features fearlessly! After all, people take pride in flaunting their new cars; they don't hide them away in the garage!

So, I get excited when I see advertisements for hearing devices that emphasize vibrant colors and a sense of pride. Because technology is cool, and younger generations are drawn to innovative options! Designer eyewear successfully erased the stigma associated with wearing glasses. It's time for hearing devices to transform even more from a basic necessity to a visionary product worthy of consumer stampedes.

Diversity extends beyond physical features. While most people acknowledge easily seen differences, such as race or gender, they often overlook the importance of diversity of thought. Yet individuals with wide-ranging viewpoints — from cultural experience, employment background, or life differences — expand and transform the knowledge base of the workforce.

I loved working at The Firm. I was good at it, too. I stayed with the company for over thirty-three years because they respected my contributions. Overall, I was treated very well and always knew my value. Sure, I encountered a few hiccups during rogue interactions, but I felt supported by the company's fairness policies. I worked hard, and opportunities followed. I hit an iconic status the day an executive vice president — a direct report to the CEO — hosted a meeting of senior leaders to consider a critical systems project and issued this proclamation: "If Rebecca Knill says it's okay [from an impact assessment perspective], then I'll approve it."

I learned this story from a senior vice president who had attended the meeting. She was gobsmacked by the high level of trust the executive leader placed in me because of my ability to anticipate and articulate risk. It was a gratifying validation. Yet colleagues who met me after the implant — long after the sign language interpreters went home, who never saw my CI processors and thought I was hearing — probably never considered my input as "diverse," even though it was a perfect example of deaf gain.

"Deaf gain" is the semantic opposite of "hearing loss." The term was coined by Aaron Williamson, a British performer visiting Gallaudet University who questioned why the term "hearing loss" was presented as a negative and not a positive spin on gaining deafness. Deaf gain celebrates the benefits that deafness can create (e.g., cultural, artistic, or intellectual) and challenges the notion that hearing loss is tragic or even second-rate. (The Kia commercial mentioned above is an excellent example.)

I think differently because I'm deaf. Having to navigate life through anticipation, based on a fine-tuned sense of probability, is a valuable skill set. In the context of my job, that meant thinking ahead ten steps to post-implementation and anticipating the next round of regulatory changes. I could foresee and accommodate future modifications within regular maintenance cycles by tweaking the initial design request, eliminating the need for a full-blown systems project next time. It wasn't quite mind-reading, but it was close enough to my childhood superhero fantasy to let me believe it sort of came true.

That top executive, a lovely woman I had the privilege of knowing for years, was aware I was deaf but probably never thought about how my skill came to be. She just knew that my unique viewpoint saved them a boatload of money and pain. She respected and valued me, as did the other senior leaders with whom I had the privilege to work.

* * *

D ue to constant reorganization at The Firm, employees frequently changed reporting hierarchies and desk locations. Almost every year, I was assigned to a different boss (and within one particularly high-energy restack month, three bosses). With each floor relocation, my managers went out of their way to ensure my workspace was conducive to my hearing. (Several negotiated even better desk assignments for me than they gave themselves.) When we moved to a new building, one leader strategically assigned the cubicles adjacent to me to people who worked remotely. Because they were never there in person, this genius arrangement reduced background noise by an additional two rows (which lasted until the next reorganization).

I genuinely loved all of my bosses at The Firm — more than twenty-five in my career — except for one. She inherited my team as part of a group reorg, and the minute I introduced myself and told her I had cochlear implants, I could practically feel her face freeze over the telephone like dark clouds ominously rolling in on a sunny summer day. She was a nice enough person and well-liked by others, but I found her personality artificial. Whenever presented with information that deviated from her viewpoint, she would turn into a plastic doll head with a blank smile, wide eyes, and eyebrows arched into her forehead, frozen.

Fortunately, that reporting hierarchy was a quick blip on my resume. The manager worked in a different building, and since my work had zero overlap with hers, we checked in by phone once a week and only met in person a few times. Also, I'm embarrassed to mention this, but she was quite tall, and twice when we met in person, she physically stooped down to my eye level, hands on her knees, as if addressing a toddler. *Who does that?*

I nicknamed her the "Inspiration Queen" (or "IQ" as I thought of her) because "inspiration" was her favorite word for issues relating to disability. On several occasions, I told her how offensive I found her pity/pedestal viewpoint, and she always waved me off, completely erasing my perspective. It actually wasn't her tendency to defend inspiration porn that was my primary objection. My issue was her hypocrisy. Specifically, she tried to brand herself as a diversity advocate yet blew off my repeated accommodation requests.

To provide some context, when my role shifted under her management, it came with a seat on the IQ's leadership team. Since two-thirds of her team worked at her site, they gathered in person in a conference room for her weekly team call, while the rest of us dialed in. Meetings via speakerphone are the scourge of telephone calls for people with hearing loss, and they only get worse with multiple attendees in a large room. The basic starting challenges are that voices naturally echo, and speakerphone mics invariably pick up the white noise of the air circulating, in addition to any and every sound present.

On the worse end of the spectrum, speakerphone calls can resemble working in a construction zone. The IQ's team meeting was a prime example of this chaos. The meeting was the equivalent of a raucous, frat-house party or a trip to the zoo, with uncontrolled background noise, poor facilitation, and no awareness of the speakerphone mic location. Even a sign language interpreter would have struggled. It was, without a doubt, the worst recurring meeting I'd experienced in my three decades of employment — a true auditory disaster.

ADA accommodations are often tangible procurements, but sometimes they're not. For example, a screen reader, a stand-up/sit-down desk, or a sign language interpreter are physical, easily acquired accommodations. However, some requests require modifications to established processes. I consistently asked to switch the meeting to a dial-in call for everyone. Dialing in separately from each person's desk would eliminate the background noise, and each speaker would have a headset microphone directly in front of their mouth.

It was a one-hour weekly status report meeting, for goodness sake, and not a free-flowing brainstorming session. Frankly, its unprofessional nature was a result of its own making. Worthy of note: I had made the exact same request to many of my past leaders (since most teams were combos of local and out-of-state members). They all agreed immediately because (1) it was a simple accommodation that cost nothing, and (2) it was the right thing to do to be inclusive.

The scenario vividly demonstrated the distinction between "assimilation" and "accommodation." The Inspiration Queen expected me to conform to her existing process, which was assimilation. However, my request required a willingness to change, which was an accommodation. My friend Danica remarked that despite the IQ's apparent interest in diversity, she probably never made the connection to being inclusive or ADA accommodations. Instead, the IQ simply saw me as a party pooper who wanted to kill her party buzz. "She probably thinks of herself as the 'cool Mom.' She's totally not doing her job."

I was so disappointed in the IQ. Simply saying, "We'll try harder," was not an acceptable accommodation. It put me in the position of policing something I'd already identified as an access barrier. Even if the meeting audio temporarily got better as she promised, it inevitably would regress to its original state, and I'd be forced to continually raise the issue to her frozen smile. By giving verbal assurances and even inquiring if things were better but never providing any actual accommodation, she was banking on me either giving up or going away.

While the IQ had the right to prefer in-person meetings over dial-in, my accommodation requests were covered by policy and federal law. She also could have suggested an alternative solution but did not. I felt the need to tread cautiously because my gut warned me that if I persisted, the IQ might reorganize her reporting hierarchy or even take away my team. Company policy prohibited trying to make an ADA issue go away (for example, removing a task from someone or moving the person to another role), but that didn't mean it couldn't happen.

Soon after that, the IQ announced organizational changes. While my job title, role, and salary remained unchanged, I was no longer part of the leadership team. It was a textbook example of what not to do. Even if the org change was coincidental, totally unrelated — because people did get moved around frequently and sometimes reported to peers — on paper, the sequence of events looked a lot like trying to make an accessibility request go away or even an act of retaliation.

Personally, I didn't think there was a straight line between my accommodations request and the hierarchy change. I felt the reporting change had been in the works since the moment we first met, as soon as I disclosed my cochlear implant to the IQ, and her tone toward me shifted like she was speaking to a three-year-old. I think she repeatedly denied my accommodations request because she already knew she was going to reorg me out of her direct line of hierarchy but needed the other pieces to fall into place first.

A lot more happened after that, but I tucked away the lessons learned. Specifically, the transformative power of inclusion stacked against the dangers of exclusion. While many profess wholehearted dedication to diversifying the workforce, true commitment often wavers at the first sign of inconvenience. But the reality is that sometimes authentic inclusion does require embracing uncomfortable

changes. That is why federal regulations were deemed necessary —
to push for action when willingness falls short.

I learned firsthand that inclusion really does matter. The Inspiration Queen knew I couldn't participate fully in her team meetings, yet she still chose to deny my accommodation requests. As a result, my employee engagement sank. Engagement surveys firmly established a correlation between top scores and exceptional employee performance. My rankings were consistently high throughout my career, a testament to outstanding managers and a great work environment. Sadly, those scores nosedived soon after I joined the IQ's team.

To be effective, commitment to diversity and inclusion has to be genuine. That assignment was an unfortunate hiccup in an otherwise positive career, and I've come to regard it like a lost weekend or a medically induced coma. Fortunately for me, the next series of inclusive senior leaders gave me a reset, and I bounced back, having new opportunities to contribute.

33

Love and Robots

I fell in love with robots in the early '90s. I was obsessed with an automated mail cart in a satellite office where I attended training classes. The boxy wagon ran on tracks, unmanned, beeped at designated stops, and halted for folks to retrieve that unit's mail. It navigated the elevator seamlessly and made the rounds between floors. It even sensed my presence and paused politely whenever I crossed in front.

From the moment robot vacuum cleaners were introduced, I was all-in, an early adopter. It appealed to my inherent laziness, and I treated it like a pet, scolding it to get away from the curtains. The experience ignited a greater hunger in me for smart technology. Plus, I wanted electronics to take on even more of my cleaning.

I have always gravitated toward machines that *do stuff* for you. Even as a kid, I got excited by the audio equalizer on the stereo, which visually represented sound by flashing corresponding colors. It was years before the personal computer was even introduced. Yet, I knew electronics in a portable, visual form — like a wristwatch — someday would be able to hear for me. (I only wish my ten-year-old self had applied for that patent.)

Automation fascinated me, especially assistive listening devices. Seeing everyday products like alarm clocks, kitchen timers, and smoke alarms adapted for sensory solutions was a revelation. Accessible products began popping into the mainstream. I still remember the moment I searched online for a flashing doorbell alarm signaling set, having forgotten the name of the one specialty store that sold them previously, and found the product on Amazon.

Likewise, television captioning happened during my lifetime. In my twenties, I considered myself a foreign film snob, only to realize that my preference was entirely due to the subtitles. Television captioning was unveiled in the '80s, and it initially required purchasing a special box resembling a DVD player that cost more than my TV. Now, closed caption functionality is automatically included in every new television set. Catering to global markets, subtitling in multiple languages is standard for streaming services.

The magnitude of Apple's[43] inclusivity efforts can't be overstated. The integration of a hearing-related accessibility menu into Apple devices was a significant turning point in my life, a personal Valentine from the technology giant. Each subsequent software upgrade has been an extended celebration with expanded options for deaf users quietly released. After respective system updates, my cell phone began vibrating and flashing an LED light for notifications. My voicemail suddenly began autotranscribing messages. Captioned voicemails started showing on the phone screen while the caller was still speaking. My brother's mother-in-law advised that Google Maps triggered my Apple Watch to tap my wrist at every intended turn.

I have always enjoyed GPS, even primitive versions I used as a visual aid that sometimes pointed me into a lake. The notion that I can drive anywhere and still find my way home is immensely reassuring. Today, Bluetooth integration with my cochlear implant processor transmits navigation instructions from my cell phone wirelessly right into my head. Driving alone in an unfamiliar town, hearing the GPS voice inside my head while my watch is tapping me for a left turn, is astounding. Both my cell phone and watch currently come close to realizing my childhood wish for portable technology to hear for me, listening for noises like alarms and dogs barking, then displaying a visual alert. Technology, man. Being able to participate, just like everyone else, is everything.

Ride-sharing apps similarly enhanced my life. They made me feel like a hipster, but more importantly, they eliminated the need to make a voice phone call for a taxi. Two decades ago, one of my biggest fears was getting lost or stranded with only audio means for rescue. Thanks to ride-sharing apps, I can now hail a ride virtually anywhere with a tap on my smartphone. This is the very definition of accessible design: The same options are available to me as anyone else, regardless of my ability to hear. In just the last few years, ride-sharing apps have come a long way in leveling the playing field for people with disabilities.

Sadly, not all electronics brands have embraced that magical thinking. For example, I upgraded my robot vacuum to one with Wi-Fi connectivity, a remote control, and the ability to return to a docking station like a homing pigeon. Thankfully, I could silence its annoying speaking voice. (I was afraid the vacuum would suddenly come alive in the middle of the night when I wouldn't hear it speaking, but my neighbors would.) I muted it dutifully, but to my dismay, there was no visual alternative. Did the designer assume that because I disabled the sound, I didn't need to know what it said? The device was controlled through an app with a written display, yet no translation was provided. Did no one test from an end-user perspective? Ugh.

* * *

Technology can foster inclusion, but it can also be an obstacle. In my workplace, network security restrictions sometimes became barriers. For example, the TTY machine I needed as my telephone in the '90s required an analog telephone line, which was against company policy and reserved solely for fax machines. At the time, that security policy became a roadblock, impeding accessibility.

Fortunately, a telecommunications manager named Mike took up my cause. He tenaciously pursued approval to install an analog line for me, persistently advocating on my behalf, and prevailed. Even in an environment that embraced inclusivity, policies could inadvertently trip up the process. With Mike's intervention, my TTY became possible.

Another source of stress for me was getting locked out of The Firm's computer network due to an expired or corrupted login password, which required calling a Tech Support hotline to resolve. Every day, I held my breath while logging in, praying that my password would work.

Since I worked in systems consulting, I had the highest level of security access to many applications. Passwords had to be changed regularly; unfortunately, new passwords sometimes malfunctioned for unknown reasons. While Tech Support offered a teletypewriter option for problem tickets, I had returned my TTY when I resumed using the voice telephone after my cochlear implants, plus The Firm had closed out all analog lines as a security precaution. For technical support outside of my work, I always chose second-level verification texts. But no such option existed at The Firm. Getting a network password reset meant struggling to comprehend overseas call center representatives with varied accents and filtering out background noise, two significant audio obstacles for pretty much anyone with hearing loss.

One fateful day, I found myself locked out of the network. My call to Tech Support was a double whammy: an unfamiliar accent and tons of background noise in the call center. Even with my CI, I understood maybe every fifth word. I finally asked the call center technician to transfer me to another rep, clarifying that I had hearing loss and couldn't understand what she was saying. My plea went unacknowledged. I asked ten times to talk to someone else. I asked very nicely, although as time passed, I'm sure the call recording captured what was essentially begging. I desperately needed to get into the network to work.

I thought of hanging up and redialing to connect with another representative. However, the calls were tracked so they would know what I'd done. Since my job required systems access, I had no choice but to comply. I hoped the rep would hang up on me like those convenient (wink, wink) disconnects from the cable or telephone company. Guessing was useless — I was required to hear the exact digits of the reset password (or rustle up a TTY, which didn't even exist on the premises). Needless to say, I didn't get the information right on the first, second, or third try. It was brutal.

Subsequently, I learned the call center reps had been trained not to transfer people who simply preferred a Midwestern accent, but that wasn't me, okay? My ability to hear was based solely on specific speech patterns (for which accents did not necessarily translate), and the harder I tried, the more challenging it got. After doing an audio version of "blink-your-eyes-if-this-is-correct" for probably fifteen minutes, I finally had my new password.

After that painful call, I received a customer survey and furiously unloaded in my email response. To my surprise, the Tech Support manager personally replied. He said he listened to the tape of my call, was hugely sympathetic, gave me his number so that I could call him directly next time I needed a password reset, and mentioned two alternatives: (1) use the TTY option to call Tech Support, or (2) have my manager make the call on my behalf.

Um, no? I told him that offering TTY as the only alternative to a voice call for a network password reset was grossly shortsighted and that requiring my boss to make the call on my behalf was demeaning. First, I hadn't had a TTY at work for over a decade and didn't even know anyone who did since the advent of texting. Besides, there were way more hard-of-hearing and deaf employees who still made but struggled with voice calls than there were TTY users!

Second, all of my managers were senior vice presidents or higher. There was no freaking circumstance under which I would have asked an executive leader of the company to call Tech Support on my behalf just to reset my password. I'm sure they would have done it in a heartbeat, but what a humiliating position to be put in! Even though my request was due to an access barrier, their unconscious minds invariably would have downgraded their perception of me as incapable of performing a basic job task. *Should I ask them to spell-check my work, too?*

I told him those were terrible choices. Further, virtually every company offered second-level verification via a text code sent to a registered cell phone. He replied that texting was a security concern. "Security concern" was just a convenient excuse to avoid accessibility, I challenged. Standard communications choices today were more robust: telephone, TTY, email, text, and preferably chat. Offering only voice and TTY stereotyped end users and micromanaged their preferences.

Since then, a few accessibility tools have entered the mainstream. For example, someone with hearing loss could probably put the work telephone on speakerphone, then open a speech-to-text app on their cell phone to read the display for subsequent verbal confirmation of the reset password, although those apps are not particularly precise either when it comes to comprehending accents. Real-time transcription service apps are available now, and I've read about promising call center translation software that converts accents into regional speech patterns since this issue is a customer service concern for many companies. Lastly, my cell phone now offers a TTY setting (it didn't back then), which might have worked, but since the mobile device was my home phone number, it also might have flagged security challenges.

The main thing I took away from the Password Reset Debacle was my vow to personally patronize only companies that offered at least visual password reset process steps to consumers, such as second-level text verification. It's worth noting that passwords are becoming less relevant with the rise of two-factor authentication security keys, so there's a new era of security on the horizon. Over time, the tech industry often resolves its own accessibility issues by inadvertently inventing the next best thing.

34

Language

At the time I grew up, speech-only was the method of communication for deaf children in hearing families. However, sign language has grown in popularity in recent years, primarily due to its use outside the Deaf community. Since infants can communicate manually even earlier than they develop speech skills, books on baby signs fly off the shelves. Who hasn't attended a pre-school production featuring signed singing?

You may have come across a poignant cartoon called *The Greatest Irony*[44] by Deaf artist Maureen Klusza. In this powerful illustration, a handcuffed, crying deaf baby is depicted next to an unrestrained hearing baby, who is happily signing "I love you." Its message is pointed: Denying sign language to a deaf child amounts to punishment and reinforces the societal belief that visible displays of deafness must be hidden. (Ahem, unless the child is *hearing*, in which case sign language is considered a trendy form of enrichment.)

I personally believe that every deaf child, regardless of hearing devices, should be taught sign language (as well as spoken language for those in oral families), and this should be encouraged for their relatives and community, as well. (Sign language is already a core value of Deaf cultural affiliation.)

Remember the video relay commercial I disliked, where a community met to learn a phrase of sign language for their Deaf neighbor? I posed a hypothetical scenario to many of the hearing individuals who told me that commercial made them cry, asking: If they had a deaf child, would they teach them sign language? Despite being moved by the advertisement's activity, they all replied no. They would want their child to speak. Even when told the child could do both, they still shrugged and shook their heads.

The debate over learning sign language has both opposition and support. Opinions are typically divided between those who follow the medical or social models of disability and whether the researchers leading the studies are hearing or deaf. There's a long-held concern in the hearing community that a deaf child won't learn to speak if they're not solely focused on oral speech. This idea seems outdated now, coming from a time when sign language was forbidden in schools. In fact, recent studies show that children with implants who also sign more readily acquire speech.[45][46]

When it comes to language acquisition, lots of kids today grow up in households where more than one language is spoken or even attend language immersion schools, effortlessly toggling between dialects. Just because sign language might be easier for a deaf child to learn doesn't mean it will hinder their ability to develop oral communication skills; in fact, it could have positive effects. For example, adult implantees are often encouraged to follow along with audiobooks for rehabilitation practice because it's a more effective bridge to training the brain to hear than simply listening to sentences. Yet, nobody questions whether using visual aids distracts the adult aural rehab path.

Introducing sign language to deaf children is affirming. While it's understood that hearing families probably won't achieve the same fluency as those within the Deaf community, embracing sign language signifies heartfelt commitment. Just as an adoptive family learns the native language of their foreign-born child to foster respect and inclusivity, teaching sign language communicates unconditional recognition and value for the child's identity. It conveys a sense of belonging that transcends linguistic walls.

Obviously, I'm biased on the matter. I didn't learn to sign until adulthood, and I feel I missed a key developmental milestone that might have positively influenced the rest of my life. Also, there are risks to consider with a speech-only approach, specifically, Language Deprivation Syndrome (LDS), which occurs when a child is not fluent in either spoken or signed language by age five, increasing the likelihood of long-term cognitive and mental health challenges.

Some parents question the value of learning ASL if they don't expect their implanted child to use it as a primary language when they're older. However, no one can predict the long-term usage of any secondary language (or playing a musical instrument or training in a sport, for that matter). Learning ASL might be a life-long enrichment or for a moment in time. Why should the time invested in learning sign language be held to a higher standard than any other childhood activity?

Signing is a tool for inclusion. It provides language options, such as being able to communicate with your child when devices are off. For someone deaf, the ability to converse in sign language greatly diminishes the fear of the Cinderella Bubble. I declined my mother's offer to come for my CI surgery recuperation in part because we had no way to communicate unplugged (that didn't involve a disproportionate amount of work by me). I can only imagine how that rejection must have felt to her.

It might surprise you that an audiologist approached me about learning sign language in third grade, and I turned him down. Unfortunately, the proposal reeked of imprisonment. First, it involved attending *summer school*, a horrifying concept for someone as grade-conscious as me. Second, the invitation was only for me, not my family or friends, which seemed like solitary confinement. Since I had no exposure to the deaf world, I was unaware of the benefits of learning to sign. After proving to the audiologist that I lipread well, I considered it a victory to be excused.

I see it differently now. It was a missed opportunity, a regrettable mistake. I didn't know what I didn't know. In the years since, I've often wondered how different my life might have been if I had learned to sign back then. It could have opened the door to talk about deafness. I would have met d/Deaf peers at an earlier age and learned from their self-advocacy experiences. I wouldn't have had to work so hard to keep up and might not have felt compelled to lie about when I didn't hear. I wouldn't have been alone.

While hearing devices are helpful tools, they're still a limited solution. Many people's hearing loss isn't extensive enough to qualify for a complete rebuild via CI, and top-shelf hearing aids must rely on damaged hair cells to process sound. Ignoring the social model of disability (which focuses on adaptation and accessibility) puts excessive pressure on someone to be hearing at all costs while disregarding issues of belonging and self-worth. How meaningful (or fraudulent) is success if someone has to be something they're not?

Because I am that definition of success. I was an ace lipreader, spoke without a deaf accent, was an Honor Roll student, and, as an adult, held a career job as a vice president at a Fortune 500 company. With bilateral cochlear implants, I achieved the highest scores on hearing tests within the sound booth. But that success came at a price: I also had to be something I wasn't, which kept me from fully connecting with others, as well as myself.

I don't regret learning to speak or leveraging hearing technology. But what I grieve, what I would exchange in a heartbeat, was the notion that I had to present as a hearing person to be considered equal, even though I was deaf. Nobody told me this outright when I was growing up. It was implicit, systemic messaging ingrained in a relentless loop of "You can't even tell" and the sharp-tongued impatience of acquaintances and strangers at virtually every crossroad. The lesson was all too clear: The world rewards imposters.

In hindsight, would I have traded success for a sense of belonging as a child, to have interacted authentically with d/Deaf peers, and communicated in ASL? While I did discover those things as an adult, it wasn't the same. It was too late to be a formative experience. I had already become who I was.

Success is hollow when you live in someone else's world. Relationships based on false assumptions are superficial and not sustainable. In that sense, I feel a kinship with closeted gays, trans individuals, biracial people, and foreign adoptees, who maybe feel they live in a gray space between who they are and who others pressure them to be.

Some days, yes, I would trade it all. But there are days when hopefulness prevails. Despite society's pushback, I'm committed now to practicing honesty and witnessing its rewards. I'm learning to embrace authenticity. However, not everyone else values that transparency. In some cases, I'm still expected to blend in or even hide. The political pendulum has already begun to swing back to one-size-fits-all. Changing that mindset is probably not going to happen on its own.

That is why technology needs to keep chipping away at leveling the playing field, thanks to adaptive solutions that have steadily transformed electronics over recent years. An era of accessible design is on the horizon.

It's coming.

It's almost here.

Closure

Something happened to me during the pandemic lockdown — the digital display on my stove went bonkers. I sent a video to the appliance store to see if it could be fixed. The service guy thought maybe it was an electrical short. He couldn't guarantee that it could be repaired or even that my stove wouldn't catch fire in the interim. The store was closed to the public indefinitely, so I bought a new one over the phone, unseen. Baking for the first time, I preheated the oven, and it beeped to signal that it was ready.

Then something astonishing happened. The oven light flashed five times! I almost fell out of my chair! I had bought a stove with an accessibility feature and didn't even know it! Even better, the flashing light was the default setting! I stood up, flabbergasted. My new stove matched my lifelong vision! Accessibility as a default, leveling the playing field for everyone!

When I was ten years old, I knew technology would translate speech for me someday. Now, decades later, accessibility options are creeping out of the woodwork. I'm happy for the youngest generation, who have grown up in an era where electronics with built-in sensory choices are all they've known. They have had the benefit of better hearing devices, cochlear implants, general acceptance of ASL as an official language, and autotranslation within mobile technology. They've been fortunate to learn about diversity and inclusion in school from an early age, and hearing loss has loosened its reputation as a harbinger of doom. The divide that once existed has been bridged, and the battle for equality has been won.

Or has it?

Disability was thrust into the public eye in 2022 with the headlines about a political candidate who experienced a stroke while on the campaign trail. His subsequent rehabilitation unfolded in the public eye as he struggled with auditory processing disorder. Auditory processing disorder required him to see words for his brain to process them completely and resulted in an occasional word mix (aphasia), a common side effect of strokes. The candidate was upfront about his progress and accommodation needs. Still, his opponent's followers pounced on his challenges, declaring him unfit for office.

Exercising his rights under the ADA, the candidate naturally requested captioning as an accommodation during media interviews and the political debate. The situation resonated with me deeply, as I regularly use subtitles for television and video conferencing.

I read the social media posts following the situation. Thankfully, many supporters emerged to defend him. However, the putdowns from detractors almost exclusively insisted he was unqualified for office simply because he *needed* an accommodation. They didn't seem to care about his performance *with* the accommodation.

A conservative pundit posted the following message on social media: "How can someone be a Senator without being able to speak or understand small talk?" After Stephen Hawking (the late, brilliant theoretical physicist and cosmologist who communicated via a speech-generating device) rolled over in his grave, perhaps she recognized the tweet as ableist (it was) because she deleted it shortly after. Her tweet was classic fearmongering, attempting to stigmatize the candidate due to his condition (again, measuring him without the accommodation). She perpetuated disability bias on a national platform.

This is why the ADA was established: to combat the pervasive stigma surrounding disability and provide people with a fair opportunity to succeed. Those who claim that diversity goals are discriminatory (that is, against people who already enjoy the benefits of majority-class standing) dismiss the fact that they have been given a head start; the deck is already stacked in their favor.

I read an opinion piece the other day scolding a government office for stating a goal to hire individuals with disabilities. The column was a vicious display of ableism, mocking the agency for seeking qualified candidates with disabilities because, the author said, a person with a disability could never be the best candidate for a job and invariably would fail miserably on the taxpayer's dime. He openly disparaged the capabilities of the deaf, blind, and mobility disabled. How dare they apply! How dare they even exist! He said in print everything those who want to roll back diversity programs think in private.

The candidate's situation vividly illustrated how society responds to differences in ability, such as auditory processing or deafness. Opportunistic remarks from the candidate's opponents served as reinforcement to those already predisposed to perceive individuals with hearing loss as inferior. This is exactly the systemic messaging that d/Deaf individuals — including children — are exposed to and absorb every day. The debate wasn't even about the candidate. The public outcry was about disability and the fact that it was visible. New waves of shame had rolled in with the tide.

I found the discussion both annoying and depressing. Mostly, I was dismayed that the commentary showed little recognition that statements putting down disability are as discriminatory as those disparaging race and gender. Diversity, equity, and inclusion are increasingly under threat as affirmative action and identity policies are being rolled back across the country; it's only a short hop until the ADA is similarly dismantled.

Maybe I was born at precisely the right time. Accommodation laws made a difference in my career. Without the bridge of the ADA, I might not have had the benefit of interpreters, and my employment options might have been limited, just as my pessimistic high school teacher predicted.

Requesting an accommodation is not a moral shortcoming; it is a right under federal law. Accessibility is not a "nice to have." It is essential. Design must prioritize accessibility right from the start and not as an afterthought.

You might argue that every piece of technology can't solve every possible issue for just a fraction of the population. However, hearing loss affects up to 20 percent of Americans now — a statistically relevant level, including youth — and will continue to grow as noise exposure swells. Productivity is lost. Human connectivity suffers.

* * *

I started to write this book twenty years ago after my first implant. During that time, the narrative changed. What started as a guide to cochlear implantation evolved into a reflection of regret for missed connections, a desire for authenticity, and a longing for community. In retrospect, I wish I'd taken ownership and voiced my thoughts, but I didn't realize them at the time. I know better now.

For those of you who have welcomed a deaf child into your world, or if a loved one or a client or even you were recently diagnosed with hearing loss, I hope you can learn from my story.

- Disability is not lesser than.
- Equality requires accessibility.
- Inclusion matters.

--- END ---

ACKNOWLEDGMENTS

Special thanks to Cyndi Stivers and Briar Goldberg at TED for their invaluable guidance and inspiration in helping shape my 2020 TED talk, *How Technology Has Changed What It's Like to Be Deaf*, which formed the basis for this book.

Thanks also to editors (in alphabetical order): Elizabeth Chadwick, Abbie Headon, and Gillian Rodgerson.

SOURCES

1. Rebecca Knill, 2020, "How Technology Has Changed What It's Like to be Deaf," filmed February 2020 in Charlotte, North Carolina. TED video, 13:49. https://www.ted.com/talks/rebecca_knill_how_technology_has_changed_what_it_s_like_to_be_deaf.

2. "Ableism." Merriam-Webster.com Dictionary, Merriam-Webster. https://www.merriam-webster.com/dictionary/ableism. Accessed January 23, 2024.

3. "Ableism." Oxford Reference.com Dictionary. https://www.oxfordreference.com/display/10.1093/oi/authority.20110803095344235. Accessed January 23, 2024.

4. Humphries, T. (1975). "Communicating across Cultures: An Inquiry into the Nature of Sign Language and the Education of the Deaf" (PhD diss., Union Institute & University).

5. Lane, H. (1992). The Mask of Benevolence: Disabling the Deaf Community. New York: Knopf Publishing Group.

6. Szasz, TS. Some observations on the relationship between psychiatry and the law. AMA Arch Neurol Psychiatry. 1956 Mar;75(3):297-315. doi: 10.1001/archneurpsyc.1956.02330210077008. PMID: 13301090.

7. Oliver, M. (1983). The Social Model of Disability, Routledge.

8. University of Washington, "What is the Difference Between Accessible, Usable, and Universal Design?" https://www.washington.edu/doit/what-difference-between-accessible-usable-and-universal-design. Last modified May 24, 2022.

9. Lanzieri, T., MD, Redd, S., Abernathy, E., MS, Icenogle, J., PhD. Centers for Disease Control Prevention (CDC), "Manual for the Surveillance of Vaccine-Preventable Diseases, Chapter 15: Congenital Rubella Syndrome." https://www.cdc.gov/vaccines/pubs/surv-manual/chpt15-crs.html. Last modified April 28, 2020.

10. Shirer, WL (1991). Rise and Fall of the Third Reich. London, England: Arrow Books.

11. National Park Service, "Understanding Sound." https://www.nps.gov/subjects/sound/understandingsound.htm. Last modified July 3, 2018.

12. National Institutes of Health, "Hearing Different Frequencies." https://www.nih.gov/news-events/nih-research-matters/hearing-different-frequencies. Last modified June 2, 2014

13. Jaslow, R. Harvard Medical School, "Scientists Regenerate Hair Cells That Enable Hearing," April 19, 2023, https://hms.harvard.edu/news/scientists-regenerate-hair-cells-enable-hearing.

14. National Institute on Deafness and Other Communication Disorders, "Quick Statistics About Hearing." https://www.nidcd.nih.gov/health/statistics/quick-statistics-hearing. Last modified March 25, 2021.

15. National Council on Aging, "Hearing Health for Older Adults." https://www.ncoa.org/older-adults/health/physical-health/hearing-health. Accessed January 16, 2024.

16. Johns Hopkins Medicine, "Age-Related Hearing Loss (Presbycusis). https://www.hopkinsmedicine.org/health/conditions-and-diseases/presbycusis. Accessed January 16, 2024.

17. National Council on Aging, "Hearing Health for Older Adults." https://www.ncoa.org/older-adults/health/physical-health/hearing-health. Accessed January 16, 2024.

18. American Osteopathic Association, "Headphones & Hearing Loss." https://osteopathic.org/what-is-osteopathic-medicine/headphones-hearing-loss. Accessed January 25, 2024.

19. World Health Organization, "Deafness and Hearing Loss." https://www.who.int/news-room/fact-sheets/detail/deafness-and-hearing-loss. Last modified February 27, 2023.

20. National Institute on Deafness and Other Communication Disorders, "Quick Statistics about Hearing." https://www.nidcd.nih.gov/health/statistics/quick-statistics-hearing. Last modified March 25, 2021.

21. Lin FR, Niparko JK, Ferrucci L. "Hearing loss prevalence in the United States." Arch Intern Med. 2011 Nov 14;171(20):1851-2. doi: 10.1001/archinternmed.2011.506. PMID: 22083573; PMCID: PMC3564588.

22. World Health Organization, "Deafness and Hearing Loss." https://www.who.int/news-room/fact-sheets/detail/deafness-and-hearing-loss. Last modified February 27, 2023.

23. Centers for Disease Control and Prevention, "What Noises Cause Hearing Loss?" https://www.cdc.gov/nceh/hearing_loss/what_noises_cause_hearing_loss.html. Last modified November 8, 2022.

24. Cari Romm, The Atlantic, "The Life and Death of Martha's Vineyard Sign Language." https://www.theatlantic.com/health/archive/2015/09/marthas-vineyard-sign-language-asl/407191. Last modified September 25, 2015.

25. Gallaudet University, "Invention of the Cochlear Implant Fans Flames of Debate on Both Sides," https://gallaudet.edu/museum/exhibits/history-through-deaf-eyes/awareness-access-and-change/invention-of-the-cochlear-implant-fans-flames-of-debate-on-both-sides. Accessed January 25, 2024.

26. Medoff, Mark (1980). Children of a Lesser God. New York, N.Y.: Dramatists Play Service.

27. Tennyson, Alfred Tennyson, Baron 1809-1892. Idylls of the King. New York :Airmont, 1969.

28. Speech for the Deaf: Essays Written for Milan International Congress, Proceedings and Resolutions. London: W. H. Allen & co., 1880.

29. World Federation of the Deaf, "International Congress of the Deaf (ICED) July 18-22, Vancouver, Canada. https://wfdeaf.org/news/international-congress-of-the-deaf-iced-july-18-22-2010-vancouver-canada. Last modified December 22, 2023.

30. Berenbaum, Michael. "T4 Program". Encyclopedia Britannica, 7 Nov. 2023, https://www.britannica.com/event/T4-Program. Accessed January 27, 2024.

31. United States Holocaust Memorial Museum, "Euthanasia Program and Aktion T4," https://encyclopedia.ushmm.org/content/en/article/euthanasia-program. Last modified October 7, 2020.

32. National Human Genome Research Institute, "Eugenics-Its Origin and Development (1883-Present)," https://www.genome.gov/about-genomics/educational-resources/timelines/eugenics. Last modified November 30, 2021.

33. Hitler, Adolf, 1889-1945. Mein Kampf. Boston :Houghton Mifflin, 1999.

34. NPR, "The Supreme Court Ruling That Led to 70,000 Forced Sterilizations," https://www.npr.org/sections/health-shots/2016/03/07/469478098/the-supreme-court-ruling-that-led-to-70-000-forced-sterilizations. March 7, 2016.

35. Kevles DJ. Eugenics and human rights. BMJ. 1999 Aug 14;319(7207):435-8. doi: 10.1136/bmj.319.7207.435. PMID: 10445929; PMCID: PMC1127045.

36. National Women's Law Center, "Forced Sterilization of Disabled People in the United States," https://nwlc.org/resource/forced-sterilization-of-disabled-people-in-the-united-states. January 24, 2022.

37. National Women's Law Center, "Forced Sterilization Laws in Each State and Territory." https://nwlc.org/wp-content/uploads/2022/01/%C6%92.NWLC_SterilizationReport_2022_Appendix.pdf. Accessed February 12, 2024.

38. University of Vermont, "North Carolina Eugenics." https://www.uvm.edu/~lkaelber/eugenics/NC/NCold.html. Accessed January 26, 2024.

39. Cowell, Sidney Robertson, Collector, and Percy Montrose. Clementine. performed by Mccready, John A 1939. Audio. https://www.loc.gov/item/2017701507/.

40. Ling, Daniel (1976). Speech and the Hearing-Impaired Child: Theory and Practice. Alexander Graham Bell Association for the Deaf.

41. NPR TED Radio Hour, Sound and Silence. Hosted by Manoush Zomorodi. https://www.npr.org/programs/ted-radio-hour/923960989/sound-and-silence. October 16, 2020.

42. Stella Young, 2014, "I'm Not Your Inspiration, Thank You Very Much," filmed April 2014 in Sydney, Australia. TED video, 09:03. https://www.ted.com/talks/stella_young_i_m_not_your_inspiration_thank_you_very_much.

43. *Radio Head Gal* is an independent book and has not been authorized, sponsored, or otherwise approved by Apple Inc.

44. Klusza, Maureen. The Greatest Irony. MOeArt.com. Cartoon. August 9, 2016. http://moeart.myshopify.com/collections/posters/products/past-work.

45. Boston Children's Hospital, "Cochlear Implant Program Activation." https://www.childrenshospital.org/programs/cochlear-implant-program/your-visit/activation. Accessed January 25, 2024.

46. The University of Chicago, SSA Magazine Archive, "Sign Language is Best for Deaf Children," https://crownschool.uchicago.edu/ssa_magazine/sign-language-best-deaf-children.html. Volume 24, Issue 2, Summer 2017.

ABOUT THE AUTHOR

REBECCA KNILL was a Vice President and business systems consultant manager at a Fortune 500 company for over thirty years. In 2020, Rebecca gave a TED talk, *How Technology Has Changed What It's Like to Be Deaf* (go.ted.com/rebeccaknill), which has several million views, has been translated into multiple languages, and was selected by the TED Editors for their favorite *Top 25 TED Talks of 2020*. She was subsequently featured on NPR's *TED Radio Hour* program *Sound and Silence*.